OUT FOR THE COUNT

DAVE HILL

OUT FOR
THE COUNT

Politicians and the People,
Election 1992

MACMILLAN
LONDON

First published 1992 by Macmillan London

a division of Pan Macmillan Publishers Limited
Cavaye Place London SW10 9PG
and Basingstoke

Associated companies throughout the world

ISBN 0 333 56312 3

9 8 7 6 5 4 3 2 1

A CIP catalogue record for this book is available from
the British Library

Typeset by Cambridge Composing (UK) Ltd, Cambridge
Printed and bound in Great Britain by
Mackays of Chatham PLC, Chatham, Kent

For Laura, Frankie and Nathan, my own dream ticket

CONTENTS

As I drove into London at dawn on 10 April 1992, I listened on the radio to Neil Kinnock making a speech from the steps of the Labour Party's Walworth Road headquarters. In it, he acknowledged his defeat in the General Election of the previous day. It was a desperately sad address, and few who heard it or (as I later did) watched it on television will ever forget the anguished enervation etched into his face or the stoical understatement of his words: 'I naturally feel a strong sense of disappointment. Not for myself, for I am fortunate, very fortunate, in my personal life. But I feel dismay, sorrow, for so many people in our country who do not share this personal good fortune. They deserve better than they got on 9 April 1992. The whole country deserves better, and we will work to ensure . . .'

At that point I entered the underpass in Marylebone and what followed dissolved into static.

A few minutes later I walked into Smith Square in Westminster where Conservative Party workers and supporters were celebrating victory outside their Central Office. With their customary grace in victory, they mocked the Welsh national anthem – 'Neil Kinnock, Neil Kinnock, what's it like to lose again?' – then went into a chant: 'We all hate the BBC! We all hate the BBC!'

These last two memories of the campaign sum up for me much of what seemed so unsatisfactory about the conduct of, arguably, the most crucial British General Election since Labour's triumph directly after the war. The Conservative revelry betrayed not only joy but also a disturbing certainty about their own, invincible virtues quite inappropriate in a party which had won by what turned out to be a modest 21-seat majority with just 42

per cent of the national vote, representing only a little over 30 per
cent of the total electorate. Yet so massive is their self-esteem they
feel justified in expressing hate for so essentially benign and
conservative an institution as the British Broadcasting Corporation on the grounds that – despite almost blanding out in its
determination to be impartial – it dares sometimes to call the
raging glory of the blue torch into doubt.

More than that, they won despite a palpable cynicism among
the people of the United Kingdom whom they ostensibly serve.
And this observation leads, inevitably, to the question of how
Labour contrived to lose. I have opinions (albeit uncertain) on the
matter which I will resist the urge to bore you with here – they
sneak out, in any case, in the ensuing pages – except to venture
that the orthodoxies established during Kinnock's period of
leadership have surely been proved a failure. Kinnock himself
may have been as close to the mark as anyone in his post-mortem
assertion that John Major's triumph represented a victory for fear
over hope. But if hope is the answer, then why, in the middle of
a seemingly endless Conservative recession, were Labour able to
provide so little of it?

The answer to that can be found in only one place – among
the voters themselves. And I suppose the underlying contention
of this book, insofar as it has one, is that voters are disillusioned
right across the board. They have good reason. It is nothing new
to hear the public moan that 'they're all as bad as each other', but
the feeling persists that the gap between the political establishment
– in which I include both politicians and the media – and those
they are meant to listen to, articulate and, yes, take issue with, is
growing wider all the time. It is not a very cheerful thought. But
it brings me to my motivation for writing this book, and the way
I went about it.

I am not an expert in politics but I believe the innocent
outsider can sometimes see things and comment on them from a
perspective and with a vigour which the insider's very involvement with his or her subject tends to preclude.

My aims were simple enough: firstly, to cover as wide and
varied a spread of territory in the United Kingdom as possible in
the period between budget day and election day; secondly, to
witness the campaign process from as many angles as I could;

thirdly to concentrate most of my attention on the points of interaction between the politicians (in person or through the media) and the voters – including me – they presume to represent. But while the theory was simple, the practice was harder. For one thing, it was so exhausting. I began with a triangular overnight train ride between London, Edinburgh and Torquay, later flew from Liverpool to Belfast and back, and drove over 5000 miles in a rented Sierra, which also served as accommodation for the four nights I slept in lay-bys. Then there was the sheer aggravation of trying to track people down and set up appointments when most of them hardly knew where they were going to be from day to day, and those who did wouldn't necessarily tell you in case you told the IRA. Add to that the need to meet the occasional newspaper or magazine deadline and you've got a schedule straight from hell. I returned home after polling day to spend a week recovering and paying accumulated bills, another week completing the unpacking of tea chests having moved house (one of precious few people to manage that lately) six days before the budget, and a third week walking in circles wondering where to start. I then completed the writing in just over a hundred days, playing back fifty hours of video recordings and twenty-nine audio cassettes in the process. I don't mind telling you, I'm knackered.

It has, though, been a valuable experience. I have always been interested in politics, but knew in my heart that the vigorous opinions I caught myself voicing on the subject were often informed as much by gut prejudice as sober thought. I wouldn't claim that pursuing this project has entirely corrected this failing, but at least the edge of my irritation – and enthusiasm, here and there – has been keened by close proximity to its object. I fondly imagine there are other folk out there who regard the political process with the same morbid fascination as I do. It is such fellow voters who will most enjoy what follows.

I owe gratitude to several people in various different ways. Bob Campbell (and his fellow diners) and Jane Winter offered hospitality. Sean French, Ian Aitken and Nigel Fountain read chunks of the manuscript, commenting generously and helpfully. Steve Platt at *New Statesman and Society* and various *Guardian* editors provided commissions which helped meet the cost of the enterprise. My publisher Roland Philipps was rich in faith and patience, and my agent Sara Fisher was, as ever, a stalwart supporter. Most of all, thanks to Nicki, Jane, Betty, Ted and Frances who bailed me out in the childcare department.

What follows is neither exhaustive nor objective nor (despite my best intentions) free from the Smart Alecry of hindsight. It is, though, a blend of snapshot, farce, obsession and artifice, not unlike the election campaign itself. I just hope it comes across as a bit more honest.

Adventures in
the Glorious Past

A routine London morning on Network South-East. At seven o'clock a bomb planted by the Irish Republican Army exploded near Wandsworth Common station, reducing a junction box to rubble and giving thousands of rail commuters a flawless excuse for being late for work. Skimming through their newspapers, those stranded travellers would have read about Alan Amos, a Member of Parliament arrested for 'an alleged act of indecency' in an area of Hampstead Heath regularly cruised by gay men craving *al fresco* pick-ups. Gazing out at the drizzle through the windows of their stationary carriages, many of these daily workers, white collar for the most part, would have reflected uneasily on the economic recession that had already corroded the comforts of Home Counties life for thousands like themselves, as businesses capsized, unemployment soared and the keys to private houses were glumly handed over to the very institutions which had so joyfully financed their purchase just a few years before.

Rule Britannia. Explosions from Northern Ireland; sexual indiscretions by gentleman politicians; the economy glug-glugging morosely down the drain – each was a smutty snapshot of Great British nationhood at the end of the twentieth century. And each was excused by recourse to a familiar repertoire of Great British denials to which the Conservative Party, after nearly thirteen years of unbroken rule, had become risibly addicted: Conservative Home Secretary Kenneth Baker denied, with slippery briskness, that the persistent Irish Republicans would ever get their way; Alan Amos, the exposed Conservative member for Hexham, had already denied that he was homosexual and, even as he announced his resignation, insisted that what the police had caught him doing in the undergrowth with a man to whom he'd not previously been introduced was just 'a childish and stupid mistake'. And so the stage was set for the Conservative Chancellor of the Exchequer, the Right Honourable Norman Lamont, MP, to make it a hat-trick in the Simon Peter class, by standing up in the House of Commons and denying there was a serious plot flaw in the Conservative government's popular capitalist epic, or anything remotely odd about handing out public money while the country was living on tick. And the Chancellor would go further: he would also deny that his second annual budget was, in essence, a stunt designed to give his boss, the Prime Minister, John Major, something to boast about to the voters during the imminent general election campaign. Everyone knew the big denial would take place between three and five that afternoon of Tuesday 10 March 1992. Only the details remained to be revealed. A nation curled its lip and held its breath.

The setting for this dubious enterprise was Westminster, where Prime Minister Major and Chancellor Lamont live and work. It is a place whose architectural and iconographic parts resonate with imagery so seductive as to transport the unwary into a Glorious Past of the imagination, a psychological, historical theme park which celebrates consoling reveries drawn from the last four centuries, the most effective filched from a continuum which starts with the crowning of Queen Victoria, takes in the two world wars of the first half of the twentieth century, and only really terminates about thirty years ago. In this mystic realm, incredible transformations occcur. A labyrinth of legend is transmogrified into an edifice of fact. The idea of a Britain that is feeble and impoverished does not arise. We British, hosannas the ambient soundtrack of the Glorious Past theme park, were the makers of the Industrial Revolution; we built an empire covering a quarter of the globe; we saw off the Kaiser; we stood alone against the Führer; we are a proud, independent people, uniquely blessed.

Voices raised in qualification get drowned out by this muzak of self-congratulation. On deaf ears fall inconvenient assertions that, as early as the turn of the century, the United States had outstripped us in industrial output; that American factories produced the bulk of the munitions with which British soldiers fought the First World War; that the resources spent defending

the empire were deployed to the neglect of industrial moderniza-
tion and left us militarily trouserless when Adolf Hitler came
along; that it was machine tools imported from the United States
that enabled the Spitfire fighter planes' Merlin Engines to be built;
that, by 22 August 1940, we would concede anything to the
Americans if they consented to save us; and that when President
Roosevelt sent a warship to South Africa to collect our last
£50 million of gold, he didn't even bother telling the British
government until it was half-way there.[1]

Most of the British, even the reluctant, spent part of their
lives in the Glorious Past theme park. Some virtually take up
residence, gorging themselves on fantastic reveries in which any
interloper making mock of Britain's vaunted virility is frog-
marched by a firm-jawed officer of the law – perhaps a Bow
Street Runner or a hologram of Sergeant Dixon of Dock Green –
directly to Parliament Square and shoved, quivering, into the
shadow of the most prominent of its many imposing statues, that
of Winston Spencer Churchill, immortalized in a mighty great-
coat, gazing intently at the far horizon for any lingering sign of
the devilish Hun. Cue 'Land of Hope and Glory'. Cue patriotism's
rose-tinted arc lights. Cue Norman Lamont?

As lunchtime approached, the subtle fabric of the Glorious
Past seemed a little soggy. The desultory rain now piddled on a
patchwork of people gathered at the entrance to Downing Street.
Peering through the black iron security gates (a recently erected
tribute to the health of our democracy), sopping foreign tourists
watched a policeman in blue overalls roll under visiting cars to
check for lurking bombs: a reminder of how the IRA had fired a
mortar bomb directly into the back garden of Downing Street,
thirteen months before, launching it through the roof of a van
impudently stationed on Horse Guards Avenue. Meanwhile, on
the apron of Richmond Terrace opposite, stood a police transit
complete with metal windscreen visor: a reminder of the furious
riot which had ripped through the centre of London two years
before, after a huge demonstration against the poll tax – a
somewhat counter-productive new method of raising local
government finance – had turned into a vicious confrontation

1. Clive Ponting, *1940 – Myth and Reality*, Cardinal, 1990.

with the police. And closer still, standing with mournful permanence in the crown of the Whitehall thoroughfare, the Cenotaph memorial was a reminder of how the two world wars had both exposed and further entrenched Britain's inexorable, century-long decline: a situation no British chancellor has been able to arrest, and certainly not the one with the Instant-Whip locks and Gothic-arched eyebrows who would shortly emerge from Number 11, complete with his bashful wife, to hold aloft the traditional tattered Treasury document case and grin gamely for the assembled cameramen.

Such was the cursed inheritance which obliged Lamont to dream up his big denial. What made things worse was the toxic fall-out from the drastic attempt to escape it, devised and implemented by Margaret Thatcher, Prime Minister Major's extraordinary predecessor. The secret to understanding her was that she had pitched a tent in the Glorious Past theme park at a very early age. She believed the Glorious Past was in no sense a romantic illusion, some placebo from the astral plane, but a real thing which, especially since 1945, had been shamefully neglected, then systematically vandalized. Her view was that its tacky furnishings should not simply be restored, but reconditioned and recycled to help construct a Glorious Present.

Central to Thatcher's strategy was an overhaul of the arcane and ageing fruit machine that is the British economy. The thing about a fruit machine is that, although its whole design guarantees diminishing returns, there's always some smart-arse convinced they can make it pay. Margaret Thatcher was such a smart-arse. She initially approached the machine with three ideas in mind: one, that the wrong sort of people shouldn't get any more turns at pulling the handle; two, that if you set about certain component parts with a jemmy, the fruit machine would work more smoothly; and three, that if you put less money in the slot, you'd have more chance of hitting the jackpot. You had to hand it to Margaret Thatcher. She was full of bright ideas.

The technique had a name: 'monetarism'. Its basis was that, if the government used its powers to reduce the supply of money into the economy, a number of impediments to economic well-being, inflation in particular, would be purged. Of course, in the way of old-fashioned discipline, the short-term consequences would be painful. But we would learn to love our punishment in the end.

For two years the ancient fruit machine squealed for mercy and refused to cough up. In the process, 20 per cent of Britain's manufacturing capacity was laid to waste, unemployment soared from just over a million to way over twice that, and the inner cities exploded into flame and fury. There was, though, a kind of imperial revivalist show, the Falklands War. Shiploads of dead Argentinians were run up the Britannia flag pole and a mesmerized populace saluted. Margaret Thatcher won a second election victory in 1983.

Raw monetarism was discreetly abandoned. Thatcher began fluttering her eyelashes and pretending it had never existed. By the end of 1986, assisted by the policy of privatization, notably of British Telecom and British Gas, she and Nigel Lawson (her Chancellor since 1983) were able to contrive a recovery fanfare. And in the 1987 pre-election budget, they decided it was cake-and-eat-it time: some extra money was earmarked for public services *and* there was a further cut in income tax. An economic miracle was proclaimed. Margaret Thatcher won her third election victory that summer. She began speaking of an end to national decline. She began acting as if she had a plot lined up in Parliament Square right next to Winston.

In the light of all this, perhaps Norman Lamont, straightening his plum-coloured tie at Number 11, was reflecting on the irony of his recent rise to fame. Maybe his boss was doing the same in the house next door. For the improvement in their statuses now coincided with catastrophes that the 'miracle' had caused.

In March 1988, the government was both nervous and exultant. The previous October an enormous stock market crash, designated 'Black Monday', had raised the spectre of a slump. Anxious to insure against it, Chancellor Lawson cut interest rates and produced a budget that made the jaws of even his most ardent admirers sag. Down still further went the basic rate of income tax, to 25 per cent. Most staggering of all, down too went the top rate for the biggest earners, from 60 per cent to 40 per cent. A boom ensued: first in consumer spending, house prices and credit; then in inflation, unemployment and debt.

A year later, Chancellor Lawson was trying to defuse it. But a looming hangover was just part of the malaise enveloping the government. First, Lawson himself capitulated, resigning on 26 October 1989 after a protracted scrap with Thatcher over the merits of committing sterling to the disciplines of the Exchange Rate Mechanism of the European Monetary System. The argument went to the heart of Thatcher's fantasy vision of This Great Nation. She believed membership of the ERM would be a big step down a European road leading inexorably to the diminution of the British 'Mother of Parliaments'.

She replaced Lawson with John Major (and Major, promoted from Chief Secretary to the Treasury, with Norman Lamont) and eventually, against all her nationalist instincts, let him take Britain into the ERM. She then continued to confront the dreadful foreigners in whatever ways were left. Poetically, it was Sir Geoffrey Howe, formerly her partner in monetarist passion as Chancellor, who pencilled in Thatcher's own appointment with the political guillotine. He handed in his cabinet cards because her attitude problem over the European Community was driving him quite mad.

Then came the revenge of Michael Heseltine. Once her dashing Defence Secretary, his own resignation had been the most dramatic of all, when he stormed out of a cabinet meeting in January 1986. His decision followed a row about who was going to bail out the latest struggling British company, Westland, a helicopter manufacturer. More fundamentally the row was about whether Thatcher knew Heseltine's job better than he did. Heseltine spent the next four years protesting that he was not after hers. He was fibbing. On 14 November 1990, he announced that he was challenging her for the Conservative leadership. When it came to the vote six days later, enough of his fellow MPs supported him to make her position untenable. She resigned as Prime Minister on the 22nd.

★

It was not, of course, Heseltine who finally replaced her. On 28 November, John Major vanquished both him and a third contender, Foreign Secretary Douglas Hurd, in the second leadership ballot. He appointed Norman Lamont his successor as Chancellor and together they inherited an economic mess which it was their job not only to alleviate, but to deny any part in making. This was a little tricky: when Lawson had delivered his contentious 1988 budget, Major and Lamont were his Numbers Two and Three. Howls of outrage from the parliamentary opposition had been met with goading speeches from these senior members of Lawson's team.

In the short term, they opted for sticking it on old Nigel anyway. After all, he was yesterday's man. But by the onset of 1992 they had set about minimizing any remaining damage-by-association by the use of propaganda. This had two dimensions. One was to go on and on about a 'world recession', claiming that Britain's woes were just an unfortunate reflection of it. The other dimension involved spending hundreds of thousands of pounds and spouting hundreds of thousands of words, spreading scare stories about how much worse everything would be if the Labour Party, their prime political opponents, formed the next government. The thrust of their attack was tax – tax, tax, tax. They produced a tendentious 'costing' of Labour's alleged 'promises' at a thumping £30 billion. They devised a visual tax bombshell, claiming that, on average, everyone would pay £1,000 more every year under Labour. They came up with a poster showing two giant boxing gloves in fish-eye close up. On one it said 'higher prices' on the other, 'more taxes' 'Labour's Double Whammy'. Pow.

They had been at it hammer and tongs ever since Christmas, a desperate defensive battle conducted with the assistance of admen Saatchi and Saatchi. The previous summer, after months of negative growth, the government had reluctantly acknowledged the economy's deterioration. The admission was made in tones of measured understatement, the political equivalent of blind men admitting to myopia, but it still left to Lamont the unhappy task of heralding dawn at dead of night while, to increasing numbers of people, it appeared that his watch was running dangerously fast. Lamont had a credibility problem. Periodically he would emerge, blinking, into the House of Commons, or beneath punishing television studio lights like some quivering noctule dragged from hibernation, to talk of 'turning the corner' or to claim sightings of 'the green shoots of economic spring'. But still the recession groaned on. By New Year even people on his own side were beginning to laugh at the miserable Norman.

The budget would be his last big throw in the protracted pre-election campaign. Precisely what Lamont might come up with had been the subject of keen speculation. A further cut in income tax had been long and loudly anticipated by those many British newspapers dedicated to licking the Conservative Party's boots. But a cut in taxes means a cut in government income, leaving less to be spent on desirable things such as schools and the National Health Service, which people were worried about. And Lamont was already up to his knees in a rising and unforeseen tide of debt. It was the sort which Thatcher's administrations had been pledged to turn back, but which now was beginning to chill the Chancellor's ideological testicles.

How shrivelled was the miserable Norman's scrotum as he said goodbye to his wife, relieved now of her role as doting accessory in the photo session outside Number 11, showing, in spite of Alan Amos, that the Conservatives were the party of traditional family ways; as he stepped into the chauffeur-driven Rover which would ferry him the short distance to the House of Commons to offer his big denial; as he purred past the Cenotaph and perhaps caught sight of the statue of Churchill, taking in these sights from behind the bullet-proof glass designed to save him should some IRA marksman step from the empire's costly detritus and try to shoot him in the head?

CHAPTER ONE

Miserable Norman and Nice John

(Tuesday 10 March)

She wore snug cotton leggings of apologetic orange, an anorak, canvas sandals, and no socks. She was from Walsall and she was wet.

'I don't see why we shouldn't get in and see them. It's our money they're playing with, isn't it?'

At half past two, the sergeant-at-arms had crossed the Commons forecourt and made thirty people happy. They had surged through the iron gateway to see the drama of the day, a file of dripping Pak-a-macs, emitting laughs of relief. But another fifty had been left waiting, their crossed fingers whitening in the remorseless Scotch mist. It was gone three and inside, having avoided assassination, Norman Lamont, the miserable Chancellor, would shortly rise, a human soufflé puffing himself up with yesterday's broken eggs. Meanwhile, the hopes of the rest of us outside, who had wished to see him do it, seemed to be sinking fast.

Ms Walsall shivered. An affable young man in cotton slacks and grubby plimsolls shivered. So did a blonde German student, hunched beneath her umbrella, a Japanese jock with a Niké holdall and everyone else in this queue for a constitutional kick. As hope slowly expired it gave way to soothing silliness. What member of the animal kingdom was Norman Lamont most like? A lemur, perhaps?

'A badger.'

'A marmoset.'

'I haven't really thought about it.'

Just opposite, a gang of uniformed schoolkids clutching flapping bits of paper chattered their way towards the X-ray security checkpoint that lies beyond the mock-Gothic Commons porchway.

'They've got invitations,' said Ms Walsall.

Bastards.

'You get them from your MP,' said Mr Affable in the slacks and plimsolls, 'but I've never had much luck.'

A pocket transistor provided both a taunt and a compensation in the form of Radio 4's live coverage. The Chancellor was speaking now, delivering his words in the meditational drone of a Buddhist bank manager, just one aspect of the public persona which had so consistently failed to excite the taxpayers at large. Lamont's long months of stodgy insistence that things were looking up had taken their toll on his opinion poll ratings. There was probably some correlation between this and more trivial matters such as the congealing of mass unemployment and the ailing performance of the pound in the Exchange Rate Mechanism, but the pollsters' findings, as always, had assumed a life of their own. Lamont lacked what media swells insist on calling 'sexiness'. It looked like being his downfall. Still, the delivery of the big denial, especially with the election looming, generated its own special frisson. The tension of the Commons, just a spit away, survived the trip along the airwaves as the Chancellor intoned:

'Over the year as a whole, GDP [Gross Domestic Product] fell by nearly 2½ per cent, ½ per cent more than my forecast of a year ago . . .'

So the recession was worse than he had anticipated.

'. . . I expect growth in the year to the second half of 1992 to be almost 2 per cent. The level of GDP for this year as a whole should be about 1 per cent higher than last.'

In other words, things were going to be less bad than they were at that moment very soon. Eventually, they would be even less bad. Clearly, there was as much to look forward to now as there had been at the same time last March.

'I suppose he might do something for us,' remarked Ms Walsall, forlornly, pinching her leggings away from her knicker line. It wasn't clear what she meant by 'something', or who she meant by 'us'. It was as if such things were meant to speak for themselves. Mr Affable was more expansive. He was a student of Parliament in his spare time, a bit of a train spotter. He leaned towards the Conservatives, but his political posture had recently straightened a bit. He was certain he wouldn't vote Labour, though he believed they were now 'less extreme' than in years gone by. But the Tories didn't seem to know what they were doing any more, even though 'John Major seems a nice chap', Ms Walsall offered plainer convictions. She reckoned they were 'all as bad as each other'.

The banality of these observations was no reflection on their authors. Rather, they expressed a balanced cocktail of folk wisdom and what might be called organic official opinion. The first gathers dully about the populace like cobwebs in a graveyard, the product, variously, of experience, prejudice and the weary cynicism of passers-by buttonholed too often by hucksters. The second is the pervasive hand-me-down of Authority as personified by Experts. These Experts comprise newspaper columnists, correspondents and leader-writers, television reporters and pundits and, of course, prominent politicians themselves. They do not function formally in concert, indeed they often argue fiercely from their various public platforms. But the point about these arguments is that all concerned are agreed on what to disagree about. This shared squabbling territory is the home turf of Authority. Anyone venturing beyond it is ignored.

Authority's Experts had long agreed about two things which chimed precisely with the views of Mr Affable: firstly, that Labour had become 'electable', a term so stuffed with assumptions about what voters were capable of wanting it effectively outlawed all dissent; and, secondly, that unlike Margaret Thatcher, John Major was 'nice', which could mean anything from contending that his policies were less crudely divisive than hers, to noting simply that people who disliked the Tories – most crucially those who had come to dislike them since 1987 – didn't dislike them quite as much now that Major was in charge. In image terms, then, the dénouement of British democracy's ultimate drama was already defined as a dust-up between 'electability' and 'niceness', to be fought out against a backdrop of deep public scepticism. Ms Walsall and Mr Affable had said it all.

That John Major was thought 'nice' by comparison with Thatcher came as no surprise. His personal style, as consumed by the public, differed dramatically from her patent blend of stentorian bombast and sledgehammer condescension. But, equally, Nice John had been carefully constructed from the moment he took over. Central to this had been his own firm-but-friendly denial that any such construction was taking place. This was not exactly a lie, because, unlike his predecessor, he had not directly employed professional image consultants to adjust the tone of his voice or his wardrobe taste. But in truth he owed much of his persona to Authority's Experts, particularly those charged with promoting the re-election of Conservative governments. In 1989 all had wanted to know what he was like, this diffident Major fellow succeeding the flash Nigel Lawson. They asked his colleagues. Nice. Very nice, came the reply. He liked cricket and football, very big on Chelsea. Never made any enemies even when he was in the Whips' office, imposing parliamentary discipline, not even when he was Chief Secretary, telling other ministers how much public money they could not have to spend. What's more, her diehard supporters emphasized, Major had remained loyal to Thatcher right up to the bitter end. Nice John walked among us. There was no escape.

With the outline sketched in, detail accumulated quickly. Much was made of Nice John's background, an intriguing blend of mundanity and eccentricity. His father Thomas Major (officially Major-Ball, though the name's second barrel fell into disuse) and his mother, born Gwendolin Coates, had spent much of their lives as travelling entertainers, working in circuses and theatres at home and abroad. Mr Major Senior plied many skills of his trade, including acrobatics. But by the early 1930s, he had changed career and started a garden ornaments business which enabled him, his wife and their three children – of whom the future Prime Minister was the youngest – to live in the salubrious and thriving south London suburb of Worcester Park. That Nice John was the son of a man who worked the flying trapeze and later earned a crust turning gnomes out of rubber moulds provided satirists with plenty of fun. But in propaganda terms it was the contravening *ordinariness* that counted for most.

Upon becoming Prime Minister, plain John Major was instantly upholstered with the mythology of free-market romance. Even allowing for the Conservative Party's history as that of the landed rich, this was all pretty preposterous. In fact, the Majors were substantially more prosperous than the average British household during the inter-war period of abject economic depression. Thomas Major was not only self-employed, but, on a small scale, an employer. Both John Major's eldest siblings were initially educated at fee-paying primary schools. During the war, like most people's, the family's income fell sharply, but John Major was, none the less, born, in 1943, into a family where material comfort and upward aspiration had been the norm and were expected to continue.

In 1954 he passed his eleven-plus examination (emulating his sister Pat, who had gained a place at the illustrious Nonesuch Girls' Grammar, succeeding where his brother Terry had failed) and went on to the nearby Rutlish Grammar School for boys, an institution which did its level best to emulate the public schools, whose disturbed authoritarian conventions so many grammar schools admired. Grammar schools remain a *cause célèbre* among grass roots Conservatives, vaunted as educational ladders of opportunity, where a particular concept of excellence is cherished, and the progeny of simple folk may dream of loftier things. So there, Nice John's cheerleaders pronounced: a grammar school boy from humble beginnings can rise through the Conservative Party to the highest office in the land. The refrain had been chorused before: the previous two Conservative leaders, Thatcher and Edward Heath, had both come up (Heath, the son of a Broadstairs carpenter, starting from the lower point) through grammar schools. However, they had also gone on to the élite Oxford University. Major, by contrast, was an academic weakling, leaving Rutlish at sixteen, at a time when ill-fortune ruled every part of his life. It was these downcast years which have retrospectively been reclaimed to proclaim his greater glory.

It emerged that during his early adolescence, Major's family had indeed encountered genuinely hard times. His father's health began to fail, in particular his eyesight. The bottom fell out of the garden ornament market. In 1955, Thomas Major decided to sell up and retire to Canada. He found a buyer for his business and agreed a sum of £3000, roughly the equivalent in property terms of £90,000 today – big money by most people's standards. However, the sale collapsed into chaos and Major Senior's

impatient creditors made the situation worse. The house in
Worcester Park was sold for £2150 and the family, pursued by
debt, moved to a dismal flat in Coldharbour Lane, Brixton.

Brixton! How respectable society shudders at its name. Setting
of an anti-police riot in 1981! Home of all those Blacks! Inspiration
for a thousand floridly pernicious headlines! And John Major had
actually lived there! Lurid anecdotes emerged about a cooker on the
landing and a toilet three floors down; about running errands for
an illegal bookmaker; about not being able to afford the proper
buttons for his Rutlish blazer and getting teased for it by sniffy
peers. Best of all, he had, for a time, been unemployed. Of
course, in booming early-sixties Britain, there were plenty of jobs
to be had. Major was simply – and quite reasonably – a little
choosy. But such inconvenient qualifications were not permitted
to besmirch the burgeoning, go-getter portrait of the Brixton
Boy Made Good. Major's past, transformed into soap opera,
doubled as a convenient moralist stick with which to beat upon
the perceived Brixton syndrome of sloth and immorality: see,
anyone can make it if they try!

Such was the window dressing that framed a politician
distinguished by his incongruity amid the bloated trimmings of
British constitutional expectation. No previous Conservative
premier lowering his rump on to the ornately carved, green-
padded pews of Westminster's opulent parliamentary palace had
seemed so perfectly, even perversely, plain.

Gawky of frame and spindly of gait, Major's personal groom-
ing maximized an impression of crushingly anodyne squareness.
His steely hair was parted obediently on his right and swept
laterally across his head with firmly utilitarian purpose: the
coiffure of a man for whom Elvis Presley might never have
existed. Beneath this sensible swathe his face was dominated by
spectacles whose rectangular plastic frames signalled an infinite
supply of practical rectitude that was, like the glasses themselves,
almost impervious to changing fashions. Any tour of his facial
features was completed by a longish drop down an upper lip
distinguished by the persistent and unexpectedly comical ghost of
a cartoon Spaniard's moustache. This terminated in the tight,
though just barely ironical, line of a mouth from which issued
taut sentences of merciless clarity on matters as unutterably

opaque as the impact of invisible earnings on the public sector borrowing requirement.

Margaret Thatcher had come across like some pushy wanna-bee invading the set of *Dynasty*. Major resembled a human filing cabinet: essentially functional, thoroughly dependable, blandly ubiquitous and ordered with winning efficiency. The only mystery was what actually lay inside. Given that his initial tasks as Prime Minister were overwhelmingly concerned with damage limitation, this was not yet easy to discover. The one distinctive signature to emerge, first from his leadership campaign and then from his incumbency, was a commitment to building what he termed 'a classless society'.

It was an evocative expression intimating a breadth of vision which masked an extremely partial definition of class. He was really referring to culture. His desire to abolish class distinction was based on a distaste for discrimination based on snobbery rather than ability. It was a meritocratic ideal expressed by an American misnomer. Far from challenging the class system as based on differential possession of wealth, status and power, it merely posited different criteria for securing access to them. Under Nice John's prescriptions the class system would prevail, stronger than ever. All that would change would be the channels for mobility within it.

Margaret Thatcher's regime had already championed such adjustments. Among their consequences was the creation of a new kind of winner and a new kind of loser, the latter a large group of people with little money, few prospects and next to no hope of improvement. John Major's pledge to enshrine such changes at the heart of his 'classless' project suggested that his 'niceness' had its limits.

Still no succour from the sergeant-at-arms. The blonde German and the Japanese jock slipped away towards Westminster Abbey. Norman Lamont kept talking, with Nice John, as the radio confirmed, sitting in his regular place at the miserable Chancellor's right-hand side.

'Even with a resumption of growth, unemployment is likely to go on rising for some time . . .'

This was uttered in the obligatory tone of regret. But, of course, Lamont and Major understood very well that unemployment has its political attractions. A dozen years of union-busting had been made easier by its creation, and organized labour had no leverage on economic policy as a result. Though she never admitted to using unemployment as a political weapon, Thatcher certainly believed that reducing inflation would be easier if the workforce was marginalized and supine. Lamont's problem was that inflation had risen sharply again, busted unions or not. So, like her, he reversed the factors in the covert economic equation in the interests of public decency: rather than unemployment helping to defeat inflation, reducing inflation would help defeat unemployment.

'Prospects for reducing it depend crucially on our success in keeping inflation down . . .'

He anticipated a drop to below 3 per cent by the end of the year. This, he reckoned, would be a good thing because when the price of goods and materials was almost stable it created:

'. . . an environment in which the decisions of businesses and consumers are no longer distorted by the expectation of a general upward movement in prices.'

Here, then, was the government's implicit definition of how the economic wheel could be made to turn again. Its smooth rotation depended on the mutual self-interest of two sets of people, businesses and consumers, both spinning the wheel in the same direction at the same, ideally increasing, speed. It was the consumers who would initially reverse the application of the recessionary brake. Despite their mortgage debts, their credit card debts, their joblessness or the threat of it, they had to be encouraged to spend. Once they started spending, businesses, craving their custom, would take steps to meet these consumers' demands. Factories would up production and, most importantly, shops and stores would order more stock. Unemployment would be cured by encouraging the employed to resume the happy slap of plastic on check-out counters. What they needed was more money in their metaphorical pockets, and a tax cut would provide it. But lower taxes meant less money for the government, which already owed plenty. How would the shortfall be met? Like a *Blue Peter* presenter,

Chancellor Lamont produced an answer he had made earlier on, constructed by recycling yesterday's rejected rhetoric:

'In a recession, borrowing will tend to rise. But there is nothing wrong with that provided that the underlying position is sound and that the account moves back towards balance as the economy recovers.'

So the consumer-led recovery would be financed by government debt. How far would the chill tide rise up the Chancellor's goose-bumped thighs?

Very far:

'I have now revised my expectations of the Public Sector Borrowing Requirement up to £28 billion . . .'

Derisive hoots and roars rose from the Opposition benches, distorting the little speaker on the pocker transistor.

'What's going on in there?' asked a dripping Ms Walsall.

'Having a good shout, as usual,' chuckled a squelching Mr Affable.

Margaret Thatcher, we had heard, was sitting a few rows to the rear of Major and Lamont, the ghost of good housekeeping past. But for the miserable Chancellor, the trickiest part of the big denial was over. He pinned back his ears and raced for redemption. There would be help, he announced, for the film, cider and car industries, the latter by reducing the tax on buying a new car from 10 to 5 per cent. Single old-age pensioners receiving income support from the State would get an extra two pounds per week and married couples, three pounds. Inheritance tax – the proportion of money due to the government from those to whom businesses and personal fortunes were passed down after their former proprietors' deaths – would be abolished in relation to most small businesses, while none would now be levied on sums below £150,000. A bit odd, that, for the government of 'classlessness'.

Then at last, the Chancellor's big sting:

'. . . having reflected carefully on the priorities for this year's budget, I have decided for the year ahead to leave the basic rate at 25 pence in the pound . . .'

Silence. Then Tory guffaws. The shock hit Labour hardest. But the Chancellor still elaborated on the iniquity of taxation levels, before dramatically concluding:

'. . . I believe that it is possible, desirable and indeed prudent to take a substantial step this year towards our goal of a 20 pence basic rate for all tax payers . . . so I propose this year to cut the rate of income tax by 5 pence to 20 pence in the pound for the first £2000 of taxable income.'

More silence. More Tory guffaws. It was instantly clear that the changes would, relative to their total income, help the worse off most. Labour was supposed to do things like that. Within a minute, Paul Boateng, one of their economics spokesmen, rushed out of the House and made a beeline for a waiting camera crew. It would be tough for him to sound indignant about a measure to help the poor. A minute later, some loud-mouth in a Bugsy Malone suit strolled out and crowed at the waiting queue, as if to a theatre line: 'It's a terrible show! Terrible show!'

Nice John and the miserable Chancellor doubtless demurred.

CHAPTER TWO

Britain's Next Prime Minister

(Tuesday 10, Wednesday 11 March)

Sitting a few feet from Nice John as the miserable Chancellor delivered his big denial sat an example of the kind of man whose votes had turned the last three elections the Tories' way. From a classical working-class background, not nearly as comfortable as the PM's, this man had made something better of himself. His achievements owed nothing to the featherbed of privilege and little more to formal study. Rather, his rise was a reward for reliance on gut instinct, to stubborn determination and to personal initiative. He was, in most things, firmly conventional, a family man who did his best for his children and was fiercely devoted to his wife. His values were earthily traditional: women, he affectionately barracked and stoutly protected; men, he thought, should always strive to be, well, *men*. To relax, he liked nothing better than a few beers with the lads. And so on. People much like him had fallen for Margaret Thatcher in 1979, perhaps voting Conservative for the first time. How curious, then, that just such an individual was leader of the Labour Party, the Right Honourable Neil Kinnock, MP.

The political cunning that informed the introduction of the 20 pence tax band left Kinnock in a tight corner. It meant that, unless his party were to take the surreal step of endorsing a Tory budget, they would have to vote against something they were in favour of, given that Labour had floated the 20 pence band idea two years earlier. In the light of Kinnock's efforts since becoming Labour leader in 1983, this would amount to a dramatic reversal of roles, because he had spent most of that time cajoling his party to adopt policies increasingly similar to those Margaret Thatcher was practising. In party terms, this was not quite the somersault it seemed. For example, the last Labour government, led by James Callaghan (who took over from Harold Wilson after his retirement in 1976), had actually pre-dated Thatcher in using monetarism as a tool of economic management. Rather the serious gymnastics had been performed by Neil Kinnock himself. His relationship with that last Labour government reveals a talent for acrobatics to rival that of Thomas Major.

The circumstance in which the last Labour government had test-driven Thatcherite economics was a calamitous sterling crisis. These are a traditional feature of Labour's periods in power, always emanating from the City of London and always fouling up the best-laid socialist plans. But their panic this time was intensified by the apparent failure of economic mechanisms that had always been held to work before. In 1975 the impossible was happening; inflation *and* unemployment were increasing together. At the Labour Party conference the following year, Callaghan made a speech which turned the old logic inside out: 'We used to think that you could spend your way out of a recession, and increase employment by cutting taxes and boosting government spending. I tell you in all candour that that option no longer exists.'

Unable to restrain the deserting currency, the then Chancellor, Denis Healey, negotiated a controversial loan from the International Monetary Fund. Healey had already borrowed from the IMF on relatively easy terms in order to keep Labour's spending programme afloat. This time the conditions were much more stringent: the government would have to pay the money back by cutting public spending and raising personal taxes. This was welcomed by the left wing of the party like a flatulent fellow traveller in a broken lift. At that time, Neil Kinnock was a big noise on the left. He held his nose and blew his top. Later, in the House of Commons, he scorned Healey, Callaghan and the rest of the Labour leadership:

'They treat the City of London as it it were some kind of winnable Tory marginal constituency . . . They think . . . that somehow there is some deal, some kind of understanding that can be reached with people who are sworn ideological enemies.'

Within ten years, Neil Kinnock was doing the same, without even being in power. Instead of pitching pebbles at the men in bowler hats, he was looking on approvingly as his Shadow Chancellor, John Smith, a sober Presbyterian lawyer, sat down with them for reassuring lunch after reassuring lunch. The precise details of their conversations remain a secret between gentlemen. But the gist of what flowed from Smith's side of the table is easy to guess: please don't be beastly to us if we win.

What the rebel Neil Kinnock would have denounced as a foul betrayal was dignified by the leader Neil Kinnock with the use of a special vocabulary. Its key terms included 'responsible', 'practical' and, so often that it made you want to puke, 'prudent'. A Labour government's putative relationship with the City (and other capitalist vested interests) was defined as 'a partnership'. Rather than sour the City's prospects, Labour would seek to sweeten them.

Kinnock's spectacular change of mind on the economy informed every element of Labour policy in 1992. There was, though, one big problem. Unfortunately, Kinnock didn't understand economics. At least, to be accurate, he didn't understand them sufficiently well to make it *look* as if he understood them when people who understood nothing about them watched him discuss economics on television. His response to this had been twofold. On the one hand, he left it to John Smith to do the talking about economics whenever possible. On the other, he tried to fix things so that when he could not avoid going on television looking as if he didn't understand economics it wouldn't be quite so obvious. This required Kinnock to execute perhaps his most testing metamorphosis of all: he would have to pretend that he was no longer Neil Kinnock and try to convince everyone that he was a completely different person: Britain's Next Prime Minister. If he pulled it off, people might stop listening to what he was actually saying.

It was a high-risk strategy which the Tories were already mocking, and evidence of its failings were manifest in the response

Labour's leader made to Norman Lamont's big denial. The difficulty was he had made the mistake – a worrying one for a Labour Party leader – of believing the Tory press. They had feverishly forecast a cut in the basic rate of income tax by one or two pence in the pound, and it was clear that Britain's Next Prime Minister had composed a provisional speech with the repudiation of such a cut in mind. But though a cut had come, it had been made at a craftily oblique angle. Adapting a script at such very short notice would have been tough for anyone, let alone a man who always looked as if he didn't really understand economics. Britain's Next Prime Minister made the best of it:

'What we needed was a budget for strengthening Britain and for promoting sustainable recovery out of the recession caused by the government. What we got was a budget to try and bribe voters with borrowed money that they're going to have to repay.'

What Neil Kinnock would once have called sound demand management, Britain's Next Prime Minister called bribery. And never mind that his accusation was justified. Unfortunately, there was a good chance that plenty of voters would put up with it. And part of the reason was that, when they looked closely at Britain's Next Prime Minister denouncing Norman Lamont for doing something Labour approved of, they thought they still saw Neil Kinnock.

People's objections to the Labour leader were of two types. The cruel irony for Kinnock was that the more he confronted one, the more credence he gave to the other. Type one was based on the belief that, despite his protestations to the contrary, Kinnock's break with the party's left wing was just a devious little ploy to woo votes, and that if he ever became Prime Minister, the screaming red would reappear. Type two held that Kinnock's conversion was authentic, so leading them to the conclusion that he was a faintheart, willing to shed his principles overnight. Whichever view was subscribed to, the upshot was the same: the man earnestly genuflecting to the voters in the garb of Britain's Next Prime Minister could not be relied upon. Neither explanation was entirely correct, nor entirely wrong. Perversely, a more accurate picture of Kinnock could be obtained by combining the elements of truth that lay in both. What emerged was an underlying strand of consistency: Kinnock was desperate to *win*.

Throughout his political career, Kinnock had been a gut pragmatist with a demagogic streak. Despite his former reputation as a maverick, he had been a Labour Party machine man all his adult life. As the child of socialist parents, (born in Tredegar to Gordon Kinnock and Mary Howells, a district nurse), as part of an extended family whose male line had all worked in the South Wales coal mines, as a Labour activist in the tightly knit pit villages, as a teacher with the Workers' Educational Association and then as an MP first elected at the unusually young age of twenty-seven, he had acquired a powerful intimacy with the part of the party that he knew. He understood and shared the scorn and suspicion felt among his own people about the rich and the posh. He knew how to speak to such sentiments from public platforms, not just in South Wales but throughout Britain, in church halls and working men's clubs. That was his cog in the Labour machine and he made it work brilliantly. Though he had been to university, he had not cultivated his philosophies very much. His were the politics of grudge and glory, of machismo and of class – real tough-boy stuff. His two-fisted rhetoric to converted audiences made him into a grass roots star. He loved the applause that he could win so readily. He loved the power his popularity gave him. Like any ambitious politician, he wanted more.

In 1979, after James Callaghan's defeat, Kinnock was offered a shadow cabinet job and accepted like a shot. For someone who had hounded the leadership so vociferously before, his haste in accepting its patronage seemed indecent to others on the left. And within a year he was defending the leadership's decision not to promise full restoration of the new Thatcher government's education spending cuts. Within two years, he was writing a violent attack in *Tribune* magazine, the journal of the parliamentary left, on its main figurehead, Tony Benn, for standing against the incumbent Denis Healey for the deputy leadership. Kinnock claimed Benn was making promises a Labour government could not hope to keep. Within three years Kinnock was describing Peter Tatchell, the gay left-winger due to fight a by-election in Bermondsey, as a 'fairy'; within four, he had succeeded Callaghan's own successor, Michael Foot, as Labour leader after the party

had died a terrible death in the 1983 election. At the party
conference that year, the scene of his triumph, he made his
inaugural speech. His theme was that a return to 'common sense
and realism' was the only way to win. In terms of policy Neil
Kinnock had stood on his hands, started walking to the right and
never stopped to look back. In terms of personality, he remained
consistent. He wanted to win, win, win, no matter what it took.

Looking back, there could be no doubting the force of
Kinnock's will. The Labour Party of 1992, taking its last, deep
breath before plunging into the election fray, was very much his
creation. Labour had become very different in organization, in
ideology and in style, from what it had been ten years ago. And
each aspect of this transformation reflected a crucial part of who
Neil Kinnock was. The changes in organization had made the
party highly centralized, with most of its muscle concentrated on
Kinnock himself, his shadow cabinet and the close team of
personal advisors he had appointed: Kinnock was a man who
liked to be in charge. The changes in ideology had been made in
response to what voters said they wanted, to the exclusion of
what they might, in the longer term, be persuaded to want:
Kinnock was a man who cherished approval and had no time for
fancy ideas. The changes in style were to make the party look
smooth and powerful: Kinnock was a man who wanted to be
Britain's Next Prime Minister.

Authority's Experts applauded these reforms. Their verdict
was that the removal of many old policies had made Labour
'moderate'. True, being 'moderate' had not been enough to beat
Margaret Thatcher in 1987, but Labour had made up ground after
starting the campaign way behind. The defeat's silver lining,
Authority's Experts decreed, was revealed in the party's management and presentation. These had helped Labour look 'professional'. In all, the benefits of Kinnock's work were pronounced
unchallengeable: 'moderate' plus 'professional' equalled 'electable'. And on the night of the Chancellor's big denial the finding
of an ICM opinion poll to be published in the next day's *Guardian*,
was that Labour lay three percentage points ahead of the Conservatives, a rating much in line with what such polls had been saying
for months. The 20 per cent tax band ploy had caused embarrassment, but, even so, past elections had shown that the challenging

party usually made ground on the government in the course of the campaign. Surely, this time, Neil Kinnock, would prove that all his fighting and fixing, all the strain and sacrifice had been worthwhile. Surely now the man posing as Britain's Next Prime Minister might turn into the real thing.

At lunchtime the following day, Nice John Major walked out of 10 Downing Street and stood before a microphone set up on the pavement. There had been a lot of opening and closing of the black iron security gates, a lot of peering through exhaust fumes for the policeman in overalls. A stream of journalists had passed through an X-ray machine and taken their places beneath a blue canopy opposite where Nice John stood. He had an announcement to make. Though too far away for us onlookers and sopping foreign tourists to hear what he was saying, the pocket transistor radio conveyed his words live. Nice John had visited Queen Elizabeth, who lived just up the road. He had gone to request her permission to dissolve Parliament and call a general election on 9 April. Happily, she had agreed. For Neil Kinnock, vindication beckoned. He was Britain's Next Prime Minister. He'd show them.

CHAPTER THREE

The Great Erasure

(Thursday 12, Friday 13 March)

Reaching the International Press Centre in Holborn for Labour's campaign launch was a test of patience, a strain on the nerves and a trial for the conscience. Another rush-hour bomb scare produced a further round of commuter grumbles and commuter fear. Two weeks previously, the IRA had bombed London Bridge station. Several people had been injured and a lavatory blown to bits. How long till the trains started rolling again? Was there really a bomb? Would it go off? How would my children cope at my funeral? Once released into the tube system, we were challenged to avert our gaze from recent, ubiquitous additions to the panoply of London spectacle. Whey-faced youngsters with skeletal dogs held out their hands for spare change. At Chancery Lane, a less diffident example of the homeless touted the *Big Issue* magazine, wearing an official vendor's bib and shouting, 'Helping homeless people help themselves!' The penetrative powers of the enterprise culture had, it seemed, no limit.

By the porch of the IPC entrance stood a television outside broadcast van and a loose platoon of police. One of them checked my credentials. At intervals London taxis pulled up, issuing a succession of men in raincoats with their ears pressed to mobile phones. The actor and film producer Colin Welland arrived, a great, grizzly man with enormous hair, rolling along in a blouson. Next up, the chalk to Welland's cheese, Gerald Kaufman, the shadow Foreign Secretary, a trim, balding figure, neatly belted in beige gaberdine. 'Good morning, gentlemen,' he said to the police, a Mekon greeting Earth security. Another policeman checked my credentials, followed by a plain-clothes goon. The

IRA, it seemed, would be almost as happy to exterminate Her Majesty's Opposition as they would Her Majesty's Government.

Up the escalator and into a large reception hall, where a technician with a stapler was having problems with an 'h'. It was a small, black 'h' and it refused to take its place in the word 'change' which concluded the slogan 'It's Time for a Change', displayed on a wide, dove-grey backdrop set up at the rear of a low platform. A campaign cliché, but a potentially potent one after three Conservative governments in a row. The image of a recalcitrant 'h', though, symbolized the biggest challenge facing Labour. Until Thatcher, voters who dropped their 'h's were the most loyal to the Labour cause. Thatcher had disturbed that habit in converting some of them, in particular skilled manual workers, known in adlandspeak as C2s. Thanks to her, many such people, especially in the south-east of England, had bought their own houses and health insurance, private pensions and Telecom shares.[1] Their lives were better as a result. Who could blame them for being grateful?

Labour had to woo these people back, and with falling property prices and rising unemployment menacing precisely these sacred Thatcher disciples, they had every reason for optimism. Given that the entire trajectory of the Labour regime under Britain's Next Prime Minister had been to satisfy such people that a Labour government wouldn't deprive them of the gains they had made, this was just as well. Indeed, the logic of Labour's policy position could virtually be reduced to a matter of raw arithmetic: they had to seduce back the former Labour voters who lived in the ninety-four most marginal Conservative-held parliamentary constituencies where Labour had finished second in 1987 – a total of around 500,000 people. Their return to the fold would end the Conservatives' control of the House of Commons, give Labour a majority of one and reflect a national 'swing' from the Tories to Labour of 8 per cent. A campaign fund of around £7 million would, therefore, be deployed to persuade just over 2.5 million out of 32 million voters that their booty would be safer in

[1]. Nationally, about 44 per cent of working-class homeowners voted Conservative in 1987, and only 31 per cent voted Labour. Since 1979, 2.5 million families had joined the ranks of those living in private homes and 5 million people owned shares.

future if they helped Britain's Next Prime Minister hump his
suitcase through the door of Number 10. As for the 8 million
who had not done so well, including the 10 per cent of the total
adult population whose disposable income was less than half the
national average and so fell below the European Community's
definition of the poverty line, well, they mostly either voted
Labour anyway or didn't vote at all. In other words, Thatcher's
losers were not the top priority except insofar as their existence
provided raw material for the odd burst of sanctimony about Tory
selfishness. And even that was less effective since the removal of
Margaret Thatcher because, of course, John Major was 'nice'.

Even more bizarre was the industrial relations background
against which these manoeuvres had taken place. Neutralizing the
trade union movement had been fundamental to the Conservatives' success in elevating the lifestyles of some 'h'-droppers and
paralysing the prospects of the rest. It had helped to ensure that
workers in the health service, in BT and in local government
services, had been either unwilling or unable to resist the Conservative tide of cuts and privatization. The Labour Party had originally been formed to represent in Parliament the labour
movement, of which trade unions were the core. The great bulk
of Labour's funds are donated by unionized workers via their
union executives. So now trade union funds would be used to
help the Labour Party quell the fears of the labouring people who
had gone upmarket thanks to the party which had engineered the
unions' demise. It did not lessen the incongruity that about a third
of trade union members appear to vote Conservative; or that
Labour's association with the trade unions had become such an
embarrassment to them that they blushed every time a Tory
mentioned it.

The IPC press conference showcased Labour's dual strategy
for circumventing these little difficulties: looking good on television, and not rocking the boat. Since it is far better to look good
on television than to look naff, the former emphasis was, in itself,
unarguable. The combined audience for the BBC's two evening
news bulletins, at six and nine o'clock, is 14.6 million, while that
for ITN's two is more than 12 million. A snappy sentence
delivered on any one of these programmes may be consumed by

two-fifths of the electorate. And if the politician looks good, it tends to ameliorate any hostile response from the viewer to what he or she has to say. This presentational objective was complemented by the substance of what Labour's leading lights were saying, things which, in the stock terminology of Britain's Next Prime Minister, sounded 'responsible', 'practical' and 'prudent'. Again, it could all be encapsulated in the unwritten maxim of Authority's Experts: 'moderate' plus 'professional' equals 'electable'.

The entire scene in the IPC hall was an elaborate homage to this rationale. Lined up before the stage where the technician fought with the 'h' were several rows of seats. On them, consulting notebooks, sat about fifty people, mainly men, like casting directors awaiting an audition. Collectively, these were what are insincerely described as the gentlemen of the press. Further back, amid coils of cable and a jungle of hardware, the television cameras stood, ready to roll. At the front of the stage, matching the dove-grey backdrop, stood a mock-Romanesque panelled buttress with a built-in lectern and a microphone mounting. The show was about to begin.

On to the handsome construction stepped a warm-up man. Normally, warm-up men dish out soft one-liners to get the audience in the mood for fun, but this particular house had not come to enjoy themselves – indeed, most were there for the preordained purpose of bad-mouthing the performers – and the warm-up man restricted himself to announcing the order of events. First, indicating to his left, he introduced a group of 'celebrities' who had come to endorse Labour. A dozen photographers pounced as the names of the 'celebrities' were read out: Helena Kennedy, QC, the noted barrister, and Anthony Scrivener, QC, former chair of the Bar Council, both sudden recipients of this stratospheric status; the magnificent Colin Welland, his rump splurging off the edges of his seat; actors Antony Sher, Carmen Munroe and Michael Cashman; and the authors Penelope Leach and Ken Follett. Obediently they sat, pretending not to be posing for the photographers who surrounded them, snapping frantically, as if they had stumbled on a troupe of fairground freaks.

The shadow cabinet would join us shortly, the warm-up man continued, indicating now to his right. Bang on cue, in filed a row of dark, double-breasted suits, every one adorned with a red rose buttonhole. Inside each suit was a politician: John Smith, sober, bald, bespectacled; Gordon Brown, the shadow Trade and Industry Secretary, jowly, solid, dark; Tony Blair, the shadow Employment Secretary, hair sprouting, mouth scooped into an excited grin; Robin Cook, 'the garden gnome' as he was unkindly called, Labour's quick and ruthless shadow Health Secretary; Gerald Kaufman, epicene, trim, ready to suck the enemy's insides out; Roy Hattersley, Deputy Leader and shadow Home Secretary, huge-headed and pale. Only three of the suits broke the rigorous, temporate colour-code, and they belonged to the women: Anne Taylor (shadow Water Minister, mauve); Harriet Harman (shadow Health Minister, lime); and Margaret Beckett (shadow Chief Secretary, emerald and azure). These were new model Labour women. Their suits said, 'I-mean-business', while their colour preferences said, 'I-am-feminine-too'. Votes, votes, lovely votes. Then finally, pride of place, in walked Britain's Next Prime Minister himself.

Britain's Next Prime Minister had his own special fascination when taking public platforms. No matter how much gravitas he struggled to project, as Authority's Experts said he should, no matter how hard he tried to look calm and statesmanlike, Neil Kinnock refused to be erased. He was there in the walk, a rolling, splay-footed, rugger-bugger swagger. He was there in the no-necked, iron-shouldered torso that spoke of scrummages disfigured by uppercuts. He was there in the mouth that grinned too quickly, in the puckering folds beneath the gleaming cheeks and the full swell of the pate. A generous cartoonist could have portrayed him as one of those scrubbed boy mascots who carry pennants for football teams. A malicious cartoonist might have drawn a glistening phallus suppressing the urge to ejaculate.

The Master of Ceremonies was Dr John Cunningham, 'Jack' as he was demotically known. Cunningham had presided over a post-budget press conference the previous day where his style had been well illustrated. His Cumbrian vowels oozing glutinously, like fondant icing from a pâtissier's nozzle, he had announced to the cameras and the party-pooper press: 'Many of you will have seen in today's papers, our advertisement highlighting the tragic story of a little girl, Georgina Norris . . .'

He had held up an example of the ad, delicately, painstakingly, like a surgeon displaying a spleen. Then he had read out the text: '"Georgina Norris died because the NHS is short of money. Meanwhile the Tories are cutting taxes to keep their election hopes alive" . . .'

The NHS was one of the things Margaret Thatcher was perceived as having damaged. Labour was anxious to show, by contrast, how very much they cared. They even had a dead child to prove it.

Now Cunningham introduced 'Britain's Next Prime Minister, Neil Kinnock'.

Britain's Next Prime Minister! Such confidence! Neil Kinnock rose and slipped straight into the mannered locutions of his alter ego. Mastering this had meant filing down the sharp edges of his hell-raiser's rasp and ironing out the undulations of his mining-valley rhetoric to leave a leavened, almost melancholy baritone less likely to disturb the ambience of life in a British sitting room. Neil Kinnock had really worked at this shit, no one could deny him that.

'Ladies and gentlemen, we shall fight and win this election with a first-class team for government, with strong policies to serve the interests of our country . . .'

Because so many people thought they could still see Neil Kinnock lurking inside Britain's Next Prime Minister's clothes, it was always wise to mention 'the team': clever Mr Smith, Mr Blair, Mr Brown and the rest. And, of course, it was 'our country', meaning everyone's. Britain's Next Prime Minister would not encourage sectarian punch-ups. He was for 'classlessness' too.

'. . . In this election, the British people will be choosing between Labour, which will back British industry, and the Conservatives, who have turned their back on British industry . . .'

Patriotism. Business-friendliness.

'. . . The people will be choosing between Labour, which will strengthen and modernize the National Health Service, and the Tories who are privatizing the National Health Service.'

The trump card. The Conservatives were making major organizational reforms in the NHS, which included introducing an element of localized competition for hospital resources. 'Privatization' was the buzz word, and a contentious one. Its very mention in the health context sent the political temperature soaring. The government insisted its use was a wilful misrepresentation. Labour knew it put voters on edge. They would be making the most of that.

Britain's Next Prime Minister continued, pointing out the soaring crime rate, the falling school standards, pausing here and there as if to marshal his fortitude while the sorry tale unfolded, before cataloguing the rises in poverty and unemployment and despairing at the waste of £100 billion worth of North Sea oil revenues and the huge government takings from selling off formerly state-run industries. With the charge sheet enumerated, the alternatives were set out. All the unpopular things would be got rid of. All the things that had gratified those 500,000 turncoat voters in ninety-four Conservative marginal seats – or ninety-five, if you threw in the City of London – and which Labour had once opposed, were not mentioned. Nor was the trade union movement. So at the end of the address, after Britain's Next Prime Minister had solemnly intoned 'it is time for Labour', and after Welland and Sher, Scrivener and Kennedy, Cashman and Leach had raised a decorous celebrity cheer, one of the journalists mentioned it for him. It wasn't even a proper question, just a great huff of historical halitosis blown in the face of Britain's Next Prime Minister:

'What about the Winter of Discontent?'

The inquiry turned the spotlight on a more subliminal part of Labour's pitch to the electorate: the wholesale disowning of its own past. Evidence of this had been strewn through the list of objectives Britain's Next Prime Minister had just read out: evidence of omission. Labour's attitude to its yesterdays was like the advice a parent gives to a child with a nasty rash: don't scratch, you'll only make it worse. History, alas, responds less readily to benign neglect.

The Winter of Discontent is widely held to have been both

the immediate cause of Labour's capitulation in 1979 and also emblematic of why it had ceased to be 'electable'. The term describes a string of acrimonious strikes in both public and private sectors effectively in the wake of the Callaghan government's measures to satisfy the IMF's loan terms. In 1975 wage restraint had already been sought through a voluntary agreement with union leaders, whereby they would not seek to negotiate increases exceeding £6 a week, and in 1978 the government's pay policy forbade companies awarding increases of more than 5 per cent a year. But the result, as inflation, taxation and unemployment rose together, had been a clear drop in living standards.[2] By January and February 1979, snow lay on the ground and all agreements fell apart as car assemblers, lorry and tanker drivers, workers in the health service and local government, perhaps sensing that the worst of the crisis was over, struck for more. The demonization of trade unions and, by extension, the contention that Labour could not control them, began with a vengeance from this time.

Labour had had to contend with this propaganda ever since. They did so by acquiescing in it. Britain's Next Prime Minister dodged the journalist's question by invoking the 'new' Labour instead. His would be a government of 'consensus, partnership and consultation'. There would be 'no special favours' offered to any interest group. But had a dozen years of such evasions been quite so necessary? Had the will been there to do it, Labour could have made a decent defence of its last period in power. For a start its crisis had been mild in comparison to the one under the 1970-74 Conservative government, when a three-day week and a State of Emergency was declared and the NUM, calling the government's bluff, helped lever Edward Heath from power. Despite inheriting the torment of the oil price rise and the hangover of Heath's own manufactured boom – the so-called 'dash for growth' – the Callaghan government had presided over unemployment which, at its very worst, was not much more than a quarter of that created in Thatcher's first term, and less than a third of that in 1992. At a high of £9 billion, the national debt, even allowing for inflation, looked quite respectable compared to the £28 billion Chancellor Lamont was now ready to sustain. And, most tellingly

2. About £7 a week for an average family. Peter Jenkins, *Mrs Thatcher's Revolution*, Pan, 1987, p. 17.

of all, average economic growth had been higher over the period from 1974 to 1979 than since. Even the IMF loan had brought short-term benefits, as foreign investment, feeling safe from socialism, poured in and the pound rose like a barrage balloon.

Labour's real difficulty with defending its record was, then, largely to do with image. The problem with borrowing from the IMF (as opposed to foreign banks) was that mighty, independent Britain was seen to be holding out a begging bowl – in the Glorious Past theme park, Britannia begs from no one.[3] But you couldn't talk about such things and look 'electable' on television because out of the archives would come footage of the Winter of Discontent, the uncollected rubbish and pickets outside hospital gates, not to mention the invincibly ignorant jibes of the Tory in the next seat. And even if you got the chance to make a case for the 1974–9 administration, or others before it, the voters might get bored and watch *Taggart* or *Through the Keyhole* instead. Labour had cut its losses on that front long ago. Far better now to wear a red rose in your buttonhole, drone soothingly on about 'partnership', and run the risk of Britain's Next Prime Minister looking like a conman, a hypocrite, or both.

And yet there was more to Neil Kinnock than either the opportunist his detractors spied, or the authoritarian, small-'c' conservative who shared so many values with working-class Tories. There was an aspect of him which, in the interests of becoming 'electable', he had doggedly suppressed along with the raw-knuckled polemic. Its absence from the repertoire of Britain's Next Prime Minister did little to alleviate suspicions about the Neil Kinnock who performed it. There is a Welsh expression which, although Kinnock does not speak the language, seems to define the principle it springs from: *chware teg*. It means 'fair play'. The Labour leader had few opportunities to reveal this part of

3. In the end, the IMF was a softer option than it might have been. The government's alternative was to heed the left and go for a so-called 'siege' economy, which would mean import controls and big defence cuts. The Americans didn't much fancy that at all, and so, as prime movers in the IMF, helped negotiate terms which were less stringent than they might have been. See Burk and Cairncross, *Goodbye Great Britain: The 1976 IMF Crisis*, Yale 1992.

himself in the quest to lure back the affluent 'h'-droppers. But on Friday 13 March he was presented with one at the Meadowbank Stadium in Edinburgh where the annual conference of the Labour Party in Scotland was being held.

In Scotland there were few of the problems Labour confronted in London and the south-east of England. The party held forty-eight out of the seventy-two Scottish seats, compared to the Conservatives' meagre nine. Margaret Thatcher's regime had been about as welcome north of the border as a fox in a chicken coop. Pivotal heavy industries had been decimated. The poll tax had been introduced there a year before the rest of Britain, making anti-Tory Scots feel reduced to the status of guinea pigs and long to bloody Thatcher's English toffee-nose. Even as they remained weak overall, Labour had gathered strength in Scotland and only two of the crucial Tory marginals lay within its borders. In Scotland, more than anywhere except his native Wales (where the electoral balance was much the same as Scotland) Neil Kinnock could afford to be himself.

He arrived at the Meadowbank Stadium at ten minutes to three. The sports centre was an assassin's paradise compared to the IPC, but if Britain's Next Prime Minister felt exposed by the relative absence of Special Branch sharpshooters, he would have been comforted by the embrace of his Scottish hosts. In the foyer he waited on a small flight of steps, firmly clutching Glenys, once his student sweetheart, now Britain's Next Prime Minister's wife. A few goons and officials clustered round him – you cannot be Britain's Next Prime Minister without a surrounding cluster of goons and officials – including his press secretary, Julie Hall, beaming beatifically like an elf in a fairy ring. For a while everyone just stood there, rehearsing their smiles. At the bottom of the steps, a band of Scottish pipers in scallops of tartan pumped up their bags of wind. Next to them, hand-held television cameras bobbed on their operators' shoulders. Fluffy, cylindrical sound booms jutted gormlessly into the air.

Smile, bob, blow. Smile, bob, blow. Then suddenly, with a grunt and a wheeze, the pipers struck up a chest-beating marching tune. They moved off towards the main hall. The goons and officials hustled in behind them, holding back the cameras and the fluffy sound booms. A great scuffling of cheesy trainers ensued as the human legs on which the technology was mounted knocked into each other, travelling forwards, pointing backwards and pushing inwards to get closer to the resplendent couple who now tripped down the stairs, radiating glory. As the beat of the marching tune prospered, so Neil Kinnock began to burst from his disguise. There it was, the splay-footed swagger, the no-necked torso and the roll of the iron shoulders straining the seams of the double-breasted suit jacket. Powdered down it may have been, but his whole head became illuminated beneath the saturating white heat of the portable TV lights, and he strode into the stadium, his arm round Glenys's waist, hugging her close till she looked as if she might break. Stepping up to the lectern, he received the packed stadium's applause with the forgivable smirk of a man hopelessly in thrall to his gratitude. Then he did what he was best at. He made a speech:

'For the people of Scotland and the rest of Britain, a Labour government is just four weeks away . . . We should have had this election more than a year ago, when the poll tax empress was overthrown in a Tory palace putsch . . . They didn't have the courage or the honesty to go to the country then because they knew they would be defeated. And so they clung to power – "rulers" – in Shelley's words, "who neither see, nor feel, nor know but, leech-like, to their fainting country cling".'

It was easy to forget that Kinnock, though not a man of ideas, was a man of poetry. Revolutionary poetry! We were reminded of it now. And also that he was a man of humour. Quoting a friend, he said of Michael Heseltine: '. . . just because he's got long hair, doesn't mean he's clever . . .'

The audience laughed. John Sergeant, the BBC correspondent laughed. So did Neil Kinnock. It didn't seem to matter now if some people thought he was stupid. He could rise above the message on the Tory election posters that had been going up everywhere, including Edinburgh. The message simply read: 'You Can't Trust Labour', and the 'L' was depicted as a learner driver's plate. To hell with it.

'. . . If the Tories hadn't kept their lingering grip on power in this last futile year, the legislation for the Scottish parliament would be law by now . . .'

Here was the third big point of difference remaining between the two major parties. Tax and the economy was one, the health service was another, and the third was constitutional reform. Scotland had been disenfranchised under Thatcher. Labour would give it its own Parliament, its own powers to rule itself. Never mind that in 1979 the rebel Kinnock had opposed such plans for Scotland and for Wales the last time Labour had advocated them (ultimately falling to defeat in a referendum). That was conveniently forgotten. He was flying, head jutting, stepping back from the lectern like an exhibitionist at a urinal. He began to speak of fear:

'Nye Bevan wrote more than forty years ago that "there is no emotion more inhibiting than fear of the future".'

Aneurin Bevan had been Kinnock's idol, a Welsh Labour rebel of the forties, a fiery speaker and hard as nails. As Kinnock moved towards his peroration, he drove home the theme of fear and how Labour would free people from it, the fear of unemployment, of falling sick or losing a home. This was almost soap box language, the sound of the downtrodden talking back. It showed that Neil Kinnock possessed what Britain's Next Prime Minister lacked. He might be sentimental, he might even be foolish, but he had at least the look of *integrity*. It was unlikely we would see much more of it in the coming four weeks.

CHAPTER FOUR

John Major's Model World

(Saturday 14 March)

It was a dirty morning in Devon, but the two ladies on the station platform were spotlessly clean. They were also extremely watchful, as if loose talk could still cost lives. On the far side of the tracks, a policeman in a fluorescent yellow bib was looking under a bench. The ladies had noticed him already, as they awaited the connecting service from Newton Abbot to Torquay. They had also noticed a lone black holdall close by them, temporarily untended.

'We have our instructions,' chirruped one.

'Oh yes, we have our instructions,' confirmed the other, only half flippantly. She turned towards me, the guilty owner. 'I was just looking at this young man's bag . . .'

It is only a Tory lady who can refer to a thirty-four-year-old male as 'young man'. Similarly, when a middle-aged female is of obvious Tory commitment she somehow demands the courtly description 'lady' rather than the more robustly egalitarian 'woman'. All Tory females over the age of forty are 'ladies'. Below the age of forty, they are 'girls'.

The Tory ladies were excited. They were heading for a big occasion. John Major was going to address the Conservative Central Council meeting some time before lunch, though for security reasons nobody had yet been told precisely when. His speech would effectively launch the Conservatives' election campaign. There would be standing ovations. There might be bombs. It was a day for teasing up the swirl of your perm, for stepping into your floral skirt, for knotting your cashmere scarf around your neck, for slapping on lots of foundation and buffing the shine of your best black shoes, the ones with the little stubby heels that were ladylike and not too brash.

The train clattered into the station. Should a young man rush forward to open the door? Or would that be over-friendly? The ladies were convivial but not companionable. Their etiquette was practised and reassuring, but of the sort that sets firm limits on intimacy: 'Oh, a journalist . . . mm.' They took a seat a polite distance away and swapped anecdotes about envelope-stuffing, the procedures for getting security passes, what they had read in the *Daily Express*. The Conservative Party has always had a place for its 'ladies'. Though condescended to, they are revered and valued. Maybe this accounts for Labour's historic failure to secure more than a minority of women's votes.

Torquay was the next stop. We all alighted, the ladies with relief. The train was old and filthy.

'They clean them every day on the Continent, you know.'

Stepping out past the comely flowerbeds, the sort only stations like Torquay's provide, they linked up with another of their species, this one dressed in a fawn two-piece that lent stature to her shoulders and discipline to her knees. She had seen Michael Heseltine speaking the day before.

'He was marvellous,' she pronounced, then added, 'as usual', as if to say, 'Damn the man who murdered Margaret.' Heseltine's appeal to Tory ladies is a rakish force of nature. Perhaps they imagine his long hair flopping forward over their faces and him surging towards a conquering coition, as if completing a company takeover.

The Conservative Council meeting was taking place at the Riviera Centre, named as if in defiance of the glamour of the French. The access road was crammed with coaches, cops and an enormous queue. A helicopter tacked overhead. Below, the eager delegates buzzed:

'Heseltine was marvellous . . .'

'Damned BBC, what do you expect . . .'

'Some Pakistani going on about all the ethnic minorities swinging to the Conservatives . . .'

The last remark was made by a middle-aged man whose mean mouth and piggy eyes suggested the price paid for generations of

—

in-breeding. He addressed it to a flashing young blade leaning on a golf umbrella who, as he was clearly keen for all to know, had recently been elected to some desirable party post. The middle-aged man concluded his anecdote with a sneering imitation of a Pakistani accent. The flashing blade snorted appreciatively.

We shuffled forward to the first security checkpoint where bags were peered into and security passes checked. Those who had applied for them late and had to collect them on the day were accompanied by a gently sardonic policeman to an accreditation office at the side of the main building.

'We had Andrew Lloyd Webber wanting to come through yesterday. "Is this really necessary?" he said. My God, did he complain.'

In the accreditation office, we supplied passport photos, produced driving licences and were extremely helpful and polite. There would be at least a one-hour wait. Forty minutes passed. Then suddenly, outside, there was action. A knot of photographers had gathered, a handful of onlookers too, and before them stood a star, Chris Patten, the Party Chairman.

He had a very important job, Chairman Chris. Twenty-four hours a day, seven days a week, he concentrated all his talents on abusing, insulting, denigrating and generally heaping derision on Britain's Next Prime Minister. For weeks he had been demonstrating this destructive gift, cleverly avoiding interviewers' questions about the failures of Conservative policy and concluding his evasions with some subtly fashioned observation implying that Britain's Next Prime Minister was a loud-mouthed, simple-minded, two-faced oik. This behaviour had rather surprised the pale pink among Authority's Experts who had previously thought of this 'Chris' as rather fun, an amusing and civilized fellow, the sort of chap one could have round to dinner, where he would delight other guests by heaping cultivated scorn on Margaret Thatcher and all the other right-wing philistines who had taken over the Tory show.

All that began to change when Thatcher kept being re-elected. By 1989, the reconciliation was complete and Thatcher offered him a big cabinet job. Perhaps it was just a coincidence. Perhaps Chairman Chris really meant it when he said he had been changed by some of Thatcher's election-winning ways. Whatever, as

Secretary of State for the Environment he was soon milking the flock at the Conservative conference and telling his leader, sitting there at his side, gazing upwards approvingly like a school marm indulging a bright new prefect, how perfectly marvellous she was. Now Nice John Major had handed him the task of organizing his election offensive. And offensive was the word.

So there he was, Chairman Chris, in his voluminous raincoat, his lank hair flapping in the wind, chuckling and being in charge. His mission was to pose in front of one of those tent-shaped, mobile advertizing floats, which bore the latest Conservative slogan. It read: 'Which Way Is Labour Blowing Today?' On the top of it was mounted a red wind sock which billowed obediently. The message marked a variation on the established theme: beware of Neil Kinnock; he is loud-mouthed; he is two-faced. The photographers wanted Chairman Chris to do something, so he held up his hands as if he had just done something magnificent.

Then the onlookers, mostly Tory ladies, made a joke, a musical one: 'I'd walk a million miles,' they choroused, 'for one of your smiles, my Ma-a-a-amy!'

All Jolson, geddit? He was holding his hands up just like Al Jolson!

Chairman Chris turned to them, keeping the smile going, and began rapidly pivoting his wrists, so that his upraised hands shook. Even *more* like Al Jolson! The onlookers, the ladies especially, loved it! At that moment it occurred to me that I hadn't been fully security-checked. No X-ray, no body search, just a glance inside the holdall. Not even a security pass. A member of the IRA could have pulled a gun out of his or her sock and shot him where he stood. Conservative Chairman Murdered During Al Jolson Impression! An improper thought came and went as the Chairman continued to thrill his public, sounding distinctly posh, a lot more posh than when deriding Britain's Next Prime Minister on television, when he betrayed a dabbler's weakness for cockney rhyming slang, perhaps hoping it would impress hoi polloi.

'Now you know how it's done, haw, haw!'

Such an amusing chap.

★

Five minutes till noon, seated among special guests beside the Riviera Centre stage. Silence fell. Then music, a starburst, a cascade.

'It's Superman!' chortled a male guest to the right. 'I hope he hasn't got his tights twisted.'

Actually, it was Purcell à la Lloyd Webber, disco-bump symphonics. A door at the back edged open and out popped Nice John's glasses, followed closely by Nice John in his Marks and Spencer suit, his wife, the dainty Norma, and the amusing Chris Patten.

'I expected a touch of ermine on the collar with all this,' said a female guest to the left, pulling a face.

'All to sell a bit of double glazing,' said the male guest to the right.

The management of Nice John's entrance looked as if it was based on the passage of a champion boxer to the ring. The music worked its way up to a pumping climax as Nice John edged his way through the spectating throng which had risen, as one, in acclamation. The big difference was, of course, that boxers act all nasty.

Having had the hems of his garments touched, Nice John took his place on the platform containing a full house of big Tory nobs. It included Norman Lamont, who had already made a miserable speech, saying how it was quite all right for the party of sound money to have plunged Britain deeper into the red. Everybody had cheered. Then there was William Waldegrave, the well-bred Health Secretary. He had made a speech in which he described little Torquay as 'the very city where we speak'. Everybody had cheered again. Blockbuster author Jeffrey Archer was there too, the party's former Deputy Chairman. He had already been enlisted into the prime ministerial entourage because he was so full of wizard jokes. A story was circulating that, on registering at his hotel, Archer had sent his personal recipe for shepherd's pie to the kitchens, demanding that it was followed to the letter. This was not so very surprising. Far more unexpected, as ever, was that young Jeffrey was wearing long trousers.

Nice John advanced to the podium and gave his audience a long, hard look. He said: 'The phoney war is over. The Battle of Britain has begun.'

Click. The fairy lights carried on in the Glorious Past theme park. But on this occasion its focal point was, on the face of it, a relatively dowdy attraction. Of course, the traditional cardboard edifices were lauded and hyped, the usual self-delusions paraded in talk of 'an independent people in an independent Britain'. But if you squinted through the dry-ice of Pavlovian patriotism, something more substantial came into view: the neat lawns and ordered brickwork of John Major's Model World.

'I want to bring into being a different kind of country. Bury for ever old divisions in Britain – between north and south, blue collar and white collar, polytechnic and university . . . We want a country in which people get on because of what they are, not who they are.'

Margaret Thatcher had been put down by learned Labour types for being a suburban bigot. The noun was accurate enough but the adjective betrayed an anthropological mislocation. Thatcher's was the mean-mindedness of the hard stone, small town fortress, not that of the post-war, big city outspill. It is John Major who is suburban. And when he journeys through the past to find the future of his imagination, he has no need to travel as far as Queen Victoria or even Churchill. He alights instead in the years of his youth before bankruptcy beckoned. Major's vision of Britain sprang from suburban resentments and, yes, from suburban ideals – the sort he believed that were sullied by socialism.

'For most of my lifetime, before I came into Parliament . . . people were expected to be dependent . . . never, however hard they worked, never independent, never in control of their own lives or their families' future . . .'

For most of his lifetime, but not all of it. Of course, government still interfered till the ration-book era was over. But then came boom time. Building sites blossomed on the metropolitan perimeters and their wider orbit. The shell-shocked survivors of Hitler's assaults set out from the broken centre to join other settlers in a greener, safer, new life beyond. It was a quiet, comfortable, decent life; a private, fastidious life, where ordinary folk could make something of themselves without anyone poking a nose in.

'We're pushing choice back to the people, because we want all of them – every single person in Britain – to have greater control over their lives and their families' future. To be the masters, not the servants, of their personal world. That's my Conservatism. To our fellow citizens I give this pledge: when the next Conservative government has completed its work, you will feel, more than you've ever felt before, that Britain belongs to you, and that you have a secure place within it. But there is one area above all in which we trust the people. To do what they wish with the money they earn, to have and to hold – for themselves and their children – a growing piece of their country which they can call their own . . .'

Sweet music this, a nineties reprise of an old reconstruction tune. A hymn to gardens with hedges, a hymn to the joys of shopping after years of shortage. More than that, a hymn to social civility.

'When I became Prime Minister, I said I wanted a nation at ease with itself. That means a government that people believe is fair. To be fair, isn't it right that those most in need should be helped most? That's the British instinct . . .'

That was a fig leaf to cover the real reason for the Chancellor's 20 pence tax band stunt, but the sort you could get away with under the prevailing economic 'common sense'.

'So how would Labour support schools? By taxing teachers. Help hospitals? By taxing nurses. Beat crime? By an assault on the pay packets of the police. It's a lunatic strategy by prejudice out of ignorance. All founded on the bogus claim that in order to build tomorrow, you need to rob today . . .'

These were the sentiments of yesterday's suburban sitting room, where conversation might be closeted, but was lit up with dreams of better things; where more tax meant waiting longer before the old, utility furniture could be replaced by something better, something smarter, something *new*; where luxury was buying your first television set and watching the coronation of Queen Elizabeth, just as John Major's own family had done in 1953. And though it was yours, all yours, and nobody else's, you could still, on special occasions, invite the neighbours in to share it, just as the Majors did, with young John politely offering everyone cups of hot English tea.[1] Those were the days of hope

1. Bruce Anderson, *John Major – The Making of The Prime Minister*, Fourth Estate, 1991, pp. 203–5.

and aspiration, before the social engineers took over. Why not revive the spirit of the best of them?

'In education, we will go back to basics and make sure they're properly taught. Where parents want them we'll open the way to grant maintained schools, free of council control . . . And, something else, there's a lasting affection throughout the land for many of our historic and familiar counties and cities. That's why we're asking the public's views on how local government should be structured, everywhere . . .'

As its name suggests, John Major's Model World prizes the idea of miniaturization. It was a signature of his premiership to convey a sense of scaling things down. It made sense for two reasons: one, because it created a clear break with Thatcher's heavy metal posturing, the difference between The Seekers and Def Leppard; two, because it simply suited his natural gifts. The concept first became apparent in Nice John's oratory. His debut conference speech as leader had been billed as 'a fireside chat' with party and nation, and it had worked out pretty well. He couldn't boast and hector like Thatcher. When he tried to shout he sounded like an angry nerd in Woolworths returning a faulty toaster. Instead, he spoke gently, and cultivated a Nice John smile.

A distaste for undue grandeur had also marked his behaviour during the Gulf War, his first big foreign affairs test as Prime Minister. Prompted by the invasion of the totalitarian state of Kuwait by the neighbouring fascist state of Iraq, the war had seen the mobilization in the Middle East of probably the most terrifying army in world history. The motivation for it was officially defined as the defence of freedom. Unofficially, it was prompted by the West's fear of losing a strategic ally and access to a cheap source of oil. Though ostensibly conducted through the United Nations, the main force of the counter-invasion was provided by the United States. Britain, as ever, came adoringly to heel behind America's President Bush, whose government, for years before, had been assiduously helping the Iraqi president, Saddam Hussein, to arm himself to the teeth. To mention this, however, was simply not the form. The Allies duly slaughtered the Iraqi army, shredded thousands of Iraqi citizens, restored the totalitarian regime of Kuwait, spared the fascist regime of Iraq and claimed a victory for freedom. Oil? Why it never crossed their minds. Nice

John had succeeded Thatcher during the build-up to the war.
When it was over, he paid a visit to the British troops in the Gulf.
Where his predecessor would have flexed like a body builder in
the heat of reflected glory, Nice John made a maidenly speech of
thanks, sitting neatly on a tank. In his bottom-warming fawn
sweater and casual summer slacks, he looked like the Airfix Boy
Modeller of the Year enjoying the star prize.

The notion of cutting bigness down to size also informed the
Citizen's Charter, vaunted as Major's Big Idea, though it was
perhaps appropriate that critics thought it rather small. The goals
of the Citizen's Charter were consistent with the mores of John
Major's Model World. In it, bigness was denounced in the public
sector services, with what Nice John described in his speech as its
'arrogant bureaucracy'. Just as 'classlessness', though misnamed,
struck a blow against snobbery, so the Citizen's Charter pur-
ported to cut Big Brother down to size. The sovereign suburban-
ite would not be talked down to in John Major's Model World.

And so he moved on to his crescendo. He spun home truths
about inflation ('We all know what it means to walk into the
supermarket and see that the price of a pint of milk or a loaf of
bread has gone up . . .'), denied he was going to privatize the
NHS, pledged himself to defend the United Kingdom against the
threat of devolution and, with a final obligatory flail of the flag,
trotted out the regulation claptrap about how Margaret Thatcher
had liberated Eastern Europe, waving a bunch of Cruise missiles
in one hand and a Visa card in the other.

The latter was just hot air for the home crowd to get high on,
to scintillate the in-bred toffs, the flashing blades and the adoring
Tory ladies who all leapt to their feet at the close of the speech
and craned their necks as Nice John, his glasses and his Marks and
Spencer suit worked their passage to an exit through a sea of
loving hands. It had all worked wonderfully. 'We'll get 'em,
John,' shouted a delegate, reaching through the ruckus to press
the premier's flesh before turning to a friend. 'There's a man of
steel behind those glasses! Fancy a cup of tea?' But it was the
distinctive Model World stuff that really mattered to the campaign, launched directly at those parts where the building sites
had flourished in the late forties and fifties, where the earliest
British television sets had taken pride of place in the corners of

immaculate, paid for, front rooms; places where working-class people had headed because they didn't want to be touching their forelocks or 'taking charity', or putting up with poverty, theirs or anyone else's, any more. Of course, back then, they'd mostly voted Labour.

Outside the Riviera Centre, an elderly toff twosome reflected on Major's performance. 'Of course,' boomed the gentleman to the lady at his side, 'there isn't the thrill of seeing leaders in the flesh now they're on television all the time. I remember being taken to see George V at Epsom races . . .'

But John Major, unlike Margaret Thatcher, was not out to borrow the clothes of pomp and mystique. With his plain fellow's empathy and boomtime recollections, he was out to steal Labour's cast-offs instead.

CHAPTER FIVE

The Beautiful Dreamer

(Saturday 14 March)

Paddy Ashdown is often described as a romantic outsider. In the clubby context of Westminster politics it is not a bad description, though you would have been forgiven for thinking it eccentric if the sight of the Liberal Democrats' leader tramping glumly through a Crewkerne car park had been your first. With the collar of his countryman's Barbour raincoat turned up, and his normally Nikon-seeking chin tucked down, Ashdown looked anything but a glamorous lone gun. Rather, he was just the leading actor in a scene of a minor political tragedy set in a miasma of sullen rain. The problem was quite obvious: Paddy Ashdown just wasn't being important enough that day.

Becoming more important was the crucial condition for Ashdown's political vindication, rather than the other way round. Plenty of Liberal Democrats were exercising power in local councils all over Britain. Plenty of people, more than 40 per cent, said they would vote Liberal Democrat in general elections if they thought the party had a serious chance of winning. But that was the big 'if' for the long, lean, outlaw plodding past smeary ranks of Cavaliers and Fiestas. In 1987 over 20 per cent had voted for the Alliance – a united electoral front between the old Liberal Party and the Social Democratic Party, which had subsequently merged into the new party Ashdown now led – and yet the Alliance had been rewarded with only 22 parliamentary seats out of 650. This meagre return, barely one quarter of the Conservatives' majority, was the reason Paddy Ashdown was not terribly important. When he stood up in the House of Commons to enter the big debates, Labour and Conservative Members of Parliament got up and left. Why stay? Whatever Ashdown said would make little difference to them.

Trudge, trudge, trudge. Out of the car park and into the rec. It wasn't as though Ashdown was alone in wishing he could be more important. So too did the motley entourage which followed him, trailing along untidily, like nursery toys pulled by invisible strings. The entourage comprised a handful of earnest supporters in an assortment of tweed caps and yachting anoraks who turned out to be Liberal Democrat local councillors; a woman reporter from the *Mail on Sunday* and a male reporter from the *Sunday Times*; two mobile television camera crews, one from the satellite channel BSkyB, the other from the BBC; and finally, trotting dutifully behind her husband, Ashdown's wife Jane, who knew more about the tribulations of being assigned to Paddy than anyone.

All concerned had long realized that nothing of much use would emerge from their jaunt round Somerset, which had been going on all day. True, soon enough, from Sundays to Fridays, it would be rip-roaring, non-stop activity as Ashdown embarked on what looked on paper like an impossible schedule of campaign travel, designed to showcase the crusading outrider of British politics as he burned up the freedom trail. But Saturdays were reserved for him to quietly tend this West Country patch, his rural Yeovil constituency with its 5700 majority. Normally, he enjoyed the job. But with the reporters and the camera crews dogging his footsteps it was as if the Messiah had come to town only to find that no one needed saving.

Trudge, trudge, trudge.

'Woo-ah!'

'Ooo-er!'

'Look 'oo's here!'

A scattering of young men, filed along the touchline, turned from the football match they were watching to plant upon Paddy Ashdown a damp slap of recognition. The legs under the television cameras scurried into position. Ashdown, having no choice, lifted his warrior's chin and swallow-dived into the void.

'Hello! Good to see you!'

There was a technique at work here. First, pick out just one nearby person, definitely not any of those cheeky herberts who had now started poking fun at your yellow rosette because its colour – sunrise yellow – was not that of the Crewkerne team. Second, be noisily familiar with your target voter, thereby imposing your domination on unpromising surroundings. Third, escape as quickly as possible. Ashdown executed the exercise like a true pro. As ever, military metaphors leapt to mind: another ambush coolly survived; another sortie successfully flown. The political satirists' exploitation of Ashdown's armed service background underlined its value to him in his present career – if they hadn't bothered to do it, it would have meant he wasn't being noticed at all. A former Royal Marine commando, Ashdown had attained the rank of captain and seen active service in Northern Ireland and Borneo. Both the epithet and the endeavour had stuck. Now he was 'Captain Paddy' or 'Action Man' and would be till the day of celestial demobilization and, depending on how important he had managed to become in the meantime, beyond.

The soccer spectators subdued, Ashdown repaired to the viewing porch in front of the wooden clubhouse. For a short while he stood quite alone. What was he thinking? Was he, perhaps, wondering what the lads down on the touchline were chuckling about? It would have been a miracle, lads being lads, if they hadn't dredged up a wisecrack or two about Ashdown's unwelcome elevation to the stratosphere of 'sexiness' a few weeks before.

'It's Paddy Pantsdown!' the *Sun* had roared, red-nosed with delight. Nightmares, nightmares, nightmares. For days, the story had been hurtling through the grapevine of the Fleet Street diaspora until, finally, on 5 February, it had broken cover and run, pink and screaming, into the daylight. Everybody stared. Everybody's eyes popped out as they read the dynamite news that six years ago, before he had become the Liberal Democrats' leader, but while he was already an MP, Ashdown, the clean-limbed, square-jawed Paddy Ashdown, had had a secret fling with his secretary. Briefly but brutally lampooned like a crimson-bummed philanderer in a naughty seaside postcard, he had learned in those few days what a terrible difference there could be between being important and just being the centre of attention.

The scandal had been humiliating for Ashdown, but he had

handled it with the dignity expected of the officer class. He hadn't bad-mouthed the former secretary, Patricia Howard. It seemed that he and Jane, who had found out long ago, had managed to make their peace. Though he had taken out an injunction to postpone the story's publication, once it broke he held his hand up like a gent. Ashdown's conduct surely accounted for his rating as a potential Prime Minister soaring by 13 per cent in an opinion poll published the following weekend. It may partly explain why the Liberal Democrats' poll standing also rose a fraction – from 13 to 15 – in the story's aftermath.[1] But a more likely and sobering explanation was that a few people had simply remembered they existed. Moreover, the discrepancy in the increase between Ashdown's personal score and that of his party added to doubts about the relationship between recognition and credibility. A big part of Ashdown's task since securing the leadership of his party had been trying to bury the reputation the old Liberals (of whom he had been a member) had laboured under as a gang of fringe exotics destined not to rule but to entertain. With his eyes-front moral posture and his craggy good looks, Captain Paddy had been doing rather well. Then his whole life had become a peep show. It wasn't fair.

Trudge, trudge, trudge. Into the clubhouse went Ashdown and fell into conversation with a beleaguered local builder wearing a shell suit and a golfing tam. The suffering of builders was the clearest rebuttal of the government's mendacious whine that Britain's problems were primarily an expression of the 'world recession'. What could be more domestic than the slump in the property trade? There was no demand for new houses to be built or for structural improvements to existing ones. The builder's family firm had a cash flow blockage and no work. What would Ashdown do if he was running the show?

There followed another of democracy's little cameos, a set-piece at the interface of politician and punter. The builder, slightly awed but fighting it, related his tale of woe in a complaining West Country burr. It was the big companies for whom he sub-contracted that were the greatest bugbear – they took ages paying their bills. Ashdown, his answer primed and ready, cocked his

1. NOP poll for the *Independent on Sunday*, 9 February 1992.

chin with mannered interest before reciting the party line on housing investment, renovation and repair. This he did in the same tone he used in television interviews and debates. It would be wrong to describe it as a regimental bark. Ashdown had always professed his dislike for his soldierly caricature, and you sensed that efforts had been made to cleanse its timbres. But they lingered. In his short. Sharp sentences. And in his air. Of command. It was the voice of a leader who had concluded that it was no use just giving orders. They had to be delivered in a way the lower ranks understood.

The builder absorbed Ashdown's crisp address without flinching and offered a not unduly deferential response. Of course, he had always voted Conservative before, but he was thinking he 'might go Liberal' this time. The Liberal Democrats didn't like being called 'the Liberals', not simply because the name was incorrect[2] but because they wanted to seem fresh and new. Ashdown, having no choice, let it pass and signed off in his habitual way: 'Thank you, my friend. I must be going.' And off he went.

Thank you, my friend. Labour people called each other, albeit increasingly discreetly, 'comrade' and electors, 'the people'. Conservatives addressed clan gatherings as 'ladies and gentlemen'. With Liberal Democrats it was always, 'my friend' or 'friends'. The practice signposted the Liberal Democrats' enthusiasm for the localization of power, to devolving it from the centre in the belief – very much in the old Liberal Party tradition – that it rehumanized political communication. Ashdown's tempering of his natural briskness when speaking to ordinary folk was a manifestation of this. Where the builder was concerned it seemed to have worked:

'I like him. He's a good bloke. He'll say hello to you in the street, but he don't know me from Adam.'

Perhaps it had not sunk in with the builder that Ashdown, in the way of politicians, will say 'hello' to anyone. But that is not to doubt that the Liberal Democrats were earnest in their dedication to a society of increased friendliness. It was, though, in many ways, a friendliness dependent on deference to a strengthened chain of command.

2. The original, unmerged Liberal Party still existed and fielded several candidates in the election.

At his speech to his party's annual conference the previous September, Ashdown had summarized the Liberal Democrats' priorities with the catch-all 'the five "E"s': the Economy; Europe; Education; the Environment; Electoral reform. Together, these delineated a policy package aimed at, as their campaign slogan had it, 'Changing Britain For Good'.

On the economy, their cry was 'private enterprise and public investment'. It was a position which endorsed the 'enterprise culture' championed by Margaret Thatcher, but insisted there should be more of it while, at the same time, its supposed benefits should be channelled for the general good as well as the individual's. The supposition was that privatization and the crushing of the unions had been of value, but the full rewards would only be reaped if more money was spent on common infrastructure – public transport, environmental improvements and so on – and if employees were given a stake in their employers' future in the form of shares and profit-related pay. However, wage bargaining would be conducted increasingly within individual firms, rather than on national, trade-based lines. Such arrangements would clearly break up union bargaining power still more. The presumption, then, was that bosses and workers could be better friends. But only the bosses were more in command than ever.

On Europe, the Liberal Democrats were the cheerleaders of British politics. Their position contrasted markedly with that of the Conservatives and of Labour. One of the first things Margaret Thatcher did as Prime Minister was to argue with the EC's other member nations about how much money Britain contributed to it – in the Glorious Past theme park, no shifty foreigners took liberties with Britannia's dosh. Neil Kinnock, meanwhile, had pulled off a dazzling reverse flip. Before the 1975 referendum on whether or not Britain should remain a Euro-partner, he had campaigned against it. Now, as Britain's Next Prime Minister, he was in favour, though what precisely he was in favour of was difficult to divine. With the Liberal Democrats it was easy: they wanted to move to a 'federal' structure, ceding some British government powers to Euro HQ in Brussels in the name of greater cooperation and, they argued, a correspondingly broader diffusion of power to the European regions. Also, they wanted to adopt a single European currency, managed by an 'independent'

European Central Bank. In other words, we should all understand that shifty foreigners could be our friends in a shared European economy. But unelected Euro-bankers would make most of the vital decisions.

There was, then, the seed of a contradiction in the Liberal Democrats' formulation of these two big 'E's: a contradiction between the decentralization and the concentration of power. The main beneficiaries of the latter appeared to be managers, bosses and bankers. The idea that comparable gains for citizens, workers and consumers would flow outwards and downwards from such concentrations depended on a belief that a common interest existed; that what managers, bosses and bankers regarded as wisdom coincided with the citizens', workers' and consumers' definition. If they did not, decentralization would hardly help them challenge the wisdoms of those at the top. Under such circumstances, friendliness might suddenly become a diminishing resource.

The Liberal Democrat policies in education and environment seemed equally predicated on the existence of a growing sense of common purpose. Education was to be a campaign centrepiece. The Liberal Democrats were pledged to put a penny on the basic rate of income tax in order to broaden and improve it, convinced that the public was united in its readiness to make a sacrifice in pursuit of a learning investment. Concern for the environment, meanwhile, was an old Liberal speciality, but it was an issue which had increasingly seized the public imagination. Like world peace and Mother Theresa, protecting the environment was something everyone could say they were in favour of. The Liberal Democrats would pursue it with a combination of market incentives and tax penalties, consistent with their mantra: 'private enterprise *and* public investment.'

These first four 'E's were advanced in the belief that the fault lines along which British society had for so long been split were now either filled in or healed, while the mystical nationalism that had united much of it against the world beyond was on the wane: that employees and employers were tired of fighting and wanted to work together; that British xenophobia towards Frogs and Dagos and Krauts was fading fast; that the traditional anti-

intellectual prejudice was a thing of the past; that heavy industrialists and litter louts alike might see the perils of pollution for
themselves as well as others. The Liberal Democrats' programme
was predicated on a belief that the old Britain of class warfare and
jingoism, of ignorance and filth was on its last legs. Only the
inception of the fifth 'E' would ensure its extinction and replacement with Ashdown's new and better Britain.

This fifth 'E' would be at the heart of the Beautiful Dreamer's
sales pitch to the nation. The nub of his proposal was that the
voting system should change from first-past-the-post to Proportional Representation (PR), specifically a form of it known as the
Single Transferable Vote (STV), though the Liberal Democrats
preferred to call what they were advocating by the snappy and
more emotive term 'fair votes'. Under PR, the mathematics of
constituency representation would change. At present only one
MP was elected for each seat, the one who got the most votes. It
didn't matter if he or she got less than half the total votes cast, as
was frequently the case, which meant that most of the constituents
were represented by a politician they didn't want. A variation of
this anomaly was echoed in the House of Commons itself. For
example, although a majority of MPs since 1979 had been
Conservatives, the proportion of the total votes cast throughout
the country for Conservative candidates had never topped 44 per
cent.

By contrast, under PR with the STV, the numbers of MPs
elected from the different parties would more closely represent
the relative proportions of the votes cast in each constituency –
which would be themselves reorganized so they were fewer and
larger – and, by extension, the country as a whole. It would also
ensure that no single party would form a majority, and so be
licensed to do pretty much what they liked, unless they got about
50 per cent of the total national vote. The effect of this in the
House of Commons would be enormous. In order for legislation
to be enacted, MPs from different parties would have to get
together and negotiate coalitions and pacts: an arrangement
which, compared to shouting insults across the green padded
benches, was infinitely more friendly, in Liberal Democrat theory
at least.

Sceptics, though, took the view that the fifth Liberal Demo-

crat 'E' might be taken to stand for something else as well as
electoral reform: Entering the Enclaves of Importance, for
instance. And in this, the Liberal Democrats' desire for 'fair
votes' coincided very nicely with their own self-interest. The
problem with their share of the vote was that it was too evenly
spread. Put bluntly, Liberal Democrat candidates seemed
certain to re-live the disappointments of the Alliance candidates
before them by coming second all over the place but having
nothing much to show for it. The 1983 election had been the
cruellest example. Then, the Alliance had taken 25.4 per cent of
the total vote, compared to Labour's 27.6 per cent, yet Labour's
share was so distributed as to give them 209 MPs and the
Alliance a miserable 23. Only in the south-west of England and
in the rural parts of Scotland did the 'third party' enjoy
sufficiently strong concentrations of support – much of it
related to religious Nonconformism – to win seats with
consistency.

     The Liberal Democrats, then, were in a no-win situation:
without 'fair votes' they were screwed, and as long as they were
screwed they wouldn't get 'fair votes'. The injustice provided fuel
for the motor of moral indignation with which they reproached
the deep unfriendliness of the Conservatives and Labour. But the
justification for its prominence lay also in a more clinical calculation based on the evenness of the strengths of the two big parties
as they entered the brutish fray of Election '92.

     With metronomic consistency the opinion polls had been
repeating the same refrain for months: Labour just ahead, Conservatives a fraction behind. On BBC television, the lanky cult
presenter Peter Snow had demonstrated in a whirr of computer
graphics how such figures would most likely translate into
parliamentary seats. Labour would have the most, but only just:
not enough to form the twenty-seat majority Britain's Next
Prime Minister was predicting. The outcome would be a 'hung
Parliament'. It would leave both big parties with the option of
forming a government only by striking a deal with MPs from the
various smaller parties who usually won around 45 seats between
them. These would include several of different flavours from
Northern Ireland and some Welsh and Scottish Nationalists. But
the biggest group of all would be the Liberal Democrats. What

would John Major or Neil Kinnock have to do to secure Ashdown's support? The Liberal Democrat leader, the masterful moral crusader, had already spelled out his central term: if you can't commit yourself to introducing Proportional Representation, 'don't even bother picking up the phone'.

There were two ways of interpreting that: either as a fearless blow for friendliness, or as a threat to attain importance by extortion.

A strange kind of rebel, Paddy Ashdown. After leaving the army, hardly a hotbed of unconventional thinking, he worked for the British government at the United Nations in Geneva. Ostensibly he was employed by the Foreign Office, though his true employer was the Secret Intelligence Service, MI6, who commissioned him, according to GQ magazine, to 'spy on the Soviet and other Eastern bloc delegations, and possibly the Chinese'.[3] Ashdown didn't sue. His involvement in domestic party politics (as opposed to any other kind) began during his Geneva tenure when he wrote to the Yeovil Liberal Party, putting his talents at their disposal. He duly won the seat for them in 1983. Previously, he has said, his sympathies lay with Labour, but he had no taste for its institutional compact with the unions. You couldn't fight a war with the squaddies crowding the officers' mess.

A great one for hierarchy, this champion of accountability. During the previous summer, the increasingly routine spectacle of inner-city riots had briefly dominated the nation's TV screens. In Newcastle, Oxford and Cardiff youths threw bricks and policemen ducked. Equally predictably, Labour and Conservative politicians stepped into studios to denounce delinquency and praise the boys in blue. Soon after, at the Liberal Democrat conference, in the bar of a Bournemouth hotel, I asked Ashdown if he agreed that such comment was motivated more by the demands of public relations than a desire to diagnose a burgeoning problem of which the police themselves, facing a crisis of public confidence, might be a part. He replied: 'I know from my time in Northern Ireland that first and foremost, you must maintain the

3. Issue of April 1992, profile by Annika Savill.

rule of law. Without that, nothing can be done.' Authority knows best.

Much the same ethos had informed Ashdown's stewardship of his party since he became its first leader in 1988. The 1987 Alliance campaign had been a débâcle. The respective leaders of its component partners, David Steel (Liberal) and David Owen (SDP), had advanced a joint platform so rickety it collapsed amid showers of splinters. Ashdown eventually rose from the ruins of an intensely destructive merger, defeating his fellow former Liberal Alan Beith in an rancorous leadership contest. During it, a document was circulated by anonymous opponents, including Liberal MPs, claiming that Ashdown was all charisma and no content. Whatever the justice of that, the Liberal Democrats' election campaign was undoubtedly going to have a different dynamic to that of the Alliance the last time round. It would be all about one handsome fellow and his vision: Paddy Ashdown, the man of principle, the man who would rise above the bickering of 'the two old parties', the man who would lead the way. The man of sex appeal, too. It would be the most purely presidential approach to obtaining power British politics had ever seen.

Trudge, trudge, trudge. Ashdown had had enough. Without so much as a 'cheerio' he stomped off to his car, Jane scurrying gamely in tow. Off they went to their cottage in Norton-sub-Hambdon, with its pine kitchen cabinets and traditional thick-cut marmalade, its spacious English garden and spotless velour sofas. Later, in Yeovil, Ashdown and his wife were due to be the star guests at a local theatre production of *The Sound of Music*. A conservative maverick indeed.

The journalists took refuge in the nearest pub where the landlord and his wife told a long tale of woe about the bad local lads, how night after night they raced their cars into the town square and made lunatic handbrake turns, and who, when they weren't doing that, were down the back alley breaking windows. Paddy Ashdown? Oh, a conscientious MP. But he couldn't do much, could he? And things would only get worse now Mrs Thatcher had gone: 'Margaret,' the landlord sighed, 'did some of the things that needed to be done.'

The woman from the *Mail on Sunday* and the man from the *Sunday Times* rang their offices to say there was no Ashdown story today. It was Nice John who had made the headlines in Torquay. He'd had a few rude things to say about PR. 'Paddy's Roundabout', he'd called it. Later, the remark was reported on BBC radio news. Following on, the presenter said: 'And we're going over, live now, to Paddy Ashdown, speaking from his home in Somerset.'

Undiminished by the static of the telephone link, the voice was chiding, long-suffering, demonstrative in its sorrow.

'The Prime Minister really cannot leave us stranded in the constitutional dark ages . . .'

A few seconds in the healing glow of the national spotlight had brought Ashdown back to life. The message was unmistakable: trust me. I'm honest. I'm strong. Please make me important too.

CHAPTER SIX

Socialist
Surrealist

(Sunday 15 March)

T aking a morning bath at his terraced house in Cricklewood was a politician who refuses to obey. His disobedience, which at times seems almost congenital, had made him a pariah in the eyes of Britain's Next Prime Minister, his ire fuelled by the knowledge that the bathing politician considered his policies useless and his methods 'Stalinist'.[1] Recalcitrance, however, can bring rewards as well as obloquy in British public life, as the bathing politician is aware. The trick is to elevate it into a style. Ken Livingstone's is to proffer neat iconoclasm in a syrup of insouciance, to articulate socialist conviction – the stuff Labour no longer mentions – as sweet reason itself. In this way, he has inoculated himself against the worst poison of his critics and, further, become a star. For some, celebrity status and socialist rigour cannot go together. But if Livingstone was less adept at squaring this purist's circle, the views of those few survivors on the left wing of the Parliamentary Labour Party would hardly be heard at all. Such was the hegemony of 'electability' under Britain's Next Prime Minister's iron rule. To breach it, you had to become notorious first.

The disclosure of Livingstone's attention to personal hygiene was made by the woman who is *not* his live-in girlfriend, or his common-law wife, but, because this was a properly egalitarian household, by his *partner*. She made it verbally, via the bathroom window, from which her head appeared in a thick halo of steam. Shortly, she opened the front door, wearing a blue towelling dressing gown and a smile. It was the smile of someone who thought being got out of the bath by a journalist on Sunday

1. Quoted in the *Guardian*, 24 March 1990.

morning was more funny than embarrassing. Norma Major, you suspect, would not have felt the same way. In the sitting room, a mug of coffee was produced: fresh, real coffee, a bit luxurious. But this was not the domicile of a Bollinger Bolshevik. The riches it contained primarily took the form of video films and books, the latter not just the dour, leftist tracts of the popular rightist imagination. For example: David Gentleman's *London*; Halliwell's *Film Guide*; a big, pictorial study of Africa; an illustrated Kama Sutra. Livingstone is a man of catholic interests.

An insistent drone began to filter through the ceiling from upstairs. In fact, a drone duet. One part was the low buzz of an electric shaver. The second was Livingstone's voice, a famously insistent vehicle for irony served through the sinuses. And soon Britain's most urbane carrier of the socialist threat had taken his place on the sofa opposite.

'Agents refer to candidates as the legal necessity,' he observed, blithely, fiddling with his necktie. 'I just do exactly what I'm told during elections, which makes a nice change, because the rest of the time I don't do anything I'm told.'

If by so acknowledging his own legend Livingstone betrayed a streak of vanity, he is probably entitled to it, if only because it is a legend based on substance. Any lurking suspicions that becoming an MP would see him abandon the unflappably impudent radicalism that made him famous during his leadership of the Greater London Council from 1981 to 1986, had quickly disappeared with his first speech to the Commons after winning his Brent East seat in 1987. The convention is to contrive something bland and obsequious, an oratorical touch of the forelock to the establishment you've just joined. Livingstone preferred to claim that Margaret Thatcher's rise to the Tory leadership had been personally managed by an enemy of the state. It didn't add to his popularity that the object of his allegation, Airey Neave, MP, had been blown up by a car bomb planted by the Irish National Liberation Army, a renegade offshoot of the IRA, shortly before Thatcher became Prime Minister.

What kind of a man, all guardians of decency cried, would say a thing like that? Their affronted emotionalism engulfed the inconvenient rationality of Livingstone's case. Neave had previously enjoyed a long career with MI6, and maintained his contacts with the secret world after becoming an MP. During the early seventies, a clique of desperadoes working for MI5, MI6's domestic counterpart, had plotted to overthrow Harold Wilson's Labour government.[2] Much of this treasonable activity had taken the form of smears and disinformation planted in the press and coordinated from Northern Ireland with the assistance of Colin Wallace, an army intelligence officer. After Wallace left the army (and before Thatcher's election), Neave requested and received Wallace's assistance in continuing this work for him, concentrating his efforts on the Labour left-winger Tony Benn who Neave feared might succeed James Callaghan as Prime Minister.[3]

How had Neave known what Wallace had been up to on MI5's behalf? The question begs the answer that Neave had known about the Wilson plot, perhaps more than just a little. Was it possible that Neave's clandestine activities, which continued up until his death, remained unknown to Thatcher during a five-year period in which he had organized her campaign to replace Edward Heath, had headed her private office, had spoken for her on Northern Ireland, and advised her on intelligence matters? Livingstone's implication was clearly that she could not have been ignorant of them.[4] Margaret Thatcher herself refused to answer such questions. Meanwhile, the Labour Party leadership resolutely declined to ask them. To Livingstone, their queasiness was pathetic. The explanation, though, is simple enough. Being 'electable' requires displays of patriotic unction before the pillars of the state, and never mind what murk is concealed behind them. Ken Livingstone, by contrast, has no time for creeping deference to such totems of the Glorious Past. The version of Britain in which he resides, intellectually as well as physically, is exemplified instead by the north-west London constituency he had risen from his Sunday morning bath to defend.

Brent East is not a perfect microcosm of the London whose greater favour it was vital for Labour to secure, but in important respects it comes close. Over 40 per cent of its voters own their

---

2. Documented in fine detail by David Leigh in *The Wilson Plot*, Mandarin, 1988.
3. Documented in *Who Framed Colin Wallace?* by Paul Foot, Macmillan, 1989.
4. *Livingstone's Labour*, Unwin Hyman, 1989, especially pp. 58–68.

own homes and more than half fall into the social category C1: broadly, the lower middle-class. Mixed into this, around 30 per cent are Black or Asian, and unemployment runs at over 15 per cent. There are eighty-four seats in the Greater London area. As Election '92 approached, fifty-eight were held by Conservatives, two by Social Democrats and one by a Liberal Democrat. Labour had to appropriate about twenty-one of these to form a majority government. They also had to hang on to a few marginals of their own, where the factors which militated most strongly against Labour in the capital were strong: firstly, the effect of inner city gentrification, whose exponents often leaned to the right; secondly, resentment against Labour local councils; thirdly, the failure by the poor to pay the poll tax, which meant likely Labour voters disappearing from the electoral roll. Brent East is just such a seat. And Livingstone had only won it five years earlier by the nerve-jangling margin of 1653 votes.

But London constituencies rarely conform to any constant archetype. In the metropolitan mind Kilburn, at the heart of Brent East, is inextricably linked with the London-Irish. Indeed, the link goes beyond the mere commonality of nationality or roots. It is, for example, quite possible to attend concerts in Kilburn's pubs or clubs where buckets are put before you with a request to donate money in memory of the IRA volunteer Bobby Sands who starved himself to death in Long Kesh prison in 1981. Livingstone himself owes part of his reputation to a particularly contentious connection he later made with the nasty little war across the Irish Sea. In July 1983 he received a visit from Gerry Adams, the newly elected MP for Belfast West and the President of Sinn Fein, the IRA's counterpart in the political realm. He justified the invitation by insisting that the British would have to withdraw from Ireland eventually, and to do so they would need Adams's help. Why not enlist it immediately? The *Sun* had already been moved to dub Livingstone 'The Most Odious Man In Britain' for his refusal to accept the received definition that the IRA were purely and simply criminals. There is no greater tribute to the visibility this earned him than his present-day role as that same paper's token red menace columnist.

Irish-related matters of a more workaday kind had to be tackled at Livingstone's first appointment of the day at a hostel and community centre called Cricklewood Homeless Concern. His role turned out to be that of mediator in a frank exchange of views between an outraged London-Irish woman called Mary (representing the hostel) and a hunter-killer Conservative Brent borough councillor called Carol (representing the Wrath of Thatcher). The hostel's primary function was to provide temporary accommodation for men, mostly Irish, who had nowhere else to go. Kilburn is richly endowed with such people, some having crossed the water in the vain search for work, others, one way or another, having simply fallen by a bleary wayside of destitution and drink. Part of its funding came from the government of the Irish Republic, another part from Brent. The latter, it was rumoured, had decided to withdraw its grant. And so the stage was set for another local skirmish in the ongoing jihad between financial supply and social demand.

Livingstone took a ringside seat and made church steeples with his fingers as the protagonists went at it hammer and tongs. Decoded and paraphrased, Mary's contention was that the Tory group, enjoying a precarious hold on council power and making the most of it, were a bunch of tight-fisted shysters who put accountancy before compassion. Likewise condensed, Carol's position was that the hostel was an ill-managed bastion of hand-wringing liberalism caught napping in the fresh air of efficiency. As a handful of local reporters took cover, Mary uttered dark allegations about how such grants were allocated: wasn't it true that one had been awarded to a new charity which just happened to be fronted by the Conservative council leader, and, what's more, it hadn't even tendered in the proper way? Carol retorted by suggesting that those the hostel served weren't all Brent poll tax payers and that, by the way, her administration had reduced the level of that tax. Turning to the press she threw out her arms like a magician's assistant and said: 'Isn't that absolutely *wonderful*?'

At this point Livingstone raised a tentative finger to speak. Cameras clicked. Biros were poised above notepads. 'Red Ken' could always be banked on for a tasty little quote. He did not disappoint. But first, he conciliated. Having learned his trade in it, he knew that local government is a cocktail of chaos and penury, responsive only to the more creative kinds of political will. Was it true that the grant was actually to be reduced rather than completely removed? It was, Carol confirmed. Were redundancies imminent? Not quite, Mary replied. All right, said Livingstone, soothingly. It seemed a bit of a waste to be closing the place when it had only been going a year. A big event, the opening, with Cardinal Hume and everything. Anyway, he wasn't impressed with the new Brent administration and not by any means out of party loyalty.

'I said the last Labour lot were a load of rubbish . . .' In fact he'd likened their reign to the regime of Pol Pot. '. . . and I think this Conservative one is a load of rubbish too.'

Nice one. A great scratching of biro on paper. Livingstone proposed a solution. He would write to Albert Reynolds, the new Irish Prime Minister, to see if he could stump up a few more punts. Meanwhile, Brent would have to reconsider.

He urged Carol, who protested a basic sympathy, to step out of line: 'I don't pay much attention to my Whips and it hasn't done me any harm. You'll sleep more happily at night if you do what you think is right.'

Duly appeased, everyone made to depart. Outside, Carol waved gaily to Livingstone as she homed in on her car, a flash of short skirt, blonde highlights and I-mean-business black tights.

'Well, at least she's a character,' said Livingstone wryly.

Hands-on experience of the sheer, engulfing torpor of the inner-city meltdown has accustomed Livingstone to encounters with zealots and eccentrics. He knows that big-league local government often boils down to the outlandish surviving the unmanageable. Government grants evaporate. Populations shift. People drift from despair into madness and walk the streets conversing with themselves. Livingstone is one of the very few Labour politicians who continues publicly to recognize the existence of a British working class. Yet he is almost alone in implicitly acknowledging its impossible diffuseness, its failure readily to fit the abstract definition accorded it by more deterministic comrades, not least some fellow members of the Campaign Group in the Parliamentary Labour Party, with its habit of resembling a shrivelled rump of diehard workerists and Little England romantics.

Off we went to meet this chaotic proletariat, with Livingstone's agent, Anne Harradine, driving the car. Our first engagement was with a drunk at a stop light. He got off the pavement

and offered his Carlsberg Special through the window. Round
the corner we parked and set off to a car boot sale, reputedly the
biggest in London. 'There's Ken Livingstone,' people whispered.
'Yes, that's him.'

Livingstone took up residence by the mobile kitchen, buying
bacon sandwiches all round: 'It's the one thing that makes all
vegetarians weaken, the smell of bacon frying.' He placed a
styrofoam cup of coffee on a grubby picnic table, together with a
bunch of official campaign leaflets from Labour HQ. He looked
around, musing contentedly, not exactly hyperactive in his pursuit of the Brent East vote. But then, he didn't need to be.
Everyone knows Red Ken. Within minutes he was communing
with the London-Irish again, though this time it was a pair of
ragged-trousered caricatures, straight out of Spike Milligan, one
of them wielding a murderous, three-pronged gardening tool:
wooden handle, blue metal trident and the words Made in
England bevelled on the socket. You don't see that around much
these days. Would Livingstone get the gardener's vote?

'Well, I don't ever vote, actually, you know.'

But if you did?

He scratched his stubble.

'Well, he might, you know, if anyone did.'

Livingstone didn't mind. He's big on both horticulture and
the human zoo, in fact natural history in general. His collection
of frogs and salamanders is one of the things that makes him
famous, especially since even his friends agree his persona is
faintly reptilian. Harriet Crawley, the Tory who pushed him so
close last time, described him as 'a charming snake'. Nor is she
the only one to make capital out of Livingstone's proximity (one
way or another), to his menagerie. On inspecting the entry by his
own address on the Brent East electoral roll, Livingstone had
discovered the name of Hyla Caerulea. The resident in question
was an Australian white tree frog, more familiarly known as
Norman. 'He's dead now,' reflected Livingstone matter-of-factly,
'but he's still eligible to vote.'

Norman had been registered by some anonymous prankster,
and it was easily done. The electoral roll is a shambles, not just
because of the poll tax and not just in Brent East. It is the Labour
vote that suffers most as a result, but Livingstone remained

confident of defeating his Conservative opponent Damian Green, a young television journalist who had worked on the business breakfast show, *Channel Four Daily*. Ms Crawley, by Livingstone's own admission, had been dynamic. She had also possessed novelty value, being unmarried and heavy with child. By comparison, Livingstone considered Green to be 'Ideal. An identikit Tory. You can be confident Damian won't get pregnant during the campaign. But I bet if you pinned him down and scoured him you'd find three sixes on his head.'

Britain's Next Prime Minister would never have been caught making a surreal wisecrack like that. To be 'electable' you had to express yourself in language of stultifying, evasive blandness, the type Britain's Next Prime Minister had vainly deployed on TV-am that morning in an effort to prevent his inquisitor David Frost from ferreting out Neil Kinnock. A piece in the *Sunday Times* had anticipated the contents of John Smith's forthcoming 'shadow budget'. The story was that Smith would propose to raise tax thresholds, the amount you can earn before you have to pay any tax. Frost asked Britain's Next Prime Minister to dismiss the report on the grounds that he had already criticized Norman Lamont for borrowing to finance tax cuts, and that a raise in thresholds amounted to the same thing. Neil Kinnock, grinning nervously on the pink house couch, said he didn't want to reveal what Smith was going to say the next day.

Frost, convivially disbelieving, persisted: 'All I'm saying is that increasing tax thresholds is a tax cut.'

Britain's Next Prime Minister replied: 'It certainly is. It's a reduction in taxes. That's certainly the case. That's a matter of fact, ah, but it's not incompatible, obviously, with the general principles we've laid down.'

'But it is a tax cut,' pressed Frost. 'You've said it's wrong to have a tax cut. You do still believe it's wrong to have tax cuts financed by borrowing?'

'Let me go through the principle again.'

'No, but that's all I'm asking.'

Britain's Next Prime Minister played an elaborate prolix-and-sub-clause defence:

'Since you ask about the general principle, I'll answer the question on the general principle. The case that we've made is that a government that will borrow for tax cuts, especially in the circumstances of an election, where its attempt to bribe is very blatant, is a government that is very careless of the public finances and the fortunes of this generation and the next generation. And so consequently, we've made the argument, that if borrowing there has to be, because of the depth of the recession, and because of the weakness in basic public services, then the strong emphasis, indeed, the total priority of any borrowing, must be on strengthening the health and education services, and in doing everything possible to encourage industry, and to get the recovery going. So that's the only basis on which we've accepted the idea, for instance, of the Conservatives leaving a £28 billion public sector borrowing requirement. None of that could, or should, be used for the purpose of cutting tax.'

Wind sock. Billowing wind sock. It was painful to watch Kinnock conforming so completely to the Conservatives' cruel caricature of him.

Frost rejoined with a confirming echo of the concluding sentence: 'None of it, for the purpose of cutting tax. So that's a clear answer on the question of cutting tax in terms of the thresholds. That's absolutely clear.'

It was also absolutely clear that the *Sunday Times* story was correct. Labour would be raising thresholds, which did indeed amount to 'a cut in taxes'. That was 'certainly the case'. That was 'a matter of fact'.

That Labour's leader was so implausible when close-questioned on television was, to say the least, unfortunate for a party so obsessed with its small screen image. It also gave cause for doubting the sincerity of Kinnock's bid to embarrass John Major during the previous Thursday's Prime Minister's Questions session in the House, by challenging him to a live TV debate. This traditional campaign *canard* had been set quacking at daybreak by Des Wilson, the Liberal Democrats' campaign director, on behalf of Paddy Ashdown. By mid-afternoon Labour were at it too, and it was ironic that Ken Livingstone led the chorus. His name had topped the draw which decides who quizzes the PM. After consultation with Kinnock's office – not a location with which he had enjoyed much intimate contact – it had been decided that

Livingstone should play the telly-joust card. Everyone knew that Major would never accept: to do so would give the appearance of sinking to his enemies' subordinate level. But this would enable Britain's Next Prime Minister the opportunity to cry 'chicken'.

'Totally contrived,' agreed Red Ken. But he had been happy to play his part in the farrago, since he approves of TV show-downs. He himself is extremely adroit at tele-communicating. A child of the mass-media age, his debating teeth were cut to sound-bite-shape and he has mastered the art of camera seduction. But that is not the only explanation for his plausibility on screen. Unlike Britain's Next Prime Minister, Livingstone was not in the business of apologizing. When such a politician emerges from the pack, it is surprising what can be achieved.

Livingstone's GLC leadership exemplified the difference between the use of modern communication techniques as a means to an end, and worshipping them as an end in themselves. For him, the point about hostile public opinion was not to service it, but to change it. So he went on television chat shows and witless radio phone-ins, not to excuse himself but to argue the case for whatever headline-making 'loony left' cause he was espousing and which, inevitably, Britain's Next Prime Minister found an embarrassing affront to his every conformist instinct: gay and lesbian rights; ethnic minority rights; Britain out of Ireland; no to nuclear weapons; cheap public transport on the rates. Not every-one was convinced, but no one was indifferent, and few were pleased to see the GLC's demise at government hands. For many Londoners the battle to save it, though doomed, provided the most exciting political time of their lives. Margaret Thatcher's decision to do away with it was, to a significant degree, the measure of Livingstone's success: Neil Kinnock she could easily deal with, but Red Ken had to go.

The GLC's abolition in 1986 removed the last institutional power base of the Labour left. The party leadership had already taken flight from the policies on which they fought the general election in 1983, a task made easier by the fact that half of that leadership hadn't believed in them anyway. The whole period of Michael Foot's leadership is one Britain's Next Prime Minister was desperate to avoid discussing, which is why David Frost chose to remind him about it:

'I guess you'd probably say Labour was unfit to govern in 1983.'

Difficult one. Inside Britain's Next Prime Minister's suit, Neil Kinnock squirmed. He was Michael Foot's personal friend and chosen political son.

'I worked for, and I wanted us to win the general election. I think that what our country went through after 1983, the inflation that came in the late eighties, the low growth, the underfunding of the health service, means that Britain would have been better off had we won the 1983 election.'

'Even with that crackpot programme?' wondered Frost. ' "The longest suicide note in history" as Gerald Kaufman [called it].'

'That's one of the descriptions.'

Dear, oh dear: nutmegged on the barbed wire of principle again. Frost went on to list the policies Labour had struck out since 1983: withdrawal from the EC, unilateral nuclear disarmament, import controls, price controls, nationalization, the repeal of Thatcher's anti-trade union laws. Neil Kinnock had supported all of them then. What did their rejection say about him today? The Labour leader burbled cringingly. Short of declaring he had been in error – which might at least have had the virtue of clarity – it was his only option. Even had he wished to, he was no longer in any position seriously to challenge the contention that the 1983 programme was all 'crackpot'. Squirming on his couch, Neil Kinnock – for by the end of the interview it was definitely he – appeared the personification of shabby equivocation. It was not very edifying.

If Ken Livingstone had been the Labour Party leader, David Frost would have had a quite different job on his hands; certainly if he had espoused the programme set down in 1989 in his book, *Livingstone's Labour*, with his customary powers of persuasion.[5] Large cuts in military spending, and increases in tax on the richest individuals and industries would have been proposed to finance a major programme of public works, in housing, hospitals, transport, roads and schools, hugely to increase the provision of education and training, and to revamp the domestic manufacturing sector; measures would have been proposed to curtail the

5. *Livingstone's Labour*, op cit, pp. 24–9.

departure of capital from the country at the City of London's whim; the renationalization of British Telecom would have been promised, along with a commitment to cable up Britain with the newest communications technology and a pledge that small (as opposed to institutional) shareholders in that industry would not lose out financially; no one earning less than £25,000 a year would be requested to pay more tax; Proportional Representation would be introduced; the pound would be devalued to improve the export performance; Britain would stay in the EC, since there was little to be gained by leaving, but withdraw from Northern Ireland; there would be a pledge to pursue full employment, not simply out of sentiment, but in the name of economic efficiency; Britain would cease to be America's aircraft carrier; the secret services would be subjected to democratic accountability. Perhaps David Frost would have described it all as 'crackpot'. If he had, Livingstone would have disagreed, and blithely proceeded to explain why.

Would anyone ever vote for such a programme? It has many similarities with the 'suicide note' of 1983, and Authority's Experts would not have the slightest hesitation in answering the question with a derisive 'no'. And yet Labour had fought that last pre-Kinnock election under handicaps which were not wholly synonymous with their policies. There were freak forces at work: the 'Falklands factor'; the destructive novelty value of the SDP; the tragic ineptitude of Michael Foot. More importantly, some of the policies represented the triumph of dogma not over 'common sense', but over the dreams of crucial Labour voters, and over the art of persuasion. An example of the former was the implicit refusal to acknowledge perfectly honourable working-class aspirations: many poorer people had always longed to own their own homes, yet Labour continued to oppose the sale of council houses. As for convincing a reluctant electorate of the need to end Britain's obsessive militarism in order to finance rebuilding its industries, or that combative unions were the effect, not the cause, of the decline of those industries, needed more than rhetoric. It needed the sustained deployment of sweet reason.

The Labour Party of the early eighties was in no state to provide it, as left and right gouged each other's eyes out. Kinnock was advertised as the soft-left compromise. He had turned out to be anything but. Where did that leave a man like Livingstone, with his impertinent perspicacity and popular charm? Having defied the party mainstream, he was punished by being voted off its National Executive Committee. He was marginalized and ostracized, reaching a wider public by sole virtue of his celebrity. Livingstone's own arrant mischievousness may account for part of this situation. More likely, he is simply the victim of Labour's spectacular loss of nerve. Whatever, it is an undeserved fate. For although Livingstone is a rogue, he has nerve, imagination, a vision for razing the Glorious Past and all the flair required for sharing it. The main protagonists of Election '92 offered nothing of the kind. By comparison with Red Ken, they were all just out for the count.

CHAPTER SEVEN

Small Change

(Monday 16 March)

An important morning for Paddy Ashdown. Better still, a morning for being important. Attaining importance in politics is a matter of projection as well as of action and, gathered in the Gladstone Room at the National Liberal Club in Whitehall Place, all the necessary apparatus was assembled: the top journalists, the ravenous cameras, the published statement of noble intentions that was the Liberal Democrats' election manifesto. Bliss, oh bliss. Second only to becoming the fulcrum of a finely-balanced Parliament, this, for Paddy Ashdown, was the closest thing to heaven.

Compared with Labour's celebrity launch – so soothing, so serene – the Liberal Democrats had contrived an ambience of burning intensity to befit their leader's elan. Terraced seating created the contours of an amphitheatre and, in its bowl, Ashdown and three lieutenants smouldered beneath the raging lights, impatient, determined, tense. Encasing them from above and from the sides, their stage set resembled a cockpit constructed from lightweight scaffolding, or recycled struts from a late-fifties magazine rack. The message was future-tech. Filing in, the journalists were handed copies of the manifesto, 'Changing Britain For Good'. The size and shape of an LP sleeve, it had the opulent look of an upgrade couturier's catalogue. Its star model gazed out from the cover, longingly surveying some beckoning horizon, in his eyes a lustrous vision, up his nose a nostril hair. The man who had slept with his secretary had redemption on his mind.

Coordinating events from the seething platform was Des Wilson, a force of nature and one tough boot. Wilson is not a politician but a professional campaigner. Born in New Zealand, he had come to England in 1960 to further his career as a journalist, but heard the call to crusade listening to John F. Kennedy's speeches on a transistor in his Earl's Court flat. He'd made his reputation as the first campaign director of Shelter, the housing action charity. Wilson's method was hard-bitten and hyperactive. He took charge of everything, starting early and working late. He learned how to handle television. He feared no one, and his irreverence was stupendous. He debated with Richard Crossman, Labour's august Minister of Housing, at an Oxford Union debate and won. He has a florid, chipmunk's face and a great, mad cackle of a laugh. His iconoclasm is irresistible. He is very good at his job.

Long a member of the Liberal Party, Wilson had never deferred to its upper crust. Show Wilson a body of complacent received opinion and his instinct is to bury his teeth in its behind. This explains his friendship with Ashdown, the glory boy outsider. Ashdown had appointed Wilson his campaign director and given him *carte blanche*. To ensure his independence further, Wilson declined to take a salary, so insulating himself against the more stately Liberal Democrats who didn't care for his style. In Crewkerne the previous Saturday, Ashdown had denied such people existed. He was lying. Plenty of Liberal Democrats found Wilson crass and overbearing. They included several MPs who did not feature in his campaign plan. Essentially, the next four weeks would be the 'Des and Paddy Show'.

After a few words from Lord Richard Holme, the Liberal Democrats' nob-in-chief, Ashdown rose, a man with a mission.

'Be warned – this manifesto may not be what you expect.'

Spot the sound bite, boxed up for transmission. Everyone present already knew what the manifesto would contain. Ashdown soared directly for the terrain he intended to fight from: the high moral ground, gazing down despairingly at his opponents kicking and gouging below.

'For forty years or more, Britain has lagged behind, trapped by old ideas, imprisoned in an out-of-date electoral system, held back by the two old parties . . .'

Journalists jotted, cameras clicked. A mobile phone began to ring.

'. . . so the first aim of this Liberal Democrat manifesto is clear. It is to break free from the past, to change Britain, and to do it for good.'

There was, of course, no applause. Ashdown's hope was for a more piecemeal appreciation in voters' living rooms later on ('that Paddy Ashdown seems a decent chap . . .').

The final address came from the fourth panel member, Alan Beith. Lacking his leader's lift-off capacity, but flapping resolutely, he took his turn at scaling the giddy heights of principle. 'We will tell the British people the truth, even if it is not comfortable . . .'

The Liberal Democrats would talk straight. Yes, they really would add a penny to income tax to finance education. Yes, they would borrow even more than Chancellor Lamont, though they would do so not for tax cuts but for investment. A Liberal Democrat government would put public money into education and infrastructure; at the same time it would break up private monopolies, British Telecom, for instance, to increase competition as the motor of industrial progress; they would grant the Bank of England independence from interfering governments pursuing crude self-interest; they would bring in devolution for Scotland, Wales and, later, the English regions; proportional representation would be introduced; they would reduce unemployment by 600,000 within two years. It was an adventurous programme which everyone knew would not be implemented, except, perhaps, for a tiny little portion if Paddy Ashdown became more important. There was only one way he was going to manage that, and it was the one thing Paddy Ashdown did not want to be frank about. Naturally, then, it was the subject of the first question from the floor: how could Ashdown say he preferred neither party to the other as a potential partner when Labour were non-committal on PR, but Major had emphatically ruled it out.

Ashdown adopted his tone of world-weary doggedness, as if to ask what else could be expected of these washed-out careerists: 'I have a feeling that what he says now will be wholly different to what he says in the lead up to a judgment day that he must be greatly fearing.'

Trust me. I'm honest. I'm strong.

The next question came from Anthony Bevins, political editor of *The Independent*. Bevins is a fine reporter and a bit of a cult figure. This is because he is prepared to be very rude to politicians. Glaring from behind his Elvis Costello glasses, Bevins was clearly annoyed. Where were the figures to go with these policies? What was it all going to cost? The Liberal Democrats' price list was only beginning to be circulated by aides.

'Oh, that's brilliant,' mocked Bevins. He wanted to go through the whole lot line by line. Wilson wasn't having that. Next!

A question about taxes. Would people stand for Ashdown putting them up?

'Let me tell you this,' began Ashdown. Normally, he would have then said 'my friend' but, in this context, it might have backfired. He continued instead, with an aching sadness caused, so it seemed, by working out what the budget reforms were worth: '. . . the Conservatives believe the British people will sell themselves for 30p a day . . .'

Ashdown insisted he believed no such thing. Trust me. I'm honest. I'm strong. Wilson closed the conference and Ashdown picked up his speech before striding off to make the best of this most important day.

Paddy Ashdown was still being important by lunchtime. Interviewed on BBC Radio 4's *The World at One* he banged home his message about the relatedness of the economy and the environment, the importance of education and, of course, how his was the only party that was telling the truth. An expert said his sums all added up and equalled a package that was quite redistributive overall. This guaranteed that the Tories, if they sensed Ashdown becoming too important, would go on and on and on about his plans to tax, tax, tax. But before that, they would do it to John Smith.

Smith's vaunted shadow budget was unveiled at two p.m. at the Institution of Civil Engineers, in a handsome building off Parliament Square, in a room lavishly lined with polished oak power-panelling and sumptuous plaster scrolling. It was the old government-in-waiting routine again. The journalists were waiting too.

'Where's the document?'

Bevins again.

After some thought, the MC replied: 'The document is in the building . . .'

What was this? A tax tease? How exciting.

'. . . it will be distributed as soon as possible . . .'

Maybe just bad organization?

'. . . it will be distributed when John Smith rises to speak.'

No. Just screwing the journalists' chances of asking awkward questions. Cue Bevins:

'Aw, come on! That's pathetic!'

It was. Meanwhile, other hacks were gossiping. ITN's Peter Allen asked the *Daily Mail*'s Gordon Greig how he rated Ashdown's prospects.

'Quite good, if there's no more philandering.'

Allen agreed: 'One more bonk, and it's goodbye.'

Eyes front. Enter Jack Cunningham. Enter Britain's Next Prime Minister, wearing his steel-framed Euro-specs and looking deep. Enter Smith, stoutly, a serious performer taking the lead role in a farce. It was a farce because a fairly small but widely-read group among the reporters present were there purely and simply to shaft him. Smith knew it and they knew it. More than that, they knew if they didn't, their editors would eventually give them the sack. Some of these editors, after all, owed a lot to the Conservatives. Years of fine and honourable effort spent insulting, denigrating, abusing, persecuting, misrepresenting and defaming the Labour Party and especially Britain's Next Prime Minister had prompted Margaret Thatcher to give them knighthoods, CBEs and big dinners at Number 10. Where would democracy be without a free press?

John Smith began his speech. Boggling intently behind enormous glasses, there was no mistaking an air of ascetic morality. He seemed the kind of man who, if a beggar knocked at his door, would take him in without hesitation and provide a warming gruel of mashed Bible and porridge oats.

'Already the present recession has lasted longer than any other downswing. Output in the on-shore economy has now been falling for six quarters in succession, a period approaching the Great Depression of the 1930s . . .'

Funny, this recession. It had all been so quiet. No union fightback, no protest marches, just a dismal, silent procession of workers collecting their cards. Smith outlined the Labour response:

'It has been assumed by the Conservatives that market forces are sufficient to ensure industrial efficiency and personal achievement. But while market discipline is necessary, it is not sufficient to guarantee competitive market success. It is the responsibility of government both to invest, and to encourage others to invest, in education and training, in research and development and in the infrastructure – the foundations of modern economic success.'

Pure Smith, this, the orthodox agenda of the Labour right; Conservative policy with a softer heart and a poor box replacing the glazed fundamentalism and casino dementia. Smith was no rebel. His power base was Parliament – where in debate his advocate's wit was crisp and cutting – and the baronial union establishment. To the horror of Labour's image consultants, he often favoured the necktie of the Post Office Workers' Union, a matrix of penny blacks picturing Queen Victoria's head. A survivor of a heart attack, his leisure hours were spent hill-walking, often with Gavin Laird, the granite-mouthed General Secretary of the Amalgamated Engineering Union. If his public image is much to go by, taking your pleasure with Laird must be like sunbathing in a fridge. But Smith was acknowledged throughout his party as a class act. Even the left respected him for not pitching in on the purges.

The preamble was over. Now came the number crunch:

'This framework will make a useful contribution to setting the UK economy on the right road to recovery, but it must be underpinned by more detailed policies. To these I now turn.'

The shadow measures were as anticipated: short-term investment incentives for industry, modest sums for skills training and an employment programme, the gradual release of money accrued by local authorities ('capital receipts') from selling council houses, which the government had forbidden them to spend. These were the main 'supply-side' proposals to help lever industry off the rocks. Smith then proceeded to state benefits and the issue to which the entire election campaign had already virtually been

reduced, personal taxation. As Chancellor, he would pay out
universal child benefit raised to £9.95 weekly; retirement pensions
increased by £5 per week for a single person and £8 for married
couples. Smith would pull in more from the highest earners by
introducing a top-rate 50 per cent income tax band on people
making more than £40,000 a year; and more from National
Insurance Contributions.

The biggest part of his extra revenue would come from the
latter. As things stood, NICs were levied at the rate of 9 per cent
of all employees' income up to £20,060 per annum. Smith
intended to remove this ceiling, and announced it, saying, 'The
unfair upper earnings limit . . . will be removed.' The emphasis
on 'unfair' suggested an unsightly growth requiring cosmetic
surgery. But the site of the operation already bore the scars of
conflict. In the preceding months, Britain's Next Prime Minister,
lunching with journalists at a plush joint called Luigi's, had
intimated that the changes would not take place immediately, but
might be 'phased in'. Frenzy! 'Labour's Tax Shambles', howled
the *Daily Mail*. Well, they wouldn't be 'phased in', after all. Stout
John Smith knew best.

Smith concluded by confirming that the new 20 per cent
income tax band would go, but revealed his intention to increase
the level of thresholds by £330 to £3625. 'As a result,' said Smith,
'740,000 people will be taken out of income tax altogether.' (So
David Frost had been quite right to badger the wriggling Kinnock
about it: 'it's a reduction in taxes, that's certainly the case, that's a
matter of fact . . .'). And Smith pledged that Labour would not,
in any budget in the next Parliament, increase the basic rate of tax
from its present 25 per cent. However, his yield would still
provide over a billion pounds to help the recovery, £600 million
for education and another billion minimum to spend on the NHS.

As Smith finished, a bunch of party workers cheered. Had
their man turned miserable Norman over, or what? Smith seemed
to think so, spicing his replies to journalists' queries with characteristically clipped strokes of wit. Then John Sergeant asked to
put a question not to Smith, but to Britain's Next Prime Minister.
Cunningham made an oozing intervention: matters of economic
policy should be directed at Britain's Next Chancellor.

'Oh, sorry,' said Sergeant, obligingly. 'It's not a difficult one.'

All the journalists laughed. Sergeant's expression said he
hadn't meant to imply, you know . . . but it was too late. For a
fraction of a second, Britain's Next Prime Minister, Cunningham
and Smith made like codfish. Then Kinnock laughed: 'Ho ho ho
ho ho ho!'

Then Smith and Cunningham laughed: 'Ho ho ho ho ho ho!'

To think that Britain's Next Prime Minister might not be able
to answer the question! Oh, what a joke it was! From the press
seats, it wasn't possible to see Smith or Cunningham's hands. It
would have been nice to know if they had had their fingers
crossed.

The excitement of the shadow budget meant Paddy Ashdown
ended the day being rather less important than when he had
started it. Smith's gambit led every TV bulletin throughout the
evening. Des Wilson cancelled Ashdown's planned appearance on
Channel 4 News as a reprisal. But the big TV event of the night
was *Panorama* on BBC 1 where Smith, Lamont and Alan Beith
argued their cases, refereed by David Dimbleby, the corporation's
heavyweight anchor. Smith was stern, Beith was earnest, Lamont
was the spook on the Ghostbuster's logo. Each played their
economic hands in the style of morality poker. Beith dealt from
the honesty suit. Lamont laid out his regular spread of tax-and-
inflation jokers. Smith's hand contained a flush of investment for
the future and a jack of social justice. But for all the steam and
indignation, the fare all three offered was meagre. From Lamont
came a wink and a nudge, and just enough loose change to make
it worth a trip to the chip shop. From Smith, more Bible and
oats. Beith, meanwhile, pointed hopefully upwards at a slice of
pie in the sky. And whichever shelf you looked on, the cupboard
was virtually bare.

CHAPTER EIGHT

The Elusive Essex

(Tuesday 17 March)

The *Daily Mail*'s headline said: 'You Make It, They'll Take It'.

Editor Sir David English remained grateful for his knighthood.

Policital editor Gordon Greig would not be losing his job.

'Labour unveiled its tax plans yesterday and revealed that despite its mask of modernity and moderation, its driving force is still the politics of envy.'

Not just misguided, these socialists, but vicious.

'The whole package presented by John Smith was designed to hit middle-class, middle-income families . . . the kind of people Labour still regards as rich.'

The entire article presented by Gordon Greig was designed to be propaganda masquerading as fact, imputing base motives for wealth redistribution without a single shred of evidence. But the *Mail*'s front page raised more subtle semantic issues: what does 'middle income' mean; who is 'middle class'; who would like to think they are, even if they're not? Burning questions, these, particularly when departing the eastern hinterlands of London, and entering the county of Essex, with its myriad representations of John Major's Model World. To drive a meandering route from inner-city Hackney to the green beyond the grime, is to journey through a terrain of symbols, landmarks on the route from bombed-out terrace to snug new semi, from public provision to private lawn: the giant Ford production plant in Dagenham; the instant, boom-built, residential estates off the trunk roads beyond Redbridge; the do-it-yourself superstores on the fringes of Romford. Each marks a crescendo in the chorus of aspiration which, vibrating through the medium of the ballot box, has decisively refreshed Conservatism's power.

Once, it was different and the political metamorphosis of Basildon sums up the change. Designated, like other New Towns under the jurisdiction of Labour's post-war government, it sprouted from the marshes like a red-brick Jerusalem, a homeland for an emigrant metropolitan working class. Basildon people were, by and large, Labour people. Not especially radical, but grateful for jobs, for indoor toilets, for the National Health Service and for lives that were looking up. For many years, the town formed part of the Billericay constituency and provided a Labour counterbalance to the surrounding Tory vote, part rural gentry, part a growing *nouveau riche*. Billericay was a knife-edge seat, an early pointer to the end result on general election nights. After 1974, boundary changes saw the old Billericay disappear into the new constituency of Basildon, which contained the small town of Billericay itself and other surrounding territories, mostly of comparable affluence. Then, in 1983, it was reduced to contain only the New Town itself, and a new Billericay seat was constructed from surrounding settlements.

Basildon proved to be a yardstick for sliding electoral loyalties. Instead of returning a Labour MP as history suggested it should, its citizens opted by a narrow margin for a Tory, David Amess. Margaret Thatcher's branded Conservatism looked a better buy to the New Town's second-generation consumers of future promise, and Amess, against the national trend, doubled his majority four years later. Labour would have to wipe that out, and handsomely, if it was to prevail in 1992.

The implications of Smith's shadow budget would significantly affect its chances, as much as for how its terms were perceived as what they actually meant in pounds and pence. To what extent did Basildon people, 44 per cent C1, but 63 per cent council housed, recognize themselves as having 'middle incomes'? As being 'middle class'? How much did they wish they had and were? The conundrum had been compounded by the recession. Unemployment in Basildon was running at over 10 per cent, as bigger employers cut back, smaller ones closed down and the self-employed went under. Home repossessions were plentiful, including of former council houses enthusiastically snapped up under the right-to-buy legislation. In Basildon, if anywhere, the Thatcherite cream was beginning to turn sour. The consolation for the disillusioned was the prospect of turfing Amess out. But just beyond the New Town's electoral boundaries, there was no comparable opportunity for those at the thin end of the wedge. In the new Billericay, they were electorally irrelevant. An axe-murderer would find a welcome there if he wore a blue rosette.

The office of the Billericay Conservative Association announced itself from above a family butcher's shop. Near to it stood a pub, and in it sat two women of early middle age. One, Janet, wore the nylon smock of a supermarket checkout clerk. The other, Brenda, was a housewife in civvies. Sipping continental coffees, an indulgence they would spin out for an hour, they were deep in one of their regular sessions of mutual, morose consolation.

'We're known as the spoiled brats,' said Janet wearily.

Though taking in the town of Billericay, Basildon District Council was Labour-run. Its municipal amenities, forcibly shrunk thanks to the attentions of the government, are concentrated in the New Town. Consequently, Janet did not feel terribly spoiled. Nor were her resentments assuaged by the fate that had lately befallen her son. The firm he worked for had gone on short time, and he'd gone out of the door. Later, they took him back, just before he came of age. But barely had he collected his first pay packet, than he got a poll tax bill from Basildon for £78. It arrived on his eighteenth birthday, a request for an instalment towards an annual £316. You make it, they'll take it. But Labour didn't invent the poll tax. This was a different 'they'. Who did Janet blame? She assigned fault non-selectively: 'All of them.'

Janet's life seemed dominated by the juggling of small change: £2.70 bought her a return bus ticket to Basildon; £1.10 bought ten cigarettes, to last at least a day. Supermarket checkout staff usually earn around £3.60 per hour, or between £117 and £136 a week. Recently widowed and with a second, dependent, child, Janet's diminished circumstances entitled her to the dubious pleasure of entering the labyrinth of state benefits to supplement

her sorry pay. There are two basic pathways through the cata-
comb, one marked 'Income Support', the second, 'Family Credit',
a new benefit introduced by the Conservatives in 1986. Janet's
manner, a cautious strain of sardonic pride, discouraged undue
prying. But her circumstances would not have differed greatly
from those of the typical hard-up family identified by the Low
Pay Unit in assessing what Chancellor Lamont's big denial was
worth.

A two-child family on £165 per week – half the national
average, but more than Janet earned for a thirty-eight-hour week
– would gain £1.92, thanks to the 20p tax band. Yet this bounty
would adversely affect their rate of Family Credit, to the tune of
£1.34. Another 38 pence would be shaved from their Housing
Benefit, a state safety net for those whose incomes are insufficient
to meet their rents. As a result, such a family would finish up 20
pence a week better off. A wealthier family, by contrast, would
gain more than £2. If Janet tucked those 20 pences away with
proper Victorian thrift, in a month she would be able to splash
out on a second cup of continental coffee when she sat down to
chat with Brenda. There was nothing Nice John Major wouldn't
do to help the poor.

With Janet's pride went propriety. She guarded her own
voting intentions jealously. But: 'You have some people round
here who discuss who they vote for. Whether they understand
why or not, to vote Conservative is the in thing – for anyone
who's dishonest.'

Billericay Conservatism has had a criminal connection. Its
MP until 1987 (who also represented the old Basildon from
1979) was Harvey Proctor, who resigned following a conviction
for the 'gross indecency' of renting boy prostitutes and spanking
their behinds. He now earns a crust selling fine shirts to proper
gentlemen from a shop in Richmond.

His successor has attracted no attention from the constabulary, but quickly achieved a different kind of prominence. Teresa
Gorman soon became one of Britain's most quotable proponents
of market forces in the raw. She approves of the advancement
of women and believes this, like all other good things, would
proceed more smoothly if the state stepped aside and let capitalism get on with it. (Just think: if supermarkets paid no business

rate or corporation tax, Janet would become rich beyond her wildest dreams.) She is spiky sweetness in a shell suit and not always appreciated for it. The displeasure of some Billericay Tories was once expressed in a satirical press release which Mrs Gorman considered defamatory. She sued and she won, and in so doing permanently reminded anyone dealing in print of her limitless integrity, prodigious talents and abundant personal charm.

Like everyone else in the country, Janet and Brenda had heard of Mrs Gorman. They spoke of her as if she was a minor pop star or a game-show hostess: glitzy, mildly entertaining and not much to do with them. The identities of the Liberal Democrat and Labour candidates were a complete mystery. They were scarcely more familiar with the contents of John Smith's shadow budget. His child benefit proposal would have made Janet two quid a week better off. Imagine the extra coffees that would buy.

Time to breathe in the richness of Billericay real estate. Janet and Brenda offered directions: down the High Street, turn right, and beware of the Neighbourhood Watch. Not that they bore any grudges:

'They're our future, the accountants, the business people,' said Janet.

She put her cup back on the saucer and headed off past the Conservative Association office back to work.

Labour's local command post for its Essex offensive was a house on Basildon's outskirts. Like everything in Basildon, it was near a roundabout and close to a stretch of landscaped municipal grass which still looked, in the weird way of New Town foliage, as if it had been planted the day before. The main office presented a collage of 'electable' Labour paraphernalia and the imprints of gut Labour activism: word processors glowered and John Potter, the candidate for Basildon and the local council leader, battered away at one of them, incarcerated in a suit and tie; on a filing cabinet someone had applied an anti-apartheid sticker and on a notice-board was pinned a reproduction of a 1945 Labour election poster, featuring an angular, constructivist 'V' and the slogan 'Now Win The Peace'. Those were the days.

Labour's candidate for Billericay was Alison Miller, thirty-eight, with jet black, terrier hair, big glasses and vermilion lipstick. Offering a Rich Tea biscuit, she related her personal history: lifelong Labour from a Labour family; dad emigrated from Hungary where he'd been a revolutionary Marxist; mum from Ireland, where she'd been active in the Transport and General Workers' Union. Raising their daughter a Roman Catholic, the Millers had had her educated accordingly, first at local state primary schools and then at a convent in Southend. At North-East London Polytechnic, she had obtained a degree in applied economics, and spent the following years doing postgraduate research and teaching. Then, in 1987, she went for a change of career and became a software engineer. She was enthused by Labour's commitment to bringing its women members to prominence. On Labour's programme in general, she was less effusive:

'Well, of course, as Labour Party candidate, I support the Labour Party policies.'

When asked exactly what she meant, she laughed.

On becoming British, Miller's father's politics had softened to reformism and he had represented Labour for the council ward of Laindon. The landlord of the Billericay pub had mentioned it. His advice: 'Watch out.' Miller regarded the area more kindly. For her, it was more like the New Town, with many council dwellings and a greater concentration of potential votes than any other part of the constituency. The rest of her attentions would be focused on the wards towards Thurrock, where owner-occupation was substantial, but not necessarily synonymous with votes for the blues.

Miller believed political leanings there challenged the popular archetype Essex Man, a flash Harry dockers' descendant who wanted to keep the blacks out and had put Margaret Thatcher in. Billericay small town itself contained such people, she said, nestling alongside more serious money, executive or landed. The difference in Thurrock was not income, but culture: round there, people did not consider that having a mortgage instead of a rent meant they were no longer working class. They clocked on at oil refineries in Canvey Island, at Ford's – either in Dagenham or Basildon's tractor plant – or at Marconi, the town's other multinational employer. A good Labour yield there would not win Miller the seat – Gorman's majority was impregnable – but it might reduce Frank Bellard, the Liberal Democrat, to second place.

It would also be a measure of Labour's national prospects. The previous evening, on the 5.40 *ITN News*, the *Six O'Clock* and *Nine O'Clock* BBC news and ITN's *News At Ten*, computer graphic depictions of the effect of Smith's shadow budget on the lives of theoretical families had lit up the screen. The Institute for Fiscal Studies had reckoned it up: if you earned more than £24,000, you lost; if less than £21,000, you gained; if somewhere in between, it all depended on how much breeding you'd done. Smith said, 'Eight out of ten families will be better off.' This appeared to be true: the average male, non-manual income is around £19,500 a year and most people earn less, some a lot less, a fact concealed by the *Daily Mail*'s term 'middle income'. But how middling was the income of the Ford and Marconi employees? A Basildon white collar worker might easily make £20,000; a skilled manual one might approach it with bonuses and overtime. Smith's servings of Bible and oats might depend on such people's altruism. Labour had to hope it was a quality which, unlike jobs and optimism, would not evaporate in a recession.

We set off for a teatime canvass. *En route*, we picked up Charlie, whose scuttling walk and cavernous vowels made it almost superfluous for him to confide, as he did with pride, 'I'm straight out of the East End.' Next stop, a front room dominated by a display fireplace, constructed in industrial brickwork, and two vast aquariums filled with dazzling fish. Twenty John Player King Size lay by a brimming ashtray on the floor. A large colour television conveyed Michael Angelis's reading of Thomas the Tank Engine to no one in particular. On the sofa lay a standard letter from Britain's Next Prime Minister. 'Dear supporter,' it began. It was the home of a ward activist with the local canvass sheets. Not everyone with a brick display fireplace and two tanks of dazzling fish qualifies as Essex Man.

We drove round the corner to sweet talk Essex Man's granny and grandad in a purpose-built, council condominium. A grey-haired female concierge showed us in, chattering frantically. The condo was a warren of whitewashed brickwork and veneered panels. Miller went into doorstep mode, pressed a bell and waited.

The door opened. The cutaway toe of a lilac slipper nudged into view.

'Mrs Stanwick?'

'Yes.'

Gently, gently.

'Good afternoon, I'm sorry to bother you. My name is Alison Miller, I'm Labour's parliamentary candidate and I'm here today to ask people if they're going to support Labour in the general election.'

Standard intro, stop for breath.

'Well, up to now I might do, yes.'

Breathe again. Then, coaxingly: 'You've got a bit of hesitation?'

'Well, you listen to 'em all saying this and saying that, but you've got to have what's best for you, haven't you, as a pensioner?'

'Yes.'

'You know what I mean?'

'Absolutely.'

Mrs Stanwick still spoke the London of her youth. The London of Charlie's youth too. We stood by a brick bulwark with an electric meter inside and a spray of dried flowers on top. In the striplight glow we nodded sympathetically as she complained about a coming rent rise and wondered when we'd get things sorted like the Germans: 'And I'm paying poll tax, paying extra for them devils that won't pay.'

Law-abiding, despairing patriot. Might be Labour. A promising floater. Miller blamed the rent rise and the poll tax on the government. By contrast, she explained, Mr Smith would give her an extra fiver. The Conservatives had pledged just two. And you had to be on Income Support. And you had to fill in a form. Yes, said Mrs Stanwick, she had heard that on the radio.

Then Charlie said: 'One thing I'll tell you. If you vote for Alison, she'll do a lot more for you than whatever Teresa Gorman tries to do. Tell you what, she even sues her own kind and gets a hundred and fifty grand.'

Mrs Stanwick was more concerned about the Germans. But for her, to be canvassed was like therapy. She didn't get many visitors. Labour would get her vote. Indeed, of twenty elderly residents canvassed, only one was pledged to the Conservatives. On this evidence, Essex Pensioner was still as solid as when Labour won the peace, even in Billericay. But Essex Progeny would decide Basildon, and they were not so sure.

CHAPTER NINE

Desperate Manifestos

(Wednesday 18 March)

'**G**ood morning ladies and gentlemen and welcome to the launch of our manifesto for the 1992 election, "It's Time To Get Britain Working Again".'

For Britain's Next Prime Minister, standing at the dove-grey lectern at Number 4, Millbank, just down from Parliament Square, it really was a good morning. A rupture had appeared in the pattern of the opinion polls. One in *The Times* (by MORI) and another in the *Guardian* (by ICM) had both shown Labour 5 points ahead. If this marked the start of a trend, then it would soon be time for Neil Kinnock to decide which items from his house in Ealing to put into tea chests and have shifted up the A40 towards Westminster.

'This election, is, of course, not only about policies. It's also a choice between values.'

His voice was tired. Perhaps it was recovering from the speech in Scotland where Neil Kinnock had emerged, sounding Welsh. Now the flat, electable baritone had returned. Only its tiredness gave it soul.

'At the core of our convictions as democratic socialists, is a belief in individual liberty. We therefore further believe, first, that for liberty to have real meaning, the standards of community provision must be high, and access to that provision must be wide. Second, we believe that those rights of the individual must, like all others in a free society, belong to all men and women of every age, class and ethnic origin. And they must be balanced by responsibilities for fair contribution and law abiding conduct. Third, we believe that for rights and responsibilities to be exercised fully and fairly, government in Britain, as in other industrialized democracies, must work to build prosperity by properly supporting long-term industrial and economic development.'

John Major could have said all that, except for changing 'democratic socialists' to 'Conservatives' and putting the points in reverse order. Even his mechanisms for achieving these broad goals were not so fundamentally different. He too was pledged to improve standards of social provision. He too insisted that all individuals should enjoy equal rights. He too believed government policy should facilitate economic development. The differences were largely of emphasis between the relative efficiencies of the market and the state in making those mechanisms work. Neither party had ambitions to build a whole new fruit machine. Margaret Thatcher had endeavoured to and failed. Labour had once wanted to, but lost hope. As Britain's Next Prime Minister put it, his vision of the country was now translated into policies that were 'down-to-earth'.

The implications were easily spotted. Anthony Bevins took one by the throat.

'Yes, Tony,' said Britain's Next Prime Minister with collegiate familiarity, picking out Bevins's raised hand. Me and 'Tony', we're professionals, we relate. Bevins had been scouring the manifesto's small print on employment. He had observed a change, subtle but perceptible, in the depth of commitment expressed to alleviating joblessness compared with previous Labour policy statements:

'You've watered that down even further. Why should we believe you give a damn about the unemployed?'

Britain's Next Prime Minister answered with characteristic lyricism: 'We want to achieve, as any responsible government would want to achieve, full employment. What we refuse to do is to give the impression that there is some magical lever to be pulled that can secure that in the immediate, or even in the medium term, in a country that begins the next period of government in weakness, in recession and is facing intense pressures in the world. We will not mislead the unemployed. We do care too much about their condition and their future to do that. What you will see is practical policies for manufacturing, for the construction industries, for house building, for transport, for training for skills, and policies which, in a host of other areas will mean first, that we stop the perpetual rise in unemployment. Second, that we start to bring a reduction in unemployment. And third, that we provide people with the means of avoiding falling into unemployment again. Of reducing, and ultimately, I hope, getting rid of any preventable unemployment in our country.'

I *hope* getting rid of any *preventable* unemployment.

The hope looked forlorn. Labour had no ambition to fix the economy to create many jobs. Full employment was yesterday's news, a goal subordinated to 'prudence'.

The relegation of full employment down the list of Labour priorities was a crucial concession to Thatcherite 'common sense'. And the remainder of the press conference arguments were similarly fought out on Conservative territory. All the questioning was about housekeeping and hidden agendas: how would inflation be controlled if the economy was refloated?; would the unions be let off the leash?; was renationalization in their minds?; how would Labour keep wages down?; how much of the billion pounds earmarked for the NHS would go towards health service workers' pay? This last inquiry related largely to Labour's most radical proposal, the introduction of a national minimum wage of £3.40 per hour. The policy had put the Tories in a state of high excitement. It would mean sackings, they hollered. There would be a wages spiral! Labour's answers to this, and all other points, were sound enough, but inevitably defensive because almost every question contained the assumption that turning back Thatcher's tide would lead to absolute chaos. And Labour could scarcely complain about that. Implicitly, they half accepted the diagnosis themselves.

The session concluded with a squib from a Tory tabloid: 'If you don't win this election, are you preparing to resign the leadership of the Labour Party?'

The shadow cabinet obliged with a chorus-line laugh.

'We are not going to lose the election. We are going to win the election,' Britain's Next Prime Minister said.

By ten o'clock, the press posse had saddled up and sauntered out of Millbank, across Parliament Square to the Queen Elizabeth II

Conference Centre, for the Conservative manifesto launch. On the stage in the main hall, four high, wide, true blue frontispieces were arranged in ranks, front to back. Behind these, John Major and the members of his cabinet would crane their necks to be seen, looking, as everyone agreed, like capitalism's answer to the Politburo. The manifesto was called 'The Best Future For Britain'. A close-up of Nice John doing his Nice John Smile radiated from the cover and in blow-up from the wings of the stage. Chairman Chris Patten prowled the apron, negotiating angles with photographers. He looked a lot less chipper than at Torquay. Opinion polls can get you down.

The house lights fell and the sound system unleashed the disco Purcell. Nice John pottered on and sat down at the front. Close by were Norman Lamont, Douglas Hurd and Michael Heseltine, whose unbelievable hair had gone all flat down one side. The press gazed up. The cabinet, barely visible, gazed down, their heads bobbing into sight like squaddies peering from tanks.

Nice John rose and proceeded to describe the manifesto as a blueprint for his Model World:

'It's a world in which enterprise creates the prosperity that enables us to take care of others. It's a world in which we can raise standards. We must roll the frontiers of the state still further back. For the sake of our future, we mustn't let the clock be turned back. And that future lies in increasing the rights and opportunities of men and women at work, not returning to the days of strikes, picket lines and the closed shop. It lies in bringing taxes down further, not shoving them back up . . .'

Of course, the days of strikes, picket lines and the closed shops had enabled more men and women to stay in work. Those were the rights and opportunities Nice John wouldn't be giving them back, though a few might be free to have some shares in a privatized British Coal. Labour wouldn't be reviving those old rights either, of course, but Nice John didn't mention that. As for taxes, Anthony Bevins had some thoughts:

'Given your statement on page seven of the document that a lightly taxed economy generates more economic growth, and given that the tax burden in this country has risen since 1979 from 35.5 per cent to 36.75 per cent of GDP, and your annual rate of growth from '79 to '91 is only 1.797, can you give us an explanation of why your record has produced neither of the things you advocate?'

Nice John's voice went nerdy: 'Those figures you quote from, Tony, are phoney figures . . .'

Bevins: 'They're your figures.'

Straight from the Treasury, in fact.

Nice John: 'Let me explain to you why they're phoney.'

Bevins: 'But they're *your figures!*'

Bevins's ears were beginning to vibrate. Nice John embarked on an elaborate rationale for why his own figures were phoney. He did not directly dispute them which, in the case of taxes, showed that if you included such as VAT and poll tax in the overall sum, most people were paying more tax than ever. But apparently it was all something to do with government borrowing.

Bevins butted in: 'But your borrowing requirement figure is now greater than it was in 1979!'

This was all a bit too much for Chairman Chris, who had a more powerful microphone than the man from *The Independent*: 'Tony, Tony . . .' (Yes, we're all friends here.) '. . . this is question and answer, not a socratic dialogue.'

Such an amusing fellow, this Chris!

Bevins, though, speaks more plainly: 'Well, answer mine then!'

Ho, ho, ho. Next!

The Tories' tax argument was garbage and their chest-beating a fraud. They didn't quite push their luck to lying in the manifesto, where they claimed, 'We have reduced *direct* taxation' [my italics], but their increases of the indirect sort were airbrushed out of history when they went on about Labour's supposed plans to tax, tax, tax. And now it was time to deploy the second prong of their heroic campaign strategy: abusing, denigrating, ridiculing and insulting Britain's Next Prime Minister. A questioner put Labour's critique of the Conservatives' plans to Nice John.

He replied: 'I'm fairly sure that Neil Kinnock won't have had a chance to read what we say, or absorb what we say, or understand what we say or make a rational comment on what we say.'

Hmmm. A bit nasty, John.

Chairman Chris, a sneer slinking across his upper lip, slipped in a sweet aside of his own, something about how you could be sure any comment would be long, if nothing else. Thank heavens the party of common civility was not resorting to personal slights. But then, of course, it didn't need to. With higher taxation, unemployment, a massive borrowing requirement, a balance of payments crisis, crucifying interest rates and two recessions in a decade to its name, it had so very much to boast about.

'We shall win this election with a clear majority,' Nice John said.

CHAPTER TEN

Don't Choose
A Stranger

(Wednesday 18, Thursday 19 March)

As a rule, Cheltenham has a gift for being both dandy and decently discreet. On its outskirts lies a racecourse but the town betrays little of the chancer's razzle associated with the turf. Like other spa towns of England, its architecture spans centuries, but stern stonework and wedding-cake curlicues of Edwardian vintage have the upper hand. Cheltenham replenishes itself by sticking tightly to this combination of solidity and genteel flourish. People of means and cultured leanings retire there, enjoy literary and musical festivals with roots in the pre–pop era and perhaps imagine themselves to have escaped the full menaces of modernity. All that went out of the window when John Taylor showed up.

The furore surrounding Taylor's selection as the Conservative candidate at the beginning of 1991 had made Cheltenham more than just a Tory marginal which the Liberal Democrats had designs on: it turned the place into a media arena for the politics of race. Taylor is from Solihull, a barrister, a former advisor to the Home Office and black, the son of Jamaican immigrants. He stood a real chance of becoming the Tories first black MP. This, in itself, made him news. But when an affronted empire-worshipper called Bill Galbraith popped out of the officers' mess tent in the Glorious Past theme park to complain that Taylor was 'a bloody nigger from Birmingham', the candidate and his adopted town became sensational.

Cheltenham's citizens, devoured by reporters and regurgitated as sound bites, were heard to respond with either the standard white English protestations of innocent colour blindness, or with prejudice dignified as arithmetic: some wished to ignore the issue, others considered that because Cheltenham was homogeneous, milky English, no dark-skinned Englishman could, by definition, know how to represent them – or, for that matter, be properly English. For John Major, meanwhile, the saga disturbed the peace in his Model World. Having just become PM and set out his 'classless' vision, a member of his own party was practising discrimination by shouting 'nigger'. In the House of Commons, Nice John condemned Galbraith. But other Cheltenham Tories were complaining too, saying that Conservative Central Office had foisted Taylor on them to as a gesture to woo the national black vote from Labour. The extent to which their gripes were informed by sentiments closer to Galbraith's was hard to prove, but harder not to suspect. As for Taylor, he became an exhibit, one whose future was far from secure. His response, like a lot of his would-be constituents, was to keep his head down and hope the storm would pass.

There was never a chance of that, and there were some in Cheltenham who knew it. With careful excavation, a Cheltenham less given to platitudes or superstition could be unearthed. A café proprietor, setting down a plate of full English breakfast, knew it because his next-door neighbour, a stalwart Tory, had remarked over the garden fence: 'Have you seen this golliwog we've got to put up with?' The story was relayed with something close to relief: at last, the chance to bend a sympathetic ear. Such opportunities, he said, came few and far between. Most people either declined to discuss the matter or were 'right-wing and racist', like the guys at the sports club he'd felt no option but quietly to resign from. To raise a voice in protest was to step dangerously out of line. 'It'll be a miracle if he's elected. This is a real racist town.'

Out on an elegant side street, an elderly woman pushed a bike with a big wicker basket on the front. You saw a lot of those in Cheltenham, spicing the flavour of throwback. Canvassed for her opinion, she clasped my hand tightly through her worn sheepskin mitt, and said with a troubled expression: 'John Taylor won't get in. I've lived here all my life – which is more than thirty-nine years – and I know what people are like. There's an awful lot of prejudice. My own sister is like it: "There's no good black men," she says.'

Her next line was delivered with a mixture of insistence and reassurance, as if the news that blackness and goodness could indeed coexist might need to be broken gently: 'I feel sorry for the man, 'cos he's nice.'

A tear trickled down her cheek.

How many people like her, or like the café proprietor, were there in Cheltenham? How would they vote? The irony was that those most angry on Taylor's behalf would also be the least keen on Conservatives, who were big on immigration controls and had an inglorious history of farming race scares to harvest votes. Only the previous year, Home Secretary Kenneth Baker had made a speech warning of floods of refugees if his proposed Asylum Bill did not become law. Baker was the Home Secretary whom Taylor had advised. Perhaps it had crossed his mind that the voters to whose base instincts Baker was appealing were the ones who might help him lose in Cheltenham. If it had, he wasn't saying so. He wasn't saying much about anything to do with blackness, whiteness or Bill Galbraith if he could help it. Interestingly, this threw him into an unspoken alliance of convenience with his rival for the seat, a local Liberal Democrat councillor, Nigel Jones.

Sitting at one end of his front room sofa, Jones was warily accommodating. He talked through his *curriculum vitae*. Cheltenham-born, he worked for the local computer company ICL, 'coming up through software', and travelling widely on their behalf, to the United Arab Emirates, Kuwait, Iraq, Sweden, Hong Kong and to Jamaica during the English cricket tour of 1990–91:

'I watched the test match that we won. I was there! The first time I went over, the manager of ICL in Jamaica said . . .' Here Jones did a mild impression of a Caribbean accent. '"We must get you over here for de test match, man." I said that sounds like a very good idea, I'm sure we can arrange a project review! And we did! It was wonderful!'

Jones's wife Kate had stationed herself supportively at the other end of the sofa. Both of them knew that I would eventually ask awkward questions about the 'race row'. I knew that they knew. Two small blonde Jones daughters in cute school uniforms eavesdropped and intervened in the way small daughters do. The house was modern, low and roomy, located in the affluent Park ward. It was thought only a Tory could ever win it at local level, but Jones was now its representative on Gloucestershire County Council, turning a traditional deficit into a majority of four. Kate, meanwhile, held a borough council seat. The Liberal Democrats had made big gains in these forums, roughly paralleling an erosion, by Jones's predecessor Richard Holme, of the parliamentary majority of the retiring MP, Sir Charles Irving, to under 5000. Irving, a gaily buccaneering backbencher, had enjoyed a strong personal following. Jones, home-grown, with a record of municipal service, and previous experience of fighting the seat himself as a Liberal, pre-Holme, in 1979, was more likely to inherit it than any outsider. But was there an Alf Garnett factor too?

'Haven't spotted it,' said Jones. He immediately changed the subject.

'What there is is a large number of people who are not Conservatives, who voted for Sir Charles Irving. You can measure that because he's on the borough council as well, for this ward, with a majority of 400, because he knows the patch.'

A cup of coffee was produced. How do you skewer a courteous host without appearing rude? Maybe this: if an Alf Garnett factor worked in his favour, would it take a little shine off his triumph?

'People don't mention it on the doorstep,' said Jones. 'Now that's all I can say.'

He changed the subject again.

'I think I know the people of Cheltenham well enough to know that they want the best man for the job. They'd prefer to have someone who knows the patch and has got a record of service to the town. We are certainly pushing that very hard.'

Oh dear. Look, was there an Alf Garnett factor or not?

'Haven't found it . . . It's the education thing. We're sensible on education, people know that. The crime thing: we've just had a 32 per cent increase in crime, the third highest in the country . . .'

The imperatives of politeness now created an impasse. The gap was filled by Jones's wife: 'What you're trying to say, you're trying to get something out of him, aren't you? But, I mean, there's bound to be certain . . .'

I protested that it was a perfectly straight question about a very important issue.

'I know, and he's not giving you a straight answer . . . people won't admit it.'

Very true.

'That's why he can't give you an answer.'

But that wasn't the real reason. Jones had decided long before to deal with the issue by ignoring it. Should he have intervened in the Taylor fracas?

'Certainly not. There's nothing to be gained by getting involved. As soon as it got announced I talked with Richard Holme about it, who's very sensible on these things, and he said, "What are you going to do?", and I said, "Keep my mouth shut."'

Jones had a point about gaining nothing by getting involved. Conversely, there was something to be gained by silence. Racist voters would undoubtably tick Jones's name in the polling booths if they wanted the black barrister beaten. That was the tainted reality created by Taylor's accession, and made worse by the rumpus that followed it. In that context, Jones had a choice: he could, in line with Liberal Democrat policy, publicly but succinctly, have repudiated racism and asserted that he did not wish Cheltenham voters to choose him over Taylor on the basis of anything other than issues and abilities; or else he could just leave well alone. For whatever reason, or lack of one, he had chosen the latter. And would, of course, reap the benefit.

The following morning, John Taylor put on his blue rosette and resumed his quest to prove to Cheltenham voters that he was not a monstrous 'nigger from Birmingham' and not a Central Office public relations plant, but a perfectly-formed Conservative who, in the buck-passing 'colour-blind' formula, 'just happened to be black'. He would be helped in this desperate task by the jovially robust Secretary of State for Education, the Right Honourable Kenneth Clarke.

The exercise took place on a small industrial estate at a firm of architectural fabricators. Outside the glass entrance door stood five white reporters (including two from national papers), five white photographers, an all-white television camera crew, some white plainclothes policemen and a couple of white Conservative party workers including the white Monica Drinkwater, chairman (not 'chairperson' or 'chair', terms preferred by left-wing trendies) of the local party, who had stuck by Taylor throughout. Inside the glass entrance door stood a little group of white company executives and John Taylor wearing his blue rosette. The white Kenneth Clarke arrived in a saloon car, fresh from a helicopter landing pad, bursting with bonhomie. Taylor and the white executives came from behind the doors to meet him.

'Well, hello John, marvellous to see you!' exploded Clarke.

Taylor said it was marvellous to see him too.

Marvellous, marvellous, marvellous.

On the pavement a wide blue ribbon had been stretched between a couple of portable uprights. Clarke, holding a pair of scissors, closed in on the ribbon. Taylor closed in on Clarke, knowing he must not be left out. The white photographers closed in on them both. Clarke then cut half-way through the ribbon and paused. Holding the scissors open at precisely the point where he had curtailed his cut, he turned and told Taylor a story about a previous time he had been asked to cut just such a ribbon and guess what?

The scissors hadn't worked!

Marvellous story! Marvellous!

While Clarke told it, the photographers clickety-clicked, gathering the indelible proof (black and white proof, no less) that John Taylor was the kind of man who could enjoy a marvellous story with Kenneth Clarke, a Secretary of State, that he would make a splendid MP for Cheltenham and just *happened* to be black.

It was time to go inside. Once there, Taylor, Clarke and the white executives completed an essential adjustment to their wardrobes. That is, they put on fibreglass safety helmets with the company logo on the front. Nobody else wore one of these helmets, not the white photographers, not the white camera crews, not the white reporters; not white Monica Drinkwater or the white wives of the white executives in their two-piece numbers with velvet collars and cantilevered shoulders; not even the white men working on the humming shop floor, some of whom were picked out to demonstrate to the white Secretary of State the more engaging aspects of architectural fabrication, while the Conservative parliamentary candidate, who just happened to be black, stood at his shoulder, agreeing with everything, and wearing a safety helmet with the company logo on it so that everyone in Cheltenham would know from the photos that he was taking an interest in local industry just like the white Sir Charles Irving had.

Watching this absurdity, a particularly grotesque example of the fakery of the democratic process, you had to wonder at John Taylor. More, you had to wonder at the fools in the Conservative Party who thought he could get an even break in an albescent Tory marginal like Cheltenham. Why had Taylor agreed to do it? Was it faith? Innocence? Duty? Ambition? Courage? Propelled towards two white employees, holding out his hand, was he wondering what they were thinking as they took his grip and smiled?

'Excellent Tory candidate'?

'Bloody nigger from Birmingham'?

He would never know.

Taylor stepped over to talk to three white lads in jeans and ski sweaters, whose wages, self-evidently, were regularly invested in getting their hair tweaked and gelled. He asked if they were interested in football. His voice was soft and coaxing, with no perceptible accent, Brum or Caribbean. The white lads mumbled a bit, standing rigid, not knowing what to say. Taylor persevered. Football was his hope for finding common ground. The other week, he said, he had turned out for Cheltenham Reserves and scored a hat trick. Boy, did his knees hurt. The white lads mumbled again. The white reporters clocked this stilted exchange, hoping to pilfer a quote. Taylor told the white lads about a charity match he was fixing up. Cyrille Regis (a black footballer) was coming. Not bad, eh? The white lads shuffled a bit. What were they thinking as Taylor probed nervously for a response:

'Excellent Tory candidate'?

'Bloody nigger from Birmingham'?

What were the white executives and their fragrant white wives thinking as they ushered him out of the door?

'Excellent Tory candidate'?

'Bloody nigger from Birmingham'?

Conservative Central Office had sent Taylor into the unknown, to a place where, like all black people venturing into genteel Little England, he was certain – even without the intervention of a Galbraith – to become a spectacle and prey to endless doubts about the veracity of such welcome as he received. His doggedness in the face of this mostly intangible adversity was utterly admirable. Yet at the factory, scuttling from one staged introduction to another, he looked almost demeaningly desperate to please. The cruellest thing was that he was assailed by attitudes which Cheltenham Tories themselves had vigorously cultivated. Sir Charles Irving knew the power of parochialism, and had used it far more emotively than – to his credit – Nigel Jones had in his campaign literature. Jones's leaflets boasted his Cheltenham birthright at the head of his list of attributes (as Liberal Democrats, the great devolvers, habitually do), but not with extreme prominence or in a way which covertly beckoned racist votes. But an Irving leaflet from 1987 had prominently featured the charming slogan: 'Don't Choose A Stranger.' Now the same voters were requested to choose John Taylor, a black man from Birmingham, an alien tribune straight from the urban nightmare.

Taylor's painful fight for Cheltenham threatened to show up the modern Conservative talk of 'classlessness' for the rhetorical flannel it was. In the wake of the Galbraith controversy, various Tory notables had publicly expressed their support for Taylor. The most conspicuous among these was Norman Tebbit, a former Party Chairman and Thatcher's Employment Secretary who, at the nadir of her recession, talked himself into folklore with his suggestion that the unemployed should be like his father who 'got on his bike and looked for work'. More recently, Tebbit had articulated an emerging Tory perspective on race relations. It became known as his 'cricket test'. The gist of it was that Caribbean or Asian Britons could not be considered loyal citizens if they cheered for touring cricket teams from the West Indies or the Indian subcontinent, and created 'problems' as a consequence.

The 'cricket test' formulation was significant because it reconciled a contradiction at the heart of Thatcherite ideology: on the one hand, it espoused the fantasy Britain of the Glorious Past, where common 'Victorian values' underpinned our greatness but which people of 'alien culture', as Thatcher had famously put it, threatened to 'swamp'; on the other, it did not negate the concept of meritocracy, the progenitor of 'classlessness', whereby it was talent, not background or birthright, which would enjoy the rewards of a free market society. On the face of it, Taylor passed the 'cricket test' with flying colours; he was British-born (ironically, the son of a West Indies test cricketer), his wife was white, his accent was English, he had made it as a lawyer. But the Tory Bill Galbraith had not caught on to Tebbit's new 'colour blind' prescription for cultural exclusivity. On 9 April we would see whether the Tory voters of Cheltenham had done any better.

CHAPTER ELEVEN

Coventry Blues

(Friday 20 March)

Standing tall in a vista of hardcore, Michael Heseltine told tales of future glory. Beneath his feet, it seemed, lay something more than the levelled site of what might once have been a factory on the outer rim of Coventry's main ring road; it was a seedbed for prosperity, in which a returned Conservative government would nurture the sweet blooms of recovery. From this very stretch of graded rubble would rise new hope in the form of a lustrous hotel and office development, covering 450,000 square feet. The desert of mud and granite chip surrounding him was, in truth, a pampas of opportunity: construction contracts would be negotiated and franchises fought for; financial service whizz-kids and sunrise entrepreneurs would clamour to secure tenancies; armies of bellboys and chambermaids would march from the dole queues to reclaim their self-respect and enjoy incomes that may even exceed a hundred pounds a week. And think of what may follow: foreign businessmen seeking export orders, virile with deutschmarks and yen; agents of corporate expansion thirsty for pools of pacified labour. Michael Heseltine could see it all on the horizon, and he just knew the people of Coventry could see it too:

'They know that the only way out of the recession is to pursue the policies of enterprise, to encourage investment and to maintain the control over the economy that we have patently got, as you can see by the falling interest rates and the control of inflation. People, I think, do see that. And they know that a high tax policy under Labour would choke off the recovery.'

Bugged by the opinion polls, the Conservatives had decided to escalate their assault. Already that morning Radio 4 had brought news of the miserable Chancellor's indignant analysis of 'Labour's phoney budget' as conveyed at the morning press conference: 'Most of the so-called gainers gain a pathetic 2p a week – or the price of a Polo mint.' The previous evening had seen further indications that Nice John Major was turning a little Nasty. Speaking to a tame audience in Manchester from a stageset costing half a million pounds, he had mocked one of the most powerful speeches Neil Kinnock had ever made. At the close of the 1983 campaign, Kinnock had hoarsely exhorted an audience in Bridgend: 'If Margaret Thatcher wins on Thursday, I warn you not to be ordinary. I warn you not to be young. I warn you not to fall ill. I warn you not to get old.' The new Nasty John intoned: 'If ever there would be a Labour government, I warn you not to be ambitious, I warn you not to be qualified, I warn you not to be successful, I warn you not to buy shares . . .' Well, it was a good try. But Heseltine was held to be the deadliest weapon in the Tory armoury. Nothing could withstand the force of his attacks: not facts, not logic, not even open derision for the outlandish assertions that poured from his mouth with barely an intake of breath:

'You're beginning to see, now, the recovery coming through . . . In a difficult world recession, Britain is fighting its way out . . . The inflation figures that are out today will indicate that we have got inflation under significant control . . . The disaster for people in the West Midlands and Britain would be Labour's politics of tax envy . . .'

The rogue grey hairs which sprouted from Heseltine's ears quivered as he blitzed the eager local television reporters. His voice, a curiously messianic cocktail of blithe assertion and flattened 'r's, held them mesmerized as it delivered its fusillade of bogus certainties. It was impossible that Heseltine really believed the recession to be other than primarily home grown, inconceivable that he did not know the fall in inflation was largely due to the desperate price-cutting of shops and companies facing collapse, and absurd for him to dismiss Labour's proposed fiscal adjustments as motivated purely by spite. But on and on he rampaged, brushing aside the recent job losses at the Jaguar plant, ignoring a questioner's lament that 8000 Coventry people had been thrown on the dole since the recession began. Today's pain would seem like nothing, he pronounced, compared to what would be in store if the country capitulated to the socialist threat. His rhetorical Exocets cruised cheerfully through the stratosphere:

'That is the one way to remove the incentives and to destroy the opportunities, to stop the process of inward investment that brings jobs to areas like this, to switch off a whole generation of young people on whom we depend for that drive and enthusiasm to build a prosperous economy!'

What a golden wonder, what a star. More than any other politician, Heseltine was his own obsessive creation, and like no other Conservative he combined the characteristics of 'one nation' wet and jungle predator dry. His career lineage mixes and matches the two strands of the party's tradition. Born into what is tendentiously known as a 'respectable Welsh' middle-class family, he was soon given a squirearchical re-fit, processed through preparatory and Shrewsbury public schools, emerging at Oxford, where he set about annexing the presidency of the Union as the first step in his intended conquest of Downing Street.[1]

He lost a fortune on the property market, made a million through magazine publishing and became an MP in 1966. By the mid-seventies he had learned how to scintillate the sleepwalkers' convention that was the Tory Party Conference with oratory that combined tycoon dynamism and cavalier dash. Since stalking out of Thatcher's cabinet he had tirelessly wooed constituency parties while firmly denying his utterly transparent intention to displace her. His failure to do so in 1990 had been greatly ameliorated by his rehabilitation in Major's government as Environment Secretary, charged with burying the poll tax. Now he was off the leash and thriving, spewing claptrap with the daredevil fury that was the core of his charisma. The words may have been weaselish, but the gist of Heseltine's message was plain: I'm rich and I'm ruthless and I'm as sexy as hell.

The next item on his programme was a walkabout in the constituency of Coventry South-West. This was the only one of the four Coventry seats held by a Conservative and John Butcher's majority was modest. Heseltine's job was to seduce the floating

---

1. See Julian Critchley, *Heseltine: The Unauthorised Biography*, André Deutsch, 1987, Chapters 1 and 2.

vote with the splendour of his presence. Down in Butts Road, Earlsden, one of the seat's busiest trading streets, the locals had got wind of the event.

'The filth generals, that's what they call them, isn't it?' said a bystander in a clammy Coventry accent, indicating a couple of cops with egg on their peaked caps. 'I hate the way they strut around, like they can do what they like.'

The bystander's name was John. He looked as if he was in his late forties and had oily, undisciplined hair. He wore a hooded nylon parka and carried a Kwik Save carrier bag, its handles crushed and rumpled from regular re-use. 'I've got anarchist tendencies meself. I think they're all a load of rubbish. I voted Green before. I might go for Paddy Ashdown if there isn't one this time.'

The camera crews which had been hovering along the pavement suddenly set off down the street towards Heseltine's exultant coiffure, which had appeared bobbing above the serried shoppers. John the bystander was not minded to follow them. Though he had been unemployed for the last five years, having lost his job as a tool fitter in the motor trade, he was not excited by the thought of retraining as a cleaner or a waiter, servicing Heseltine's global entrepreneurs. He would rather stay home and listen to Radio Caroline. The pirate stations were his passion and he had even travelled abroad to 'free radio' conventions. 'The Continentals, they're rolling in it, aren't they? The food's all rubbish here, isn't it? Over in Belgium, they cut the fat off the bacon.'

Heseltine's determined stride was bringing him steadily closer. Squalls of damp wind set his suit jacket flapping, pinioned only by a middle button secured over a blue lambswool sweater and a vaguely military tie. His shoes were sleek, black slip-ons with glinting gauds at the bridges of the uppers. It was the rig of a gentleman alligator. He offered his hand to shoppers with rapier thrusts as the cameramen zoomed.

'I used to get all the papers, you know,' said John. '*Morning Star,* the *Daily Worker* and the *Telegraph.* That's a good mix in'tit? Dennis Skinner, he used to be okay, but what's he done lately?'

It was true that the diehard leftist had been reduced to comedy cameos where the national scene was concerned. But what about Dave Nellist, over in Coventry South-East?

'Oh, I like him, he's a man who's stuck to his principles, but look what they've done to him. What can you do?'

Nellist was a sympathizer with the Militant Tendency, a Trotskyist grouping within the Labour Party, and had been expelled because of it. He was standing as an independent. Labour's top brass were desperate to beat him.

Heseltine was closing in, Butcher scurrying in tow. John the bystander said he was off. His wife had joined him now. She wore an orange coat buttoned to the neck and spectacles with plastic wings. What did she reckon to the great man?

'Oh, not my type at all.'

Together they crossed the road, John's wife pulling a PVC shopping bag on wheels. As they did so Heseltine homed in on a woman pushing a baby in a buggy.

'Hello, Michael Heseltine, supporting the Conservative candidate.'

'Hello, I'm the wife of the Liberal Democrat candidate.'

'Oh . . . Oh well, very good. Very good.'

He turned in my direction, jabbing out a paw.

'Hello, Michael Heseltine, supporting the Conservative candidate.'

'Hello, I'm the press, I think we've already met.'

'I see. I see. Very good.'

Looking on, another Coventry voter, Brian, reflected on the state of the national battle. He was a small businessman, a 'diehard Conservative', but Labour's behaviour was engaging him.

'A lot of the old values have gone, haven't they? They've gone middle of the road, terrifically middle of the road. In their manifesto they didn't even use the word socialism, did they?'

It was true. Brian wasn't impressed.

'I get the feeling it's all rather superficial. What they are showing is an attractive side. Both the parties are very careful about what they show. They're all getting a professional, slick way of presenting it, a commercial way of presenting it . . . Well, it is sad, isn't it, I suppose? They just want to get voters and they don't seem to care how they gain them, that's the point, isn't it? I think there's more apathy about than ever before. It should be about getting all these people back in their jobs, shouldn't it? But people see this recession as bigger than the political parties can solve.'

Brian looked on amused, as Heseltine surged into a chip shop. Where others had collapsed into confusion before the gaze of his gimlet eyes, the counter staff remained unfazed.

'Will you be having any chips, Mr Heseltine?'

'Not today, thank you. We've got John Butcher, the Conservative candidate . . .'

'I'd have got in some extra fish if I'd known.'

Heseltine eyed the battered aquatic corpses on display.

'Can we tempt you, Mr Heseltine?'

'Very good! Very good!'

Woosh, he was away.

The cashier raised his eyebrows. He had ruled out a Tory vote. However, he was still in a quandary over the alternatives.

'I can't decide. I want to vote Labour really, but I'm not too sure.'

His misgivings could be reduced to a single name: 'Kinnock . . . Kinnock only actually. The fact that he's changed his mind so often to gain votes, and I don't like any politician that changes his real views just to gain votes. I mean, I would forgive him if he had to do it to get in power, and when he got in power, he went back to his true beliefs. I would forgive him for taking the opportunity. But if he wins power and he sticks to his present views, that's not the real Labour Party.'

Changing the subject, he pointed across the street to a photography shop. 'Have you seen over there? They've got this great big portrait of Butcher in the window.'

Butcher and Heseltine had gone over to admire it. Nearby, a pair of women traffic wardens were beaming.

'He came over to talk to us, Michael Heseltine. He's very nice, very nice.'

'Yes, very nice, very nice.'

Terrible shoes, though.

'Well, you can't judge a man by that.'

But if Butts Road revealed anything, it was that appearances do count. To its voters, Labour appeared insincere. Michael Heseltine, well, he'd simply appeared, a triumphant force of nature. When credibility leaves a vacuum, charisma has a way of filling it.

CHAPTER TWELVE

Coventry Reds

(Friday 20 March)

Carbolic clean and wearing a wide dark tie with enormous white spots, Roy Hattersley arrived at police HQ on the edge of Coventry's precinct centre looking as if he had been dressed by his mother to meet a maiden aunt: hardly the personification of vengeful misanthropy Michael Heseltine had invoked on the building site three hours before. On the contrary, Hattersley exuded utter contentment. The Labour Party was as close to what he wanted it to be as he could ever have reasonably hoped: right-wing, conformist, committed to the economic *status quo* and to modest handouts to the poor in common decency's name. His prospects of becoming Home Secretary appeared to be improving. With luck, he would soon be meeting senior police officers, not as their guest but as their boss.

And yet, paradoxically, for all his satisfaction with Labour policy, Hattersley's style and demeanour chimed with his party's pink executive look like an old church bell in a synthesiser orchestra. Plump of build and fulsome of phrase, his incongruity had been rudely illustrated at the end of the last Labour conference, when proceedings had closed to the sound of Queen's 'We Are The Champions' blasting from the public address system. The wondrous sight of Hattersley linking hands with shadow cabinet colleagues and chorusing words sung by a promiscuous bisexual glam rocker – the late Freddie Mercury – showed just how far from the Ragged Trousered Philanthropist the guiding imagery of democratic socialism had come – and how much Hattersley's hadn't.

He stepped into the foyer and re-emerged in half an hour, armed-by-association to join the farcical Law and Order fray. The

Conservatives' record on crime rivalled that on unemployment as the measure of their special genius. Thatcher had won in 1979, promising to reduce both. Within two years, the jobless total had doubled and in seven it had trebled. Echoing this, the period till 1991 had seen spending on law and order increase by 450 per cent while reported crime had almost doubled. An advanced knowledge of criminology is not required to make a link between crime – particularly crimes of violence and theft which had risen the fastest – and want. Nor, in reality, was the relationship lost on Hattersley. However, to cock an ear to this hollering truth was to contradict prejudices doubtless held by many of the 500,000 voters in those ninety-four key marginals. The popular view, rarely contradicted by the Conservatives who cynically benefited from it, was that the way to beat crime was to be more 'tough' with criminals. The rational view – that thugs and thieves multiply in conditions of poverty and social fracture – was therefore held to be 'soft'. Since Labour had as good as admitted that it could make no real dent in unemployment, since in any case you cannot be 'electable' if floating voters think you're 'soft', and since Labour had long ago abandoned all attempts at challenging erroneous perceptions, the only option left was to peddle the government's fictions under a subtly different cover.

On the step outside police headquarters Roy Hattersley proceeded to do just that. The Chief Constable of the West Midlands, he explained, had asked the Home Office for over 120 more officers to walk the streets. He had been allotted only eleven. Labour would do better, and next week Hattersley would let us know how he was going to pay for them. The trick was in the packaging. Hattersley's emphasis was on the need for more officers on foot. In the Glorious Past theme park – where Conservatives do not enjoy a monopoly tenure – private property and public serenity is maintained as sacrosanct by the affable, chuckling presence of 'bobbies on the beat'. A small increase in their numbers on the reprobate streets of Britain would make us all feel better, despite producing next to no reduction in our chances of being mugged or robbed.

That it had fallen to Hattersley to shift these shoddy goods was appropriate. His discomfort with the decor (as opposed to the 'moderation') of Labour's 'electability' had its roots in his attachment to a past which was less idealized than his political opponents' but was clung to no less fondly. He is a clever man, much cleverer than Britain's Next Prime Minister with whom he didn't really get on and whom he regularly shamed by comparison when called on to deputize for him at Prime Minister's Questions. Hattersley is big on *bon mots*, and among his prolific writings is a book-length account of *A Yorkshire Boyhood*, his own, full of down-to-earth Labour folk committed to assisting the deserving poor. These folk are portrayed with a remembered affection which flirts too closely with condescension, but seems to personify the kind of doughty virtues for which a Hattersleyesque Labour Party would stand. There would be a proper suspicion of Fancy Dan marketing techniques such as those deployed in the previous night's Labour election broadcast, in which panoramic footage of Our Great Nation was alternated with mood-lit talking head shots of Smith, Brown, Beckett, Blair, Taylor and Cook plying restrained promises about how they would – though not straight away, of course – make it greater still. Britain's Next Prime Minister got a word in at the end, but Hattersley was conspicuous by his absence. Maybe it was because he had broken ranks. Unlike the others, he had declined the attire of a banker's boardroom, or to erase words such as 'socialism' and 'equality' from his vocabulary, arguing that without adhering to the principles they denoted, Labour had as good as given up. As a result, he entered the election sounding more left wing than any of his peers, despite being to the right of most of them. There is no greater illustration of the presentational contortions 'electability' had required.

Hattersley completed his communion with the press and slipped into the passenger seat of a smooth green car. Next to him sat a chauffeur. The back seat was shared by myself, Hattersley's agent and one Jim Cunningham, a long-serving city councillor and current leader of the local Labour group. Cunningham said little, though he was a contentious figure, the man selected to fight the expelled Dave Nellist. The car set off round Coventry's interminable tangle of flyovers and one-way streets. Above the purr of the engine, Hattersley reflected on two photographs of him that had appeared in that day's *Guardian*. Taken on the pitch at Leeds United Football Club, the biggest showed Britain's Next Home Secretary in suit, tie and polished brogues, essaying a stiff-legged prod at an awkwardly bouncing ball. It was not a spectacle of enormous elegance, but Hattersley affected sanguineness: 'I was quite pleased. Quite pleased.'

We were sinking now into the soft furnishings of Hattersley self-parody, a comfortable setting from which to observe the small absurdities of oneself and others. It was the view from which Hattersley addressed his typewriter when writing his humorous columns for *Punch* and for the *Guardian* itself. The creation of this distance enabled him to advertise plebeian enthusiasms, such as supporting Sheffield Wednesday, with a cultivated amusement befitting the world of letters to which he had ascended. It was also the measure of the temperamental chasm between himself and Neil Kinnock.

'They told me,' he said, referring to the second photograph, 'not to risk heading it. It has a tendency to make you screw your eyes and face up in a rather unflattering way . . .'

The second picture showed Hattersley squinting and grimacing as if suffering a heart attack.

'. . . Unfortunately, someone crossed the ball at head height and I couldn't resist having a go at it . . . I just couldn't resist it.'

Forever the Yorkshire Boy, Hattersley with team in tow arrived at the local campaign office, a house at the end of a terrace normally used as a trade union base. There we were joined by Bob Slater, Labour's challenger to John Butcher in Coventry South-West, who, with his fixed crest of black hair, rakish moustache and glutinous smile, brought back misty memories of Dickie Davies. Cunningham, a Rothmans smoker, looked pale and worn. Suddenly, one of the entourage doubled back agitatedly. A photographer was encamped on the doorstep. This small emergency required a rapid reorganization of the red-rosed trio. The plan seemed to be as follows: Bob and Jim would act natural and continue on the original route, while Roy would nip in through the side entrance and answer the other two's knock. The photographer could then pounce on a perfect pack shot as Roy opened the door! The manoeuvre was executed beautifully. Its purpose was anyone's guess.

Inside the campaign office, Cunningham, lighting up, set out his credentials: Lanarkshire-born, engineer by trade, worked as a shop steward and senior steward of the Manufacturing, Science and Finance Union for twenty years. Though he had lived in Coventry for three decades, his Scottish accent was undiminished. He had a gristly toughness about him. Cunningham had served his time. Gruffly, he considered his opponent's reputation for sticking to his guns:

'I've always found Dave Nellist's principles a little bit hard to define. I've seen a lot of protest politics. In terms of achievement, that has been more illusory in my view.'

There had been disquiet over Nellist's expulsion. He was conscientious and definitely human. When asked on to TV chat shows, he accepted and behaved like a gentleman. Whatever his principles were, it looked as if he had been picked on for standing by them. But Cunningham was not ready to accept the role of soggy compromiser.

'The difference between Dave Nellist and I is that I've got experience of doing things, whereas Dave has got experience of raising issues, but hasn't had the experience of actually delivering the goods.'

Nellist was what the post-Fordist theoreticians of *Marxism Today* would call old-fashioned: he talked about 'struggle' and mobilizing the working class, which wasn't 'electable' talk at all. Cunningham, though, also declined to be outdone when it came to proletarian cred:

'I represent the working class as much as Dave Nellist does. I have had my achievements within the Labour movement. I've certainly been involved in factory occupations; I don't know whether he's ever occupied a factory.'

Such insurrections, though, had revealed the limits of class confrontation: 'Once you've got that sort of experience, you know how far you can go and how far you can't.' This defined the difference between himself and Nellist, who is 'basically Marxist or hard left'. Generously, Cunningham cited Russia as proving that Marxism didn't work. He preferred that to getting personal.

'I think in a number of instances Dave Nellist is maybe misguided. I don't know the individual that well to call him wicked.'

Calling Nellist 'wicked' would not have been smart. He had

become a minor celebrity, and Cunningham acknowledged his 'strong personal following'. So successful too was Nellist the Personality, that the national press couldn't be much bothered with Cunningham, with his air of graft and realism. They were far more intoxicated by the whiff of revolution.

In a soulless office, a hundred yards from the police HQ Hattersley had visited, Dave Nellist, sacrificial victim, prised a sandwich from its plastic shell and reflected on the fallout from his purging:

'I've had the best part of a thousand letters from Labour Party members around the country, saying that they were tearing up their party cards. I had twenty-five quid from a doctor in Huddersfield yesterday, fifty quid last night from a union bloke in Coventry, hundreds of pounds from union branches. The local chairman says about a hundred people have left the party. Just a minute . . . A quick bite of the sandwich.'

Nellist had got so into the proselytizing groove, he was even commentating on his own mastication. He had just returned from a photo session in the cathedral at the request of the *Daily Telegraph*. Making the journey by foot, he said he had been 'stopped twenty times in the road by people to wish me good luck'. In the first forty-eight hours after the election was announced he and his supporters had been on a 'poster blitz'. During this, he said, he hadn't spotted a single Tory flyer, just one for the Liberal Democrat and eighteen for Cunningham. By contrast, 'We've got about thirteen hundred up. We've got hoardings eight foot by eight foot on the outside walls of people's houses, including the house right by the gates of Coventry City, who are playing at home to Oldham tomorrow. We've got estate agent-type boards by front gates, about three dozen of those. It's like a by-election within a general election.'

Britain's Next Prime Minister had decided to get Dave Nellist because he thought there would be votes in it. He never said as much, of course, but there was no other plausible reason. Nellist had been one of Labour's most industrious and successful MPs, increasing his majority in Coventry South-East from a narrow 2500 in 1983 to a solid 6653 in 1987. He was admired in his constituency and respected by many in the House of Commons.

But for Britain's Next Prime Minister, the advantage to be gained by getting rid of Nellist outweighed any other consideration.

Nellist's sin was his association with the *Militant* newspaper which advances the perspectives of the Militant Tendency, a largely self-contained organization, formerly known as the Revolutionary Socialist League, whose intellectual guru was Leon Trotsky. Throughout the eighties, and before, they had carved out a niche in the Labour Party while denying their own existence as a distinct political entity. In 1985 Britain's Next Prime Minister had discovered to his pleasure that publicly battering Militants could prompt a few more people out of every hundred approached by public opinion pollsters to say they thought he was a fine fellow, and would continue to think so for at least a fortnight. His famous attack that year on the Militants who dominated Liverpool City Council had been rerun as a key part of his 1987 election campaign, at the end of which three more people out of every one hundred decided to vote for him than had for Michael Foot four years before. With such a bounty to be had, it was obviously worth devoting large quantities of his and other people's time to battering Militant further. Thus, Nellist and his Liverpool MP comrade, Terry Fields, had been investigated, tried, pronounced 'member' of Militant and dispatched from the Labour Party. Another triumph for 'electability'.

In response, a small army of partisans was rallying to Nellist's cause. These included many from the local party who 'think we've been stitched up. They feel that it's been unfair.' Also: 'I've got a letter from a fella saying he's got a caravanette, just tell him where to park. Yesterday, I had a seventy-seven-year-old woman from Nuneaton phone up and say she's got a car, she can give me one day next week, three days the week after and all day polling day. We had a big fuss in the paper last week because a twelve-year-old was organizing some work with his school mates . . .'

Another bite of the sandwich. A telephone call to take. Between interruptions Nellist conversed in West Midland timbres of hyperactive reassurance, implied protestations of innocence spiked with hustings adrenalin. In appearance, he differed from archetypal Militants whom Hattersley – who despised them – loftily derided in an article written in 1982 as 'short-haired youths in sleeveless pullovers wearing training shoes'. True, the lads answering telephones and exercising the photocopier in the room next door broadly fitted that characterization. They had, too, the tight lips and hunted look routinely assumed when tolerating the presence of the bourgeois press. Nellist, though, looked sharp. Sandy-haired and neatly-bearded, his shirt was crisp and Persil-white, his tie advertised solidarity with the National Union of Mineworkers, while his suit was a revelation, a sharpster's delight in chequered tan. Celebrity Militants always seem to favour hipster-chic. But Nellist's differences with his executioners were, of course, more than sartorial:

'Most things that the Labour Party opposes, I'm with 'em a hundred per cent. It's what it *pro*poses that I find too modest. In '87 we stood on a platform of a million jobs in two years. In '83 it was a return to full employment. Today there isn't any target: things will get done "as the economy allows it". Now, I was against the Gulf War and the Falklands War, but I don't remember Thatcher or Major saying, "Hang on Galtieri, hang on Saddam Hussein, we'll have a war with you as soon as the economy allows it." Labour ought to have the same attitude towards the three and a half million unemployed, the millions who live in damp houses or don't have holidays each year.'

The first hint there, though caressed with gentle shrugs, of the Black and Decker Trot didactics that automatically presuppose in outsiders a hopeless capitulation to capitalist propaganda, and push up sales of paracetamol. But there was, too, the stuff of questioning political will. Militant may not go much for elegantly barbed innuendo, but they are mustard-hot when it comes to getting off their arse.

Nellist, sipping a coffee and eyeing a Twix, produced a draft of his personal manifesto, some of which he briefly paraphrased. Where tax and benefits were concerned, he made John Smith look like Scrooge: minimum wage not £130 a week, but £185 for thirty-eight hours; pension promises matching those of '87 were useless when a retired couple had lost 'the best part of twenty-five pounds' since 1980; he had stood by a three-pound increase in child benefit – more than Smith was offering for first children – way back in '83. Generous, then, the Nellist agenda. However, his proposals signified not a greater predilection for philanthropy, but an aspiration whose fulfilment was dependent on a fundamental realignment of power in the economy. He repeated a time-honoured revolutionary homily: 'It's not about getting a different slice of the cake: it's about who controls the bakery.'

The way to achieve that was nationalization, but not on the post-war model. Under the heading 'A Socialist Economy', Nellist's draft manifesto read: 'The economy is owned and controlled by a small minority of people. The wealth we produce is directed into increased dividends for shareholders and inflated salaries for directors . . . How could ordinary people direct the spending of the wealth they produce? Only through the owner-ship of this wealth being in the hands of all the community.'

It went on to quote from an article published in *Labour Monthly* in December 1974:

> While everyone apparently shares the belief that we should abolish poverty, homelessness, slum schools, hospital waiting lists . . . It must now be clearly apparent that none of this can be achieved at the speed or with the breadth that we demand if we are to rely on capitalism to pay for it. Privilege will defend itself, and by that defence deny even the existing facilities to the underprivileged. There is no need to be apologetic about the extension of public ownership or the establishment of workers' control. They are now the prerequisites of the economic survival of Britain . . . There is no alternative in the capitalist system – it is a failure.

These were not Dave Nellist's words. They were Neil Kin-nock's. Nellist not only agreed with them, he remained convinced that, with faith and application, the notions enshrined in them could turn people on.

'The ideas I put forward in Coventry, if somebody reports them in a newspaper down south, and then you go and ask people what you think of what this bloke's saying in the paper, I would not be surprised if nine out of ten people said 'the bloke's a lunatic'. But if I go round Willenhall, an area where I've lived in and represented for over ten years, you'll get a lot of support for it. We've got roots round here. Those ideas are part of the fabric.'

The sandwich eaten, Nellist made ready for his next media appointment, a local radio interview. I headed off for Willenhall in search of the working class. It was knocking-off time, and Coventry's citizenry was heading home from work. Not all that much of it was heading for Willenhall, though. Whole streets of tatty terraces and heart-chilling weather-greyed council blocks bore the invisible, yet smothering pall of unemployment, deprivation, hopelessness. Only one thing lightened the load: regular punctuations, sometimes merging into unbroken lines, of livid pink rectangles, bearing a one-word message: 'Nellist'.

It was a bad time to buttonhole Willenhall's denizens. The day was cold, most people were heading home and it was too early for the pubs to be buzzing. But some impromptu vox pop bore witness to the permeation if not of Nellist's ideology, then certainly those roots he talked about.

A young man at a bus stop: 'He's a good bloke, stuck to his guns.'

An older man leaving a paper shop: 'I suppose he's a bit extreme. But he takes a bit of interest. Can't fault him for that.'

A woman on the pavement, bending into the wind: 'He's a lovely fella. You'll put that in, won't you?'

A couple of cheeky lads: 'No poll tax! No poll tax!'

The campaign against the poll tax defined the difference between Militant and 'electable' Labour with a heavy line. The All-Britain Anti-Poll Tax Federation was the Trots' creation (dishonestly sexified in the Tory press as 'a Militant front') and it introduced insubordination to people who had surrendered quietly all their lives. The bottom line was 'can't pay, won't pay' and millions took that advice. Nellist was ready to go to prison, but had his bill paid by the well-heeled right agitators – and Thatcher soulmates – of the Freedom Association, fearing martyrdom in the making. (Fields did endure incarceration, in Liverpool's stinking Walton jail. His expulsion took place within a month of his release.) Militant worked to legitimize non-payment as not delinquency but dissent. They were largely successful.

'Electable' Labour, meanwhile, bemoaned the tax iniquity of the tax in the House of Commons but urged the populace to pay up. At the height of the revolt, the party's popularity soared. Was that because of, or in spite of, the non-payment campaign? For Nellist, there was no doubt. What is more, he thought, the demise of the tax proved the case for the tactics and the class analysis

Militant espouses: 'It's the Tories who actually practise class struggle, by cutting benefits, by allowing unemployment to rise to mass levels. They are the ones who are taking on the working class. All I go out and say is if you *stick together* you can defeat things. That is an old lesson, and I think it is still appropriate in the nineties.'

It was an assertion depending on one or two challengeable assumptions: for example, that of the 95 per cent who do not own the great bulk of the nation's wealth have a common interest in defeating very much of what had happened in the previous twelve years; for example, that the black and Asian British, the women who work at home, the sexual non-conformists, the punks and the house-proud pensioners actually recognize themselves in the image of muscular working-class self-organization depicted by Hattersley's 'short-haired youths in sleeveless sweaters and training shoes', the lads answering Nellist's telephone. Arguments about such matters lie at the heart of ongoing struggles about the future of the left.

But one thing you can say about Militant: if everyone had paid up, the poll tax would have stayed. In mobilizing to force its removal, they inflicted more damage on Margaret Thatcher than Neil Kinnock, Roy Hattersley and the rest of 'electable' Labour had managed in eight years.

CHAPTER THIRTEEN

Valley Boys

(Saturday 21 March)

Balloons, yellow balloons, and printed on them in red: 'Neil Kinnock'. By their presence the pedestrians on Risca High Street were informed of excitement to come, but the best some of them could manage was wry curiosity tinged with amazement: 'I've never seen so many police in Risca.'

This from an old man with his hands wedged in his blouson pockets. He nodded towards the top end of the road. 'That police station down there, that's shut at night now. It's a burglar's delight round yere.'

His mate, short and wiry, with a daft dog on a leash, chimed in like an echo chamber: 'It's a burglar's delight.'

The first man continued: 'You don't see a policeman round yere now, that bad it is. They're afraid to walk up through yere, the women ones, at night.'

The second man said: 'Up through yere, the women.'

'If you report a robbery now,' said the first man, ''e's either got to come from Abercarn, that's four miles away, or from Blackwood. By the time they get yere it's a waste of time.'

'A waste of time,' said the second man.

A sleek red saloon pulled in to the kerb at the point where the balloons bobbed most copiously. In went the photographers, in went the cameras, in went the press. Out got Britain's Next Prime Minister or, as it proved, this being his home turf, out got Neil Kinnock, and through the rumpus we caught glimpses of his pale, beaming face.

The first man sighed: 'I don't think he's really up to it, you know. I think that Ashdown would be better.'

So what was the problem with Neil?

The first man cocked his head and tutted: 'He's like a little boy, isn't he?'

Risca and the adjoining Crosskeys together comprise the biggest settlement in the Islwyn constituency. Its population is less than 12,000. Until quite recently probably eight out of every ten men living there, as in Islwyn as a whole, depended on collieries for their living, if not as coal face workers, then as fitters, technicians or railway workers. But even before the strike of 1984–5, there were only nine working National Coal Board (now British Coal) pits in the whole of South Wales. Now only three remain and none of them are in Islwyn.

'The railway jobs that went yere when the pits closed down was unbelievable,' said the first man. 'They lost everything.'

'Everything,' said the second.

The miners' strike had been the worst nightmare of Kinnock's leadership. He thought the NUM president Arthur Scargill was a demagogue and his methods suicidal. Kinnock had spent the year of the dispute impaled on a fence dividing gut sympathy from political embarrassment, as picket line violence escalated (blamed, naturally, on the miners and never on the police) and the defeat he had always anticipated became inevitable. When the miners finally capitulated, Thatcher's triumph over organized labour was effectively complete. What was left was still more unemployment, something Kinnock had spent from then till 1992 gradually concluding he could do next to nothing about.

'It's been terrible,' said the first man.

'Terrible,' said the second.

They meant it. Ten per cent of Islwyn's population was unemployed.

Neil Kinnock – his exuberance confirmed that it was definitely him – was trying to get into a cake shop. His attempts to execute this manoeuvre gave new meaning to the expression 'bunfight' as the media menagerie, his aides and his supporters all converged on the doorway at once. Then came an unexpected visitation. Gangling and bespectacled in a long, black overcoat, he might have been a church beadle but for his enormous blue rosette. His name was Peter Bone, Islwyn's Conservative candidate.

'Mr Kinnock,' he called, with edgy politeness, craning over the scrum. 'Er, Mr Kinnock.'

Kinnock looked up. He was a foot shorter than Bone and three times as wide.

'Oo are you?'

The hostile tone suggested he had already worked that out. Kinnock's supporters were catching on too.

'Look out, Neil! He's an Essex Man!'

Not exactly, but he was a man from Essex. Bone had moved to South Wales from Southend after selling his electronics business and setting up in Gwent with help from the Welsh Development Agency, a government body designed to encourage an influx of new industry. He now ran a travel agency in Newport, renting condos in Florida. As such, he was a creature from another planet.

'I'm the Conservative candidate . . .'

'Oh,' said Kinnock, sarcastically, 'I thought I would have recognized you.'

Great hoots of laughter from the Kinnock supporters. Their man was sounding more Welsh than at any time in the campaign.

Bone persevered: 'Why won't you debate with me in front of the Islwyn electorate?'

'Why should 'e?' rasped a furious female voice.

'You're not worth it!' growled a male one.

Any lingering resemblance Neil Kinnock had to Britain's Next Prime Minister disappeared. Jabbing his finger, he replied with menacing emphasis: 'Listen. *You* go, and get *your* boss to debate with *me* on television . . .'

The rest was lost in raucous applause. Bone turned and stalked away. Kinnock's supporters, mocking Margaret Thatcher's famous goading of Michael Foot, chanted: 'Frit! Frit! Frit! Frit!' as the Conservative candidate, shaking perceptibly, headed for the massed sound booms and the prospect of a consoling quote on the local news.

They don't like Tories in the valleys. Mention of Winston Churchill, strictly an English hero, has been known to prompt older people to spit on the floor. Conservative attitudes to miners also inform this dense history of antipathy. When they strike, it is the Tory custom to brand them as deranged subversives and respond accordingly. For example, in 1926 when Welsh miners came out for six months against wage cuts, Stanley Baldwin sent battleships to patrol the Cardiff coast.[1] So when Thatcher denounced the NUM as 'the enemy within' she was retooling a sound bite from the Glorious Past. In keeping, the riot police she sent to neutralize the pickets were armed with batons and plastic bullets, and trained in crowd control techniques developed by the army in Northern Ireland.

The second man in Risca High Street, the one with the daft dog, recalled this blue militia escorting lorries bulging with imported coke brought in to Port Talbot docks to undermine the impact of the strike: 'They broke all records,' he sighed. No policeman on the High Street at night, though. Perhaps Roy Hattersley would put that right.

Islwyn, then, was Labour and seemingly solid for eternity. Kinnock took over 70 per cent of the vote in 1987. Still gazing quizzically from the pavement, the first man said: 'Labour could put up a monkey down here and they'd vote for it.'

'A monkey,' said the second man.

To Bone, such affinities were beyond understanding. 'It's tradition,' he had supposed, correctly, a few weeks before, but without much inkling as to what had brought the tradition about. He had one worthwhile observation though: 'If Islwyn was on the other side of the Bristol Channel, it would be a Conservative seat.'

A big 'if', but worth considering. The last Islwyn pit, just up the road in Oakdale, closed down in 1989. It marked the end of a long pit decline, partly alleviated by new, light industrial employers. An Aiwa factory is perhaps the most significant example of this 'inward investment'. There had been other Conservative-prompted incursions, too, into this Labour heartland of slag heaps gathering grass. A comprehensive school had decided, with the support of parents, to 'opt out' of local authority control under Conservative legislation, leaving the Labour-run Islwyn Borough Council helpless and dismayed. The ex-pitmen, meanwhile, took redundancy money. Most then signed on and hoped. A few enrolled for further education. The previous year I had downed pints with some of them at the Oakdale Rugby Club bar. None

1. See Raphael Samuel's Introduction to *The Enemy Within – Pit Villages and The Miners' Strike of 1984–5*, Routledge & Kegan Paul, 1986.

had yielded during the strike, yet all stuck by Kinnock who sometimes joined them for a drink, to tell stories and crack jokes. These ex-miners at least sympathized with his sidesteps to the centre. What else, they asked, could he do? Canvassing in '83 they'd heard it on the doorsteps of their very own village: 'How can we risk getting rid of our nuclear weapons?' 'We can't keep the pits going for ever.' Kinnock is not soft. He listened. He trimmed. He decided he would have to risk looking like a faintheart or a fraud.

Returning to the red saloon, waving and clasping hands, Kinnock rolled up to Blackwood, just a mile away, for more of the same. He covered the upward-sloping terrain of the Saturday morning market inch by inch, his minders engineering snippets of screenplay as best they could: into a covered fruit stall, looking healthy, accepting a good-luck card, homemade by children. 'I'm worried,' said Charles Clarke, Kinnock's managerial fixer-in-chief, clutching his mobile phone. 'I'm terrified someone's going to get hurt.' Camera crew directors hustled for advantage: 'Julie! Julie! Can we get Neil over this way?' Ms Hall smiled her elfin smile.

The gladhanding was over by lunch. Time for Kinnock to get back to Cardiff for an appointment at the Arms Park. That morning in the Welsh capital he had addressed a press conference on the subject of Labour's proposed Welsh Assembly. In 1979 he had led the campaign against devolution on grounds of working-class unity, attracting the wrath of his local party for the first time. Now he was in favour of devolution. He was in favour, too, of symbolic associations with his roots, hence the trip to the Arms Park, cathedral of Welsh rugby, and a showdown with the Scots.

Later, back in Risca, in a free house called the Cuckoo Inn, a few of the lads in a teeming lounge bar spotted him slipping into his VIP seat as they gazed at a monster TV screen, eight feet across. They had all heard about it, the fuss in the High Street that morning, though it was dead again down there now. Mooching in from the drizzle-soiled housing estate across the municipal green, they had squashed into plastic banquettes, resting pint glasses in their groins, desperate for an end to the shortage of national rugby triumphs almost as acute as that of

Labour governments. For once, they were not disappointed. Wales won by 15 points to 12. The celebrations spread to every pub in Risca and there were a fair few of those. The Cuckoo Inn was not the only one to cradle a jarring combination of valley community sentiment and the engulfing blandishments of mass-tech entertainment. In another, the lads – and they were nearly all lads – who patronized it considered their lot with a mordant stubbornness which also appeared to dictate the way they voted: 'Labour, always Labour. Well, what have the Tories ever done for us?'

As the night wore on the thump of processed funk increased in intensity; ashtrays filled to brimming, and lager ('the amber nectar, man!') eased down eager throats. The rugby result was discussed with satisfaction : 'Magic, man, magic!' But jobs were described as temporary phenomena, liable to disappear overnight. There was none of the binding pride with which the former pitmen had remembered their lost industry. One lad was a dogsbody at a printing firm. Another, a becalmed painter and decorator. A third, a dismantler of public telephones. Some earned less than three pounds an hour. Most were sleepwalking towards their middle twenties, still living with their parents, partly, the way they told it, out of apathy, partly because they had no other obvious choice.

Two nights before, Kinnock had made a big speech in Birmingham. The segment picked out on television showed him at his best, in full flight, recalling with his whole body the Wales of his youth: 'The kids I grew up with, and the previous generation, when they were hit by slump, when the collieries closed, when the steel mills closed, where did they find refuge, where did they go to get jobs? They came here, to the West Midlands. It's no good them doing that now, because there's 10 per cent unemployment, quarter of a million unemployed. What a terrible price is being paid.'

None of the Risca lads had seen that fragment of speech, but it told them nothing they didn't already know. Maybe they would try to leave one day. There again, maybe not. Neither option held much promise. What they held on to was the echo of a way of life of which the pit strike had been a last-gasp defence. Never mind what the papers said, that strike had not been foisted on its participants by a satanic Scargill and a coterie of thugs. Though varying from field to field, the miners' resistance – in South Wales as much as anywhere – was not motivated by blind obedience to their leader up in Barnsley but by their own, localized desires to preserve something: a way of working which was more than just a matter of clocking on at the start of a week and getting paid at the end. It was about cooperation, about mutual dependency, about loyalty to past generations. The same applied to voting. Peter Bone, the Tory candidate, found it inexplicable: 'They say "if I don't vote Labour, my grandmother will turn in her grave".'

The Oakdale Miners' Institute building has been transplanted brick by brick to the museum of Welsh Folk History near Cardiff. It has left behind an emotional investment still strong but of diminishing returns. A Welsh rugby win was a consoling novelty. A Labour government led by a Welshman would be much the same: 'Kinnock can't do much if he does win; but he's a good bloke. He's one of ours.'

CHAPTER FOURTEEN

The Mongrel Bark

(Sunday 22 March)

'Hello Cardiff? I thought I'd lost you then for a minute. I'd hate to do that.'

Sitting in a self-operated radio studio, Dafydd Wigley was sending himself up. Plaid Cymru, the Party of Wales, has never come near to winning in Cardiff, so the prospect of losing it did not arise. But Wigley, the party's president and best known MP, had embarked on the election trail intent on changing that, if not on 9 April, then by the end of the century. 'Towards 2000' was the name of Plaid's manifesto, declaring the millennial landmark by which time they aimed to secure 'self-government' for Wales. The British Broadcasting Corporation in Bangor was a useful means to that end.

'. . . Some 12,000 are literally homeless, sometimes sleeping in the backs of cars . . .'

This was the English version of Wigley's election broadcast, on the subject of his country's housing crisis. He had already reeled off the Welsh equivalent, reading from a hand-written text, in which only 'okay', 'SNP' and 'London' were intelligible to the unschooled ear. 'London' accidentally became 'Lindon', but Cardiff let that pass. Mispronounced or not, the English political capital's culpability for the dearth of council dwellings in Wales was made plain enough.

Heading out through the foyer, Wigley glanced at the television in the corner. The pictures, beamed by satellite across continents, showed the English cricket team – containing one white South African, one white Zimbabwean and three black Englishmen of various Caribbean descents – engaged in a knife-edge struggle in the semi-final of the Cricket World Cup.

'159 for 4, could be close,' observed the MP knowledgeably, one of the men John Major had had in mind when he had referred in Torquay to 'the threat to the union that has served this country well'. And the reason for that was the bubbling new confidence of the Welsh and Scottish nationalists – if 'nationalist', in Plaid Cymru's case, is quite the right word.

'We're a mongrel people in Wales,' asserted Wigley, settling into a couch at his next destination, the chintz-and-stained-wood lounge of a hotel on the bank of the Menai Strait. A picture window offered a gorgeous view of rushing water, the Menai Bridge which straddled it, and the rocky apron of Anglesley beyond. 'We don't want to see an inward-looking, narrow Wales, but one that can play a role in the world as a whole, shoulder our responsibilities towards the Third World and the rest.'

Across the room, three men in jeans and trainers were easing the hinged sections of the portable Plaid Cymru telly backdrop out of cardboard cartons. Four of these had been made at the shoestring cost of £3500; one for Cardiff, one for Swansea, one for London and one for here in Bangor at the intersection of three constituencies in the party's north-west heartland. Over the water, Ieuan Wyn Jones had prevailed in '87, suitably becoming the first Plaid Cymru MP to represent the island seat in the first election since it had been renamed Ynys Mon out of deference to the area's majority first tongue. A few yards, literally, to the west, Wigley's own seat of Caernarfon began. Bangor itself, meanwhile, fell within the boundaries of Conwy, which was held by a Tory.

The voting variegations in these three seats suggested a tactical character to electoral loyalties which it was Plaid Cymru's task to standardize to their advantage. Since the last war, as Anglesey, Ynys Mon had had a Liberal, a Labour and a Conservative MP before Jones; after first winning Caernarfon in '74, Wigley had annexed the Labour vote so completely that they were reduced to fourth place; in Conwy, conversely, Labour were a close second, leaving Plaid a poor last. In each case, anti-Tory sentiment had expressed itself pragmatically, with gut nationalist voters ready to back Labour and vice versa. The latter had helped Plaid's third member, Dafydd Elis Thomas (who was bowing out as an MP this time) in Meirionnydd Nant Conwy. Yet the whole situation created a paradox: Plaid's victors owed a great deal to pragmatic

Labour voters, yet the fulfilment of their historic mission required seeing Labour off, not just in the north-west, but throughout the country. With an all-Wales fighting fund of just £25,000, they were setting about this massive task by urging the Welsh people to look outwards, beyond their own boundaries and neglectful London, to a benign greater Europe unfolding before their eyes.

'The only separatists now,' said Wigley, 'are the Little Englanders in the Tory party who want to pull out of Europe and remain an offshore island.' His voice was a galloping, managerial Welsh baritone. An accountant by trade, he had started out at Ford's in Dagenham, gone on to be chief cost accountant with Mars in Slough and returned to Wales as financial controller of Hoover in Merthyr Tydfil, down south in the Rhondda Valley: 'We employed 5500 people then,' he sighed. 'There's 1500 there now.'

The shrinking of this famous Welsh industry was grist to Wigley's anti-Labour mill. His point was that Wales's overwhelming Labour loyalty had done it little good. A 5 per cent swing across Britain from Tory to Labour on 9 April would, he calculated, reduce the Tories from having six Welsh seats out of thirty-eight to just three, yet still leave them as the biggest party in Westminster. What Plaid ultimately needed was a mass Labour defection from Labour, giving them a mandate to negotiate self-government and set up a proper Welsh Parliament, with tax-raising, law-making and economic-planning powers, as well as assuming all the social and infrastructural prerogatives presently held by the Welsh Office, with its £600 million budget, deployed as the Welsh Secretary, David Hunt – whom the Welsh people didn't want and who didn't even hold a Welsh seat – saw fit. 'There's a touch of the governor-general about that.' As for the Welsh Assembly Labour proposed, that would be 'a talking shop'. It was time for the 'mongrel people' to assert themselves.

It was not a glamorous self-definition, but you could see the sense of it. Not only did it do justice to the yesteryears of migration – particularly from England – of both wage labourers and entrepreneurs that had accompanied industrialization in the south, it also described the dog's dinner of the north's economy. Tourism, an alien contagion in the eyes of mystic nationalists with arson on their minds, is as permanent a feature of the landscape (from what the English call Snowdonia to Llandudno by the sea) as struggling sheep farms (ignored by the Ministry of Agriculture, complained Wigley) and deceased slate quarries, once the primary source of local employment, now down from 20,000 jobs at the time of World War One to about 300. The old industries that might once have been a pressure cooker of aspirations for change have gone. 'I have more people working in the independent television and film industry in my constituency,' Wigley observed, with one eye on the backdrop construction, 'than are working in coal in the whole of Wales.'

Anxious to supervise the erection of his set – a problem rival party leaders did not have – Wigley slipped off momentarily to ensure that the whole lot wouldn't fold up on him when he came to address the cameras. In his plain grey suit and sensible specs, this documentor of the 'Welsh democratic deficit' was the frontman for an ideological coalition which wedded idealistic fervour and appeals to indigenous identity carefully couched to outlaw glib xenophobia. 'Towards 2000' offered a shrewd cocktail of accountable soft socialism, rurally-focused environmentalism (in some seats, Plaid had joined forces with the Green Party) and autonomy not as a chippy little nation state, but as a progressive region within a future federal Europe committed to the concept of 'subsidiarity', by which decision-making would be as downwardly-localized as feasible within the broad EC embrace.

With this formulation, Wigley was convinced Plaid Cymru were poised to clean up, as the cultural fabric of Labour-dominated Wales wore away to create a demand for something new.

'I think what is happening in Wales is that there is a change from the politics of the place of work to the politics of the community in which you live. That is a perceptible change. When the slate quarries came to an end, the grip of the Labour Party also came to an end, and then your politics revolved around questions like, "What facilities do you have in the community in which you live?" And it is a change which is now happening in the coal-mining valleys of Glamorgan and Gwent in the post-Scargill era. How that works through in political terms will be fascinating.'

Wigley's vision of a Wales of enhanced independence and prosperity in an evolving 'Europe of the regions' sat quite comfortably with his party's continuing commitment to bilingualism as the keystone of cultural tradition. Champions of a devolved, federal, European future see the regional model as a way of reconciling nationalistic desires within existing nation states (such as the Basques' in Spain) with the countervailing forces of greater mobility, global shrinkage and cultural uniformity in a hi-tech, transnational world. In other words, marginalization need not be the price paid for regional particularity. For such a dream to become reality would require both institutional evolution at the centre of Europe and cultural evolution in the meaning of 'community'. Of the first, Wigley was optimistic. The last European summit at Maastricht had set up a Charter of the Regions. He believed it could lead to 'a second chamber of the European Parliament that acts as a decentralizing force to put a brake on the first chamber that inevitably wants centralization.' As for a community outlook that is not based on (sometimes sour-faced) parochialism, that could be a tougher circle to square.

The predominance of Welsh as the area's first language remained the biggest purely positive reason for Plaid's buoyancy in the north. About two thirds of Wigley's constituency mail is written in the native tongue, while 'about 80 per cent' of surgery conversations are spoken in it. His campaign newspaper, *Herald Ni*, was a four-sided, reversible feast, delivering its message in both Welsh and English, to be folded according to taste. Wigley disputed, though, that linguistic attachments are Plaid's sole serious electoral asset. In the valleys and urbanized south, the native tongue had ceased wagging years back and Plaid's general election vote was minute. But they had councillors, even in Islwyn, where the nationalist candidate Helen Jones, a former Greenham Common partisan, all-purpose collectivist and cultural humanist, had fiercely described Labour in Wales as 'corrupt' and 'bankrupt'.

Wigley looked into the future and saw a weakening of Westminster's reach in a Labour vote that is 'incredibly soft, compared to what it was. Labour is either going to fail to form a government again,' he continued, 'in which case it could disintegrate, and we must be ready to pick up the bits, or Labour will come in, give a Parliament for Scotland, won't do anything for Wales, get into the sort of economic mess all governments do in mid-term, and I tell you,' he concluded, reaching a barely-suppressed crescendo, 'we're going to take Labour to the cleaners in those valleys then.'

Off he went then to deliver his text as the Menai coursed behind him. It was mid-morning. In Australia, England were still battling it out with South Africa. In the ex-slate village of Rhiwlas, just inside Wigley's constituency, someone in a front room may well have been watching it, since they had a satellite dish mounted on the outside of their house. Though squashed into a hillside crevice, Rhiwlas's properties were mostly unremarkable post-war bungalows which disappointed romantic – and, of course, absurd – expectations of ancient granite hamlets. A few people were stepping out to buy their Sunday papers. The newsagent carried the full range of British Sunday titles, broadsheets as well as tabloids, evidence that the intelligentsia has planted its feet pretty firmly in the Bangor foothills. It is, after all, home of the University of North Wales, where irate indigenous undergraduates have set up a Welsh student union to rival the official National (meaning British) Union of Students branch.

Fleet Street's metropolitan wits read pretty incongruously on a cropped and craggy hillside, from which emerged no sound save the occasional gormless bleat of a hardy sheep. Collectively, the up-market journalists had done their best to lampoon the thunderous fatuities of the party leaders' itineraries in the preceding days, with their staged 'events', witless photo opportunities and no-score telly-draws. The Tory poodles, of course, devoted vast acreages to frightening people with graphs and tables purporting to prove how Labour would tax, tax, tax. One in the *Sunday Express* didn't even bother to cost in their proposed increases in state pensions and child benefit, so abject was their slavering at the Conservatives' feet. The big pictorial splashes, though, heralded Margaret Thatcher's re-enlistment into the ranks. Four out of five opinion polls published that morning showed Labour still ahead, in one case by 5 points. It seemed the Tory campaign believed a chorus of Rule Britannia to be in order.

On the Welsh hillside, a sheep sent out another plaintive cry. If a bleat can be un-British, that was surely one. A man who had just bought a copy of the *News of the World* whispered that he would be voting Conservative: 'But you keep that kind of thing a secret around here.'

CHAPTER FIFTEEN

Broadly Flat

(Monday 23 March)

Nice John, Chairman Chris and the gorgeous Michael Heseltine took their seats behind a bulwark of cornflower blue at Conservative Central Office, Smith Square, Westminster. They had a problem: Authority's Experts thought the Tories had 'lost' the first full week of the campaign. The basis for this assessment cannot have been scientific, given that the BBC poll of polls still showed Labour only fractionally ahead, just as it had almost constantly since the budget and for weeks before. As much as anything, the criticisms were aesthetic.

The previous Wednesday, the first Tory TV election broadcast had gone out, preceded by hyperbole of an intensity normally reserved for feature films starring Sylvester Stallone. The comparison is not entirely ludicrous, since the broadcast had many familiar ingredients of a cinematic epic, compressed into a ten-minute personality puff: a title, 'The Journey'; a famous-name director, John Schlesinger; an implausible plotline; and an outsider hero who prevails in the face of overwhelming odds. Much of the broadcast depicted Major revisiting his Brixton 'roots', buying rootsy kippers in the market from rootsy black traders, and loitering in his car without being questioned by the police. At one point he peered through the bullet-proof glass to express his amazement that the less seedy Brixton dwelling he had moved into after leaving the infamous Coldharbour Lane flat had not been knocked down: 'Is it still here? It is, it *is*.' Unlike the sets for most bad movies, the building was not prefabricated, but the dialogue made up for that.

On Sunday lunchtime, Major had been questioned live from Downing Street by ITV's star political interviewer Brian Walden.

This important television appointment had been brought forward at the Conservatives' request in an attempt to enhance their leader's profile in the light of fears that he was not making much of an impact. For fifty minutes, Walden had worried away at the issue of whether Major could convince undecided voters that he was sufficiently 'caring' about the public services and the unemployed, against the background thesis that perceptions of 'caring' would be decisive. He got nowhere. For all his preparation, and for all his persistence, Walden was quite unable to prevent his interviewee from making the points *he* wanted to make: about the increases in NHS funding which the Conservatives had, indeed, made (though the issue, not covered, was whether it was enough); and the need to 'incentivize' – a grotesque new piece of jargon – middle-income professionals in health (like consultants) and education (like secondary school head teachers) by putting more money in their pockets through tax cuts. To do otherwise, Major insisted, would persuade lots of them to leave the country: 'What sort of message is it to young people to say "go and train to be a doctor, be successful, become a surgeon, and at the end of doing all that and providing a service that we desperately need, there isn't an incentive for you, there's a penalty for you"?' The gist of Walden's approach concerned floating voter perceptions. What it yielded was a classically firm but friendly Nice John riposte, far more convincing than the awful party election broadcast.

Another Tory device for pumping Major's homely profile was unveiled in the preceding days, the first two of a series of meet-the-people stunts 'in the round'. Supposedly based on the famous tank-and-squaddie session in the Gulf, it involved the PM in his shirtsleeves perched on a stool, surrounded by positively-vetted stooges. They fed him flattering lines about government policy, which Nice John smilingly fielded and returned with self-flattering replies. Little bits of these exchanges were duly regurgitated on television, for which they were solely designed. Chairman Chris and his team clearly believed there was no kind of bullshit the British public wouldn't swallow. Authority's Experts, though, were more choosy about their diets. 'Lacklustre' was a favourite put-down. In response, Chairman Chris's licensed leakers had spread news at the weekend of a change of tactics: Nice John was going to get nastier; and the battalions flak-attacking on tax, tax, tax would lower their sights from 'middle-income' or 'middle-class' voters to target the sacred C2s.

The Monday morning press conference was intended to reflect this redeployment. Happily, it descended into chaos. There were two related reasons for this: the first was a front-page story in the *Guardian*; the second was another disrespectful intervention by Anthony Bevins of *The Independent*. The *Guardian* piece was written by its economics editor, Will Hutton, and his colleague, Ruth Kelly. Basing their findings on a close reading of *The Red Book*, the manual of detailed Treasury figures published at every budget, Hutton and Kelly sought to demonstrate the impossibility of a re-elected Conservative government, or any other, being able to meet its spending promises without either raising taxes (which the Tories were, of course, pledged to cut), breaking their spending promises or increasing borrowing from £28 billion to around £40 billion, a debt which, for Norman Lamont, would amount to emasculation by freezing tidal wave.

Nice John dismissed all that with robotic emollience: 'The most important suggestion in the *Guardian* article is that current spending in future wouldn't be covered by tax revenues. That is wrong.' But his circuitry was not programmed to cope so efficiently with Bevins. Sitting in the front row, Tony the Tiger (with the *Guardian* story, doubtless, in mind) began by asking Nice John to 'give us a pledge that you won't increase the tax burden in the next Parliament, please'.

Behind Nice John was an upwardly-revised 'tax bombshell' trumpeting that a Labour government would take not just the additional £1000 a year in tax as previously claimed, but £1250. In front of Nice John, there now rose a thin semantic smokescreen: 'As you know, Tony . . .' (We're all friends here, you know.) '. . . direct taxes have come down substantially in recent years and we are continuing to reduce, er . . . and we are continuing to reduce, er . . . er, direct taxes. We have done so repeatedly over recent years. The one way you can be certain the burden of tax will rise, Tony . . .' (Me and Tony, we understand each other.) '. . . is to have a Labour government . . .'

Another reporter began blowing the smokescreen away. He put it to Major (as Bevins had at the manifesto launch) that the *overall* tax burden had actually *increased* since 1979. The underlying point was that people have to pay VAT, other excise duties (on cigarettes, alcohol, and so on) social security contributions and the poll tax to the government as well, and when they were included in the calculation, the total tax take as a percentage of Gross Domestic Product was, indeed, slightly higher than in 1979.[1]

Nice John's mouth went slightly rigid. He responded evenly: 'The tax burden is broadly flat . . .'

Broadly flat? Small groans begin seeping from the normally deferential gentlemen of the press.

'. . . despite the fact that we've repaid a vast amount of debt over the last twelve years.'

Bevins counter-punched: 'Look at your own borrowing requirement now, it is now bigger than you inherited from Labour.'

Chairman Chris, spotting a socratic dialogue, tried to intervene: 'I am sure that . . .'

Nice John said: 'The figures aren't accurate . . .' He began spewing statistics, saying the national debt under Labour had been 'on average' the equivalent of £40 billion today.

Bevins followed up: 'The borrowing requirement you inherited from Labour was less than what you are now leaving behind you.'

Chairman Chris: 'As you well know . . .'

Bevins slugged on: 'You've got a bigger borrowing requirement now than you inherited from Labour.'

Nice John began: 'As you well know . . .'

'Well, it's true,' smouldered Bevins. 'I've got the Treasury table. Do you want the Treasury table?'

He began flapping a piece of paper at Nice John who responded with some flapping of his own, in his case with a hand, as if repelling a troublesome wasp. We were entering slapstick country: banana skins were materializing under feet; trousers were falling to ankles, revealing spotty undershorts. Nice John's face was covered in custard pie. Once again the Tories claim to be the party of lower taxation was shown to be rubbish, never mind reductions in direct taxes. Nor would Major give a firm pledge in response to Bevins's initial question about the total tax burden. As for the borrowing requirement, there were different ways of

1. 34.75 per cent in 1978–79 and projected to be 35.75 in 1992–93.

looking at it. If you defined it as a percentage of Gross Domestic Product, then Labour's in its last year in office, 1978–9, was 5.5 per cent, while the Conservatives', as set in the budget for 1992–3, was only 4.5 per cent.[2] However, the Treasury table Bevins was waving stated that in real terms, at 1990–1 prices, Labour's borrowing in 1978–9 was £23.2 billion – less than the Tories',[3] and a great deal less than what it might end up being if the *Guardian* story was right.[4]

So there it was: linguistic fig leaves were withered, if not ripped away. And yet what would be the consequences? It was probably not so much the content of the exchanges as their *tone* and that of their accompanying body language that brought a puce flush of suppressed panic to the cheeks of Chairman Chris. The popular papers, the Labour-loyalist *Daily Mirror* excepted, could be relied on to ignore these exposures. The real worry was how *untidy* it would all look on television that night.

At teatime, in a Chinese takeaway in Hackney, a handful of electors prepared to make a donation to Her Majesty's Customs and Excise. For every chicken chow mein at £2.70, 40 pence (VAT at 17½ per cent) would be Norman Lamont's – or maybe John Smith's – to do with as he and his henchmen saw fit. As they awaited the appearance of their silver cartons, from the television mounted above the counter ITN's *News at 5.40* served up a digest of the day's campaign events. For John Major, there had been more unwelcome statistics in the form of the trade figures for February. As usual, Britain's industries and consumers had been buying more imported materials and goods than had been exported, and the difference, though smaller than in January, was still worse than expected. A spokesman for each party was then shown offering an assessment.

2. Treasury figures.
3. Treasury budget briefing note, Public Finance Statistics – Historical Trends.
4. The story began: 'The incoming government will face the worst crisis in public sector figures since records began, implying that the next administration could have to raise the standard rate of income tax by up to 5p in the pound . . . Public sector current spending will exceed current revenue by £11.3 billion in 1992–3.' Further down it said: 'Mr Lamont was only able to introduce his tax-cutting budget by ignoring the deterioration in the underlying fiscal position.'

Nice John appeared, saying: 'The important point about the imports is that the greatest growth is in the import of capital goods. That rather reinforces the view that the recovery is on the way.'

Britain's Next Prime Minister popped up, declaring: 'What is really concerning about them is that we've got an economy which is at best flat and possibly still slipping backwards and nevertheless we've got a growing balance of payments deficit.'

Finally, Alex Carlisle, a gnarled and dishevelled Liberal Democrat, loomed in close up, to declaim: 'Lord Snooty and his pals at the Department of Trade and Industry, Peter Lilley and his ministers, have failed this country and they should have been sacked years ago.'

Major's point was that if companies were buying new plant and machinery, it meant they were gearing up for recovery. Neil Kinnock's remark implied that a recession-weakened pound should improve the performance of exports over imports, not the other way round. He was invoking the tendency of exchange rate fluctuations to provide a partially self-correcting mechanism to trade balances. This has been a regular Conservative line of defence, so at least he was being consistent. Carlisle, meanwhile, was just putting the boot in to the least-known cabinet minister of all, a diehard Thatcherite whose fair and boyish looks were of the type some gay men adore. Carlisle's jarring presence in this sound bite beauty contest came almost as a relief, although Des Wilson might have felt differently.

The customers in the Chinese takeaway watched, dully magnetized. 'Listen, guy,' said one, blowing out his jowls with distaste. 'Them is all crazy. Crazy, crazy, crazy.' He made a rotating movement round his ear with his index finger, picked up his box of pork ribs and left. Another, amused by this display of contempt, began paying closer attention as highlights of the Conservatives' morning press conference came on. There was Anthony Bevins storming, and Nice John flapping. They were followed by the regular roadshow reports. Britain's Next Prime Minister had been in Redditch, though what we saw was Neil Kinnock wally-waltzing with a woman in the market square and grinning from ear to ear. Paddy Ashdown was seen talking to sheep in Brecon, then vaulting a wooden fence *en route* back to his helicopter. 'I suppose they put them up to that, don't they?' said the customer. 'I mean, I don't suppose he actually *wanted* to jump over a fence.'

I offered an alternative explanation: Ashdown may or may not have wanted to jump the fence, but his decision to do so would probably have been influenced by a desire to be filmed doing it. The camera crews would have been pleased – the vault made great pictures. At that level, the media and the mediated shared a strong mutual interest.

The customer frowned and thought for a minute: 'It's all bollocks, isn't it?'

It was hard to argue with that. Straight after, having contributed to the consumer-led recovery, I watched the next mid-evening bulletin, the BBC's *Six O'Clock News*, at home. Jennie Bond commentated on Kinnock in Redditch, the same visit as ITN's correspondent had covered twenty minutes earlier: 'This is the heart of a Tory-held constituency and not considered marginal. But the local Labour Party had done its job in spreading the word . . . for most, though, the press of people meant they'd seen little of the man himself.' There followed quotes from two women regretting that they had been unable actually to speak to the Labour leader. The second of them concluded by remarking, wistfully, of the camera crews: 'There's too many of you. In the old days it used to be just the BBC.' Bond concluded: 'But this is the way modern elections are fought. And tomorrow, Mr Kinnock and his entourage will move on.'

It was an assiduous text: while complementing the pictures, it also explained the stage-management that had gone into creating the scenes they recorded. The next report, on Paddy Ashdown, filed by Justin Webb, employed a similar technique: '. . . Many of the seats the Liberal Democrats want to win are in rural areas and it's important that Paddy Ashdown is seen as the farmer's friend.' Webb also underlined Ashdown's determination to push education up the campaign agenda. The film showed him saying a few words on the subject to the Welsh farmers: '. . . and we tell you where the money comes from, my friends . . . It's gotta come from you and I.'

Trust me. I'm honest. I'm strong.

Webb concluded: 'The visit ended at a school. Where else? The children played their part to perfection.'

This was conscientious reporting, virtuously angled to expose the manufactured nature of the events described. At the same time it was, inevitably, 'all bollocks'. Television is about pictures, images. No amount of verbal scepticism floating through the speakers can completely subvert the love affair between eye and screen. And there was another problem with these reports. At a deeper level, what the public was seeing was evidence of the triumph of 'balance' over journalism, and of personalities over issues.

By what criteria had the ITN and BBC editors judged it appropriate to send their crews and reporters to document these farcical 'events'? Or to follow Major, Kinnock and Ashdown at all? In the end, they are a mixture of statutory demands, existing convention and fear of harassment. Broadcasting bodies are bound by law to allocate airtime (including that set aside for party election broadcasts) to political parties in proportions which broadly reflect the public's predilections for supporting them, thereby ensuring against blatant bias through the overt promotion or exclusion of any one party in relation to others on grounds other than their level of popular support. It is, too, the habit of parties and broadcasters to coordinate their activities with the aim of making sure that the latter get smooth access to the day's main events, and the former have those events covered.

This relationship serves a mutual professional interest. Whether it serves the public's is a matter for debate, for the senior partners in this collusion are not the broadcasters but the party managers. It is they who, in concert with the politicians, 'set the agenda' by choosing the topic for the morning news conference and organizing the day's liveliest itineraries around his leader. It is the broadcasters who, by and large, follow. And the statutory requirement for 'balance' demands that whatever preposterous assertions a politician makes in the course of that day are reported straight-faced and challenged only by some equally outlandish declaration from representatives of the other parties. For a journalist to make a *judgement* about the relative veracity of the different parties' claims is to invite a ferocious ear-bashing from whichever party manager has been offended and the threat of reprisals in the form of withdrawing access to the politicians and their 'events'.

Of course, the broadcasters could always tell the party managers to stuff their press conferences, their photo-opportunities and their star interviewees, send their camera crews and reporters somewhere else, and forgo 'balance' in the interests of the relentless detection of untruth. But this is a democracy, so that would never do.

Later that evening, at Liberal Democrat headquarters in Cowley Street, Westminster, five party volunteers, a keen and fresh-faced crew, clutched stopwatches and stared at a row of screens. Each screen was tuned to a different television channel, and each volunteer was charged with timing and assessing every fragment of election coverage that passed before them. The hour between eight and nine was the quietest for news. On one screen a woman flitted through a wine cellar. On another, a panda chewed a stick of bamboo. Only ITV carried an election-related programme, a *World in Action* investigation into how the erasing of poll tax non-payers from the electoral roll might decide key marginal results. But from nine it was action time. The main BBC bulletin led on the trade figures. A linear collage of comment and imagery unrolled: a repeat of the comment from Major; a repeat of the comment from Kinnock; no comment from Ashdown in rural Wales, unless he was addressing it *sotto voce* to those sheep; a new comment from Gordon Brown; then Carlisle again, though less aggressive than he had been on ITN. Time for a different item, Labour's manufacturing manifesto: Kinnock, at his lectern, bathed in a pink glow; Lilley, denouncing it (tax, tax, intervention, tax, tax, tax); the 'broadly flat' Tory press conference; eventually, a word from Alan Beith.

And so it went. The Liberal Democrat volunteers watched, listened and pressed their stopwatch buttons. They made notes on duplicated forms under column headings: 'Lib Dem visual'; 'Source'; 'Effective?'; 'Why?'. All would be collated and scrutinized. Evidence of temporal under-exposure, or policy misrepresentation would prompt a prickly phone call from Des Wilson to the guilty editor. Inelegant settings would be marked out for future avoidance. Ashdown expounding from the lower rungs of an aluminium ladder elicited murmurs of unease; but they liked it when he vaulted the fence.

A telephone rang, and was answered by the young and sprightly volunteer-in-chief. The call was from a female floating voter and she was in a tizz. The cause was Ashdown's address to the Brecon farmers when he told them where his £1.9 billion for education would come from: 'My friends, it's got to come from you and I.' The termination of this sentence's construction, it seemed, was a grammatical inexactitude, and deserved the loss of a vote. The irate floater declared herself for Major and hung up. 'Totally barmy,' said the volunteer-in-chief, replacing the hot receiver.

As the *Nine O'Clock News* concluded, myself and the volunteer-in-chief moved to a different room to watch *Panorama*, devoted to the first of David Dimbleby's big interviews with the three main party leaders. Opposite him, on the other side of a lagoon of polished desktop at the National Liberal Club, Ashdown wore a suit of soft dun and a look of deep concern. Dimbleby pressed Ashdown on taxation. Ashdown insisted that 'middle managers' on £27,000 a year should be spared the disincentive effect of falling into the 40 per cent tax band, when uncapped NICs would effectively bump it up to 49 per cent. Under him, people earning over £30,000 in taxable income would only pay 33 pence in the pound (with a 41 pence band for those earning over £46,000 above their personal allowance). He and Dimbleby circled around that topic for a bit, before taking to the floor for the hung Parliament tango. How could Ashdown presume that such a result would make him more important? Minority governments have struggled on alone before. And if he intended to carry out his threat to vote down a Labour Queen's Speech containing many things he approved of, but not a commitment to PR, how would that square with his professed desire to secure stable government? Gamely, Ashdown held on to his halo. Remarking on the morning's *Guardian* article, he said: 'We are the party that went into this election, incidentally, saying that this situation was much tougher than the other parties recognized. And so it has proved to be. Now under those circumstances . . . I don't believe . . . that government, on a minority basis, would either have the authority or the *stomach*, to do what was necessary.'

Trust me. I'm honest. I'm strong.

It was a chess match, a brisk but gentlemanly duel. The lucidity of the protagonists, their evident knowledge and debating poise, was enviable. Dimbleby could probably claim to have tarnished the beautiful dreamer just a touch. But not that much. For by the end, just as at the beginning, Ashdown remained on the screen, looking handsome and calm, the beneficiary of a forty-minute free commercial. 'All bollocks' might be overstating the case, but television's election coverage was looking to be wider than it was deep. At best, like the tax burden, it was 'broadly flat'.

CHAPTER SIXTEEN

Big Boys and Glamour Girls

(Tuesday 24, Wednesday 25 March)

In a sumptuous conference room near the top of the Liverpool pierhead's Mersey Docks and Harbour building, Big John Prescott got to his feet. 'Most of us who've sailed out of this great port,' he said, nodding towards the river estuary, 'remember this building, the Liver building and the Cunard building, which was where I had my first medical examination to go away to sea. So I'm delighted to be here with my comrades today.'

He's a magnificent beast, Big John. It was hard to picture him stripped to his skin while a man in a white coat inspected his genitals for germs. A former waiter on the *QEII*, now MP for Kingston-Upon-Hull East and shadow Transport Secretary, Big John is wide all the way up; his stance, his girth, his face. Even his manner is wide, like a bingo-caller in a glitzy northern nightclub. He's got everything except a suit of lights. No wonder Labour's top brass were desperate to keep him off the television – too proletarian by half.

Joining Big John for the launch of Labour's maritime policy programme were Big Sam McCluskey and Big Pete Kilfoyle. Big Sam is a giant Scotsman and leader of the National Union of Seamen. He had a coarse beard and smoked a huge cigar – not really Britain's Next Prime Minister's idea of a vote-catcher either. With Big Pete, though, relations were sweeter, despite the fact that he too smoked a huge cigar, and had a Nashville cowboy's moustache. Big Pete had led the persecution of Militant in the Liverpool constituency parties, a process which culminated in his victory over a covert Militant candidate in the Liverpool Walton by-election. That campaign, and the acrimony it unleashed, was just the latest bout of bloodletting in the gory political history of a city denied its rightful franchise in the Glorious Past theme park for being too true-to-life.

Liverpool's heritage is Britain's, compressed and concentrated in one besieged city-state. All the mercantile grandeur, all the far-horizons opportunism, all the internal neglect are concretely documented in the handsome waterfront piles, the shells of empty factories and the wretched housing estates. Once the empire's second trade metropolis, its prosperity has leaked away like a receding Mersey tide, leaving a heavy silt of gallows' mirth and working-class defiance. Its pungent richness clings to your shoes the minute you arrive. Big Pete was the only native among the assembled man-hulks, but Big John and Big Sam looked well at home.

When visiting Liverpool, it is important (and respectful) to separate reality from myth. This is never very easy, because the two have an incorrigible tendency to coincide. 'You could get mugged in 'ere,' Big Sam's local apparatchik had said on the way to the press conference, as we all wedged into a lift, its doors sliding shut on a magnificent expanse of marble floor and high walls of lavish masonry. He wore jeans and a grubby anorak and half-cupped a burning cigarette in his hand behind his back.

In the conference room, a constituency worker had introduced himself, confidentially: 'It's all happening in Wallasey, you know,' referring to the Liverpool constituency of that name. 'Scandal. Sex and drugs and rock and roll. It's a two-woman fight, if you know what I mean.' Later he'd be knocking on doors, until a specific point in the evening: 'We stop when *Coronation Street* starts.'

Labour's Wallasey woman, Angela Eagle, was absent, but Neville Bann was there, the candidate for Mossley Hill. He and Eagle were the challengers in Liverpool's only two relatively middle-class and non-Labour seats, and both were expected to win. Present, too, was Jane Kennedy, the 'electable' replacement in Broad Green for expelled Militant Terry Fields who, like Dave Nellist in Coventry South-East, was standing in his own right. A slim, pretty woman, she stood out among the Big Boys like a pot pourri in a meat-packing plant.

'There were 1400 ships in our merchant fleet,' Big John went on, in the blunt-sensible, half incredulous tone that Authority's

Experts found common in the extreme. 'It's now around 400. We don't have a fleet now to serve what is basically an island nation.'

The problem with marginalizing Prescott was that, one, he knew his subject and, two, in the previous few years people had kept dying on boats, in cars and on trains in a series of transport disasters. So he was forever on the telly, wide and ungrammatical, filling up the screen. He had a grasp, too, of what Liverpool might require if it was ever to revive. 'Traditionally traffic has come here, in from the west, from America, into here.' But the trading magnet's arrow had swung east. Big John, racing on, addressed himself to the implications: 'There's been a lot of talk of land bridge . . .' He sketched in a putative electrified rail link, starting with a loop around Liverpool, straddling the Pennines to his own home seaport town, linking across Europe 'and eventually joining up with St Petersburg in Russia'. It would be bait for investing multinationals and wouldn't break the bank: 'It cost something over a hundred million pounds to widen the M62 [the motorway from Liverpool only as far as Manchester]. We can electrify the whole Pennine route for that.'

This was 'partnership' talk, Euro-esperanto imported into what Britain's Next Prime Minister had decreed the citadel of unelectability. An odd conclusion, on the face of it, for such a loyally Labour city, but the ascendancy of Militant had been embarrassing. The crunch came in 1985, when the city council, driven by a Militant caucus fronted by sharp-boy Derek Hatton, shook its fist at Westminster, refusing to implement spending cuts in the face of slashed government grants. As if the prologue hadn't been crucifying enough: 65,000 jobs gone in six years; 25 per cent were unemployed. The council itself became the biggest employer in 'this great port', and yet had been deprived of £350 million since Thatcher came to power. Pre-poll tax, the shortfall had been shored up with rates increases, which the government – as ever, committed to reducing state interference – promptly 'capped'. The showdown's overture took the form of farce, as the council hired a fleet of taxis to deliver redundancy notices to its 31,000 workers, whom they claimed could not be paid. It was a stunt, but a wounding one and it was Neil Kinnock who howled. His speech to the Labour conference that year, scourging the

Mersey Trots, became 'electability's' guiding text. Even the Tory press liked it, so it must have been all right.

Not that it did very much for Liverpool. Nor, before that, had Michael Heseltine who, in his previous stint as Environment Secretary, had pared down the grants in the first place. In 1981 he had stomped through the ashes of Toxteth and the heroin slums of Croxteth, cameras in tow, doing his one-nation number with a bus full of bankers following. Businessmen were urged to join with municipal bodies in the name of enterprise and job creation. Few showed the slightest interest. A short walk from the Docks and Harbour building stood the main monument to Conservative government initiatives, the 'urban regenerated' Albert Dock. It was an imperial toy town with shops. At the right time of day, you could linger at the water's edge and watch a man in a picture pullover leap around a pontoon outline of Britain, predicting the weather for daytime television. Another attraction was a Porsche showroom, where the young unemployed were free to go and look through the windows and dream of ownership or, maybe, theft.

But that was the image problem again. It is quite unfair to think of Liverpool, as its smug detractors do, as a city crawling with light-fingered scallywags, bent on liberating anything of value that isn't nailed down. Yet there are plenty of Liverpudlians more than willing to make sport of their own reputation, for skulduggery, for mischief, for fixing backstairs deals. In a pub downtown, a trio of red-nosed tipplers, their accents thick with phlegm, reflected on the city's recent political past with all the self-glorying machismo that makes up Liverpool's unstoppable stereotype.

'You gorra hand it to Derek, he was a personality.'

Hatton, inevitably, dominated. Since fleeing local politics, he had been had up on fraud charges and made an appearance on Terry Wogan's chat show. At the end, the audience cheered.

'The thing about him was, he always gave yer an answer. Even if you knew it was bollocks, at least he gave yer one . . . old Degsy.'

'Degsy' was Hatton's nickname. He'd had his car number plate personalized to celebrate it: DEG5Y. During his time as the council's frontman, he had gone in for big, box-shouldered suits and chatting up the female office staff. He was dreadful. He was irresistible.

Two of the trio of tipplers had been out of work for months. They could, of course, have applied to be telephone sales assistants or security guards, but, as one of them said, he didn't have the legs for the first, or the muscle for the second. The third tippler was in employment, self-employment in fact, as a licensed taxi driver of the sort Hatton and Co had employed for what Kinnock had called 'the grotesque chaos' of the council's distribution of redundancy notices. Liverpool has more black cabs per head of population than anywhere in Britain, some say the world. A long rank of them regularly stagnates on the dip leading down to the famous Adelphi Hotel, a landmark in the grand style dating back to the lost age of plenty. The writer Tony Lane put this abundance down to Liverpool still being 'a city with the habit of the seafarer ashore after a voyage – spend it while you can because the world might end tomorrow'. The tipplers, lining up more pints, seemed to subscribe to this philosophy. They looked back on the Militant period with a kind of reckless affection: it might have been mad, but it was entertaining. As for the general election, they knew who they'd be voting for: 'Ken Dodd.'

From the battlefront to the tellyfront. Tuesday night was the big one, Labour's NHS election broadcast, watched on the in-house TV of a cheap hotel by Liverpool's Lime Street station. It began with a caption introduction:

> The story of two girls with the same problem
> One can afford private treatment
> The other can't

They both sat in a hospital waiting room with their mothers, grimacing, with a hand pressed to an ear, as the broken blue voice of B. B. King began to moan soulfully. The one who can't wore a blue, fleecy-lined quilted anorak with the stitching starting to unravel. The one who can had scholarly spectacles and a regulation school blazer and tie. Clips from their contrasting fates were intercut in a parallel narrative. The one who can't went to an ageing Victorian school building, endured her lessons in pain and ended up crying in the toilet. The one who can disappeared under anaesthetic and woke up to kisses and flowers, a corrective grommet successfully inserted. The one who can't had eight months to wait. The melodrama concluded with the one who can's mother writing a cheque. B. B. King's lament reached its conclusion – 'that someone, who really cares, is me' – as a second caption rolled:

> It's their future
> Don't let it end in tiers

Britain's Next Prime Minister appeared, washed in sunlight, sitting in a straight-backed, pale blue chair. '. . . If the Conservatives win, they'll continue to privatize the National Health Service . . . it's time for a change. It's time for Labour.'

It was a naked appeal to profound emotions, executed with extreme expertise. And yet it was more than a message about NHS underfunding, 'two-tier' systems and waiting lists. The broadcast enshrined core values advanced in the Labour campaign and also the gift-wrap in which they were presented. 'Caring' was perceived in opinion polls as a Labour virtue. They might be incompetent, visionless and untrustworthy, but their faint hearts contained trickles of liquid gold. The election broadcast was a caring cavalcade, soft-focused and 'feminized' in keeping with the new Labour image.

The next morning, in a conference room at the smart Crest Hotel, the same version of Labour, the gentle one that really cared, prepared to launch its 'Manifesto for Merseyside'. No Big John, no Big Sam, just Big Pete from Tuesday's three Big Boys, wearing his red rose buttonhole, Roy Hattersley representing Britain's Next Government, and Liverpool's 'electable' candidates. Jane Kennedy, attired in business black with a floral scarf knotted across her breastbone, was a vision of Labour's aspiration to 'professional' sensitivity. Not that she was all public relations and no soul. She was prepared to acknowledge the existence of the 'other' Labour candidate in Broad Green, and did so with refreshing irony: 'I've got to say there isn't one, haven't I?'

Though not born in Liverpool, eleven years of residence had ingrained in Kennedy something of the native knowingness. She

had come to the city from Cumbria to study chemistry at
Liverpool University and now worked as a full-time official with
the National Union of Public Employees, 'so I have got some
street cred.' A Broad Green constituency party member ever since
coming to Merseyside, she knew Fields and agreed he had a
following. His poster campaign, she said, was centred around
Old Swan, an enclave known for its soured tenements and
poverty: classic Militant territory. Kennedy admitted there was
'some sense of loyalty to that macho image of a man who was
prepared to go to jail to fight the poll tax'. But she felt his stance
rebounded on him more than it helped: 'People feel very angry
about the fact that they're having to pay a huge surcharge.'

Poll tax non-payment in Liverpool had, predictably, been
near the top of the national league. It did little to contradict the
city's reputation for lawlessness. Kennedy agreed and elaborated:
'It's a particular image of Liverpool but the vast majority of
people want to shake that off. They cringe when they see it
portrayed in the media.' The other day, Paddy Ashdown had
come to town. The cameras caught him having problems with
his friendliness offensive: 'I'm not your friend,' spat an angry
young man. 'Well perhaps you might be,' Ashdown replied.
'People say, "why did they have to put that on the telly?"' said
Kennedy. '" We're not really like that."'

The struggle in Liverpool to impose 'electable' Labour on
Militant Labour – or 'Real Labour' as Lesley Mahmood, the
Militant candidate beaten by Kilfoyle in Walton had called herself
– threw into the relief the contradiction between the party's new
appearance and its reality. During the Walton campaign, official
Labour apparatchiks had taken photographs of Mahmood supporters – many from the national Militant network Dave Nellist
was drawing on – as they went about the streets for use as
evidence in future expulsions. If that looked like witch-hunting,
Kilfoyle could live with it. 'They stand for Militant, they stand
for the Mormons and they stand for the Muppets.' The same
Wrath of the Moderates had seen the removal of Fields. Gentle
Jane Kennedy now rowed her boat across the bloodbath towards
the Commons benches.

You had to wonder about Labour's 'feminization'. On the one
hand, more women MPs would be an obvious benefit. And there

was plenty to be said for their effect in diminishing the party's enduring association with dog-eared men sipping cold tea in smoke-filled rooms and, for that matter, the unyielding puritanism of Militant. But if an influx of womanhood might be expected to dilute the worst excesses of most male-dominated clubs, it hadn't done much to curtail the authoritarianism of the Kinnock regime. And within this paradox lay another: the softness sales-pitch – in the form of red rose buttonholes, of dove grey backdrops, and of smart, sensible women – signalled precisely the opposite about the party to what those women's progress said about them. The women's advance spoke of struggles won. Labour's exterior was designed as a representation of 'moderation' – or what some, maybe including Big John Prescott, would call defeatism. Feminism had been appropriated as a tool with which to brand shirtsleeves activism as extremism. It does not say much for a progressive party when it appropriates feminine virtues to conceal its retreat.

An avuncular Labour worker came to hurry Kennedy along: 'Come on, Jane, it's starting. We need you for the glamour, love.'

Kennedy smiled indulgently. At least he didn't call her 'queen'.

Time to get back on the motorway, heading north. The 'Manifesto for Merseyside' had been launched with the standard polish. Hattersley spoke of 'partnership between private business and the community', of a 'coordinated transport plan, land bridge, rail link' bringing 'a new age of prosperity to the people of the region' and a city which 'has never lost its sense of humour and has never lost hope'. Needless to say, the manifesto pointed out that the land bridge would become a reality 'as resources allow'.

But much more exciting was the news coming over the radio. Radio 4's *Election Report* conveyed highlights of the morning press conferences. They were totally dominated by reaction to the health broadcast. Britain's Next Prime Minister said: 'This is the election which will decide the future of Britain's National Health Service. Indeed it's the election which will decide whether our country continues to have a National Health Service of the kind the British people want and need.' Robin Cook said: 'Labour created the NHS and for forty years the National Health Service has served the British people well with dedicated care. Now the NHS needs Labour again.' Smooth Jack Cunningham said: 'Our party political was prompted by the real experience of a father and his child. It was well-researched, the father remains resolute in his determination to have what happened to his child in the National Health Service under the Tories exposed.'

Comment at Conservative Central Office was rather different: 'Despicable,' said Michael Heseltine.

'Shameless,' said Employment Secretary Michael Howard, a man for whom the word 'supercilious' might have been invented.

Already there was speculation that the emotional charge of the broadcast might be backfiring. 'Moderate', 'professional', 'electable' Labour had a bloody great fight on its hands.

CHAPTER SEVENTEEN

Independent Thinking

(Wednesday 25 March)

The colour on the TV was turned up high, the volume, right down. On the silent *Nine O'Clock News*, Chairman Chris Patten looked sour. Jack Cunningham looked grim. The row about the health broadcast had set the media election campaign alight.

'It wasnae very clever, if you ask me, especially as the mother is the daughter of a Tory mayor . . . Do you take sugar?'

I didn't, but John the janitor did, and so did his workmate, George. We sat together in a bare anteroom in the Palace of Arts in Bellahouston Park, Govan, south of the River Clyde in Glasgow. John brought over the tea. He had caught most of the details of the health story as it had broken like wildfire throughout the day. Neil Kinnock was heard, at Labour's only morning press conference, telling Peter Hitchens of the rabidly pro-Tory *Daily Express* on *The World at One* that the party election broadcast had portrayed 'a genuine case'. Unfortunately, by then, the child's mother had already been quoted in the equally rabidly pro-Tory London *Evening Standard* (whose first edition is out by mid-morning) denying it. And, yes, she was the daughter of a Tory mayor, an ex one anyway. She had also been interviewed on *The World at One*, saying: 'There are many differences between what was shown and my child's case. It isn't my child.' The mayhem had been sparked when the child's full name was revealed that morning in both *The Independent* and (by Hitchens) the *Daily Express*: Jennifer Bennett. It emerged that her father, John Bennett, had written to Robin Cook in January, expressing his concern at the length of time Jennifer was having to wait before having her operation, and the broadcast had been based on the contents of his letter. Mr Bennett was also interviewed on *The*

World at One. He professed himself content with the broadcast which, he said, 'showed a situation which is all too real to parents'. Embroiled in this confusion, Labour appeared defensive, while the Tories were basking in sanctimony.

John the janitor had followed all this with some cynicism. It was his cue for relating the way his own political allegiances had evolved. During the seventies, he had spent eight years in the army with the Royal Artillery until medically discharged, diagnosed as temporarily epileptic. Admitted to Glasgow's Southern General hospital, he was shocked, he recalled, to find nurses out on strike complaining about low pay and long hours, 'and this was while the *Labour* Party was in office. There's been thirteen years of Toryism, but people have got short memories.'

He had come to the conclusion that neither Labour nor the Conservatives (he didn't mention the Liberal Democrats) could do much for Scotland. But he wasn't exactly holding it against them. With John, it was more a matter of human nature: 'People complain about decisions made in Westminster. But at the end of the day, if you're a Scot, you have to come round to thinking there's about fifty million English and there's only about five-and-a-half or six million Scots. So obviously, you go by the majority. If there's all those English saying, "Well, we don't want x, y and z," why should five million Jocks say, "yeah, but we want it"? And why should the English give them it? I know if I was an Englishman I'd be saying, "Why should six million Jocks tell us how to run our affairs?" And for that reason I think the Scots should vote for independence.'

Had Jim Sillars, MP for the Govan constituency and Deputy Leader of the Scottish National Party, been present to hear John speak, he would have applauded the destination, but queried the choice of route. He would have agreed about the failings of the British parties (though it is part of Sillars's political legend that he was a Labour MP during its last spell in office) but denied the right of the English to complain about the Scots' share of the Union cake. On the contrary: the SNP's conviction that Scotland can sustain itself as an independent nation state rested heavily on the view that it is the English who have had the best out of the Union, especially in the last thirteen years. In their manifesto under 'Action for Jobs', the SNP were claiming: 'Since 1979 £100 billion of our North Sea oil and gas revenues have been wasted by Westminster, with £40–50 billion forecast for the nineties.' And then there were the fish stocks: about one third of Europe's total lies in what would be held as Scottish waters under independence.

John, though, did not even mention those natural resources which fuelled much separatist sentiment. His was a more cultural nationalism, and seemed predicated on a particular conception of the Scottish character and the failure of the English to appreciate it. He was not, for example, grudging about the disproportionate numbers of Scots who fought for Britain in the Gulf: 'It's a Scottish trait. We're a fighting people and we're proud of our heritage as far as fighting for the United Kingdom and Great Britain is concerned.' And yet: 'We were really pissed off when Mr King[1] spoke for the British Army and let the Jocks be slaughtered first.' His machismo had long been offended in this respect: 'It gets right up my snitch all this England, mother England. Like the song in *Dad's Army* – "Who do you think you are kidding, Mr Hitler, if you think old England's done?" Scottish and Welsh boys died in their thousands. It's an anti-British song.'

Another paradox to exercise the mind of Sillars. With his leader, Alex Salmond, the MP for Banff and Buchan, he had brought the SNP round to the kind of left-wing policy platform which gut nationalisms by their nature frequently conspire against, and which included an aim immediately to 'withdraw from the UK's Trident [nuclear submarine] programme, and [to] order nuclear weapons and installations off our soil.' Throughout, the SNP's ambitions were considerably more socialist than those of Labour. Their 'medium-term recovery strategy' contained a commitment to 'fund full employment', through investment in training, infrastructure, research and development and boosts in exports. They were committed to providing 'education for life', a 15 per cent increase in health spending and big improvements to municipal housing. Like Plaid Cymru, they laid great stress on a future within the EC, but were more assertive than their Welsh counterparts. They did not speak mildly of 'self-government' by

1. Tom King, the Defence Secretary.

the end of the century. They demanded independence *now*, and believed themselves a nation state in waiting, fit and ready for the Euro-embrace.

The SNP entered the election full of confidence. An opinion poll published at the turn of the year had suggested that half the Scottish people favoured independence. This poll had since proved to be a freak. But the SNP's popularity still hovered in the high twenties, above both Tory and Liberal Democrat ratings. Their prominence had elevated the election in Scotland to a higher plane than that 'south of the border'. In Scotland, people were not quibbling over public spending pittances. They were discussing *politics*.

Earlier in the day, Sillars had addressed a meeting of pensioners in the main hall of the Palace of Arts. For his audience, having an SNP MP would still have been a novelty. The party's strongest territory was not the inner cities but the rural north-east where Salmond, Margaret Ewing and, further south, Andrew Welsh, held their other three parliamentary seats. Sillars had got in at an amazing by-election in 1988, turning a deficit to Labour of well over 19,000 into a majority of 3554. He is the SNP's Mr Charisma, a streetfighter to Salmond's technocratic smoothie; tall, with a nest of black curls, a defiant, dimpled chin and a rhetorical style that was both caustic and intellectually acute. Govan is the Glasgow seat most associated with shipbuilding and an attendant history of working-class militancy. Sillars's capture of this Labour fortress was the stuff of nationalist dreams.

His pensioner audience had been full of pertinent questions: how would an independent Scotland meet their needs more fully? Could Scottish industry cope on its own? How would an independent Scotland be run? Sillars answered with customary precision, and addressed their fears on the last point about a one-party state. If the SNP won a majority of Scottish seats, thirty-seven or more, they would consider it a mandate to negotiate independence. They would then call a Scottish general election, under a PR system, open to any political party. Within a year, they hoped, a freely-elected Prime Minister Alex Salmond would be leading a free Scottish people into a new dawn.

Sillars considered this prospect with relish, despite opponents raising the spectre of instant private capital disinvestment. He offered me a biro to take down details of his appointments the next day. It had 'Royal Bank of Scotland' embossed down the side. 'They take good care of me,' he grinned before rushing off to his campaign office, leaving the pensioners to chatter in huddles. Though animated, their conclusions did not bode well for Sillars. The prospect of independence disturbed their conventional instincts. It all seemed so strange and unknown. Change, in the abstract, was automatically associated with threat. Crime preoccupied them – that was one thing that was different from their remembered youths. They would have liked to have talked some more, but had regular habits to honour. 'We have to go home and make our teas,' a woman in a fluffy hat explained. She would not be voting for Sillars: 'How can we manage on our own? Unity is strength.' The others seemed to agree.

John and George the janitors were less fearful. To them, the prospect of Scotland standing alone offered hope of reversing the same tide of immorality the pensioners touched on. For John, the Labour movement in Scotland had been a corrosive influence. 'We let ourselves down badly, as far as the Scottish working man was concerned. We were the biggest skivers under the sun.' George had worked for five years in the shipyards, till 'GEC came in and cut 5000 jobs on the spot', but he too blamed the unions for the decline of the yards. Folk memories of 'Red Clydeside' held no attraction for him.

Glasgow itself John described as 'a fucking shambles – excuse my language – and the Labour people keep telling us, "We only get enough money to do this and that."' They were scornful of the vaunted revival of the city and its promotion by the Labour council as a cultural capital. For them, this was nancy-boy stuff, an example of 'money wasted' to be lumped in with other nonsense like renaming a square after Nelson Mandela or championing 'frightening' causes like gay rights. 'Us common, so-called working-class people, we didn't get any access to what came in, or where it was spent,' when the roads were a mess, hundreds of houses were scarred with damp and there was a cardboard city under the Clyde Bridge. 'We're only supposed to vote these people in, then let them rule our lives without them asking us "Is this OK?"'

In the past, the SNP had been denounced by socialists as

'Tartan Tories'. It was a jibe which Salmond and Sillars were turning on 'electable' Labour with relish. Yet here were two committed SNP voters speaking the language of Tory populism and at the same time seeing the 'Nats' as their salvation, as 'Scottish through and through. They'll stand up and they'll fight tooth and nail for you.'

The extended *Nine O'Clock News* was coming to a close. John turned up the volume. Chairman Chris Patten had said that 'this sleazy, contemptible broadcast' had 'raised serious questions about Mr Kinnock's fitness for public office'. Smooth Jack Cunningham had accused Patten of making 'sanctimonious, dishonest and abusive attacks upon Neil Kinnock'. The health broadcast story, it was clear, would run and run. But sitting with the janitors in Govan, it was like a message from another world. The party election broadcast on health hadn't even been shown in Scotland. They had had one about devolution instead. And meanwhile, a headline in Glasgow's *Herald* newspaper read: 'The nation will never be the same again.'

CHAPTER EIGHTEEN

The Modern Bannockburn

(Thursday 26 March)

On the road to Edinburgh, the car radio conveyed the voice of Alex Salmond assuring the people of Britain that he had no plans to be mean to the Queen. His platform was the BBC's *Election Call*, a daily weekday morning phone-in, transmitted simultaneously on television and refereed by Jonathan Dimbleby, David's younger brother. It was easily the best of the regular campaign programmes. In contrast to most phone-ins, the callers asked questions which were shrewd and, unlike the media professionals who normally cross-examined politicians, they had no vested interest in 'balance' or congeniality. They just got stuck in. It was a tribute to Salmond's arguments as much as to his guile that he wasn't being skewered. It was also an indication of the nature of the Scottish debate that a man whose party was advocating nationalization, full employment and the break-up of the United Kingdom did not seem in fear of being upbraided as an imbecile. Meanwhile, in 'mother England', everyone was still squabbling over Jennifer Bennett's ear.

The scrap was gradually changing from one about credibility to one about conspiracy, from grommet surgery to Grommet-gate. Britain's Next Prime Minister had begun the day condemning whoever had leaked the child's details to the *Daily Express*. Immediately, a reporter informed him that Julie Hall had revealed Jennifer's forename during an 'off the record' briefing on the day of the broadcast itself. Britain's Next Prime Minister said: 'That contradicts all of my information.' Straight away, the press secretary then contradicted him. In a dramatic break with precedent, she stepped up to a microphone and confirmed that she had indeed mentioned the name 'Jennifer', but denied with passion that the family could have been traced as a result of that or anything else she had said. There then followed a splendidly fractious exchange, caught by a BBC reporter's tape recorder, between Peter Hitchens and another journalist (who turned out to be the *Daily Mirror*'s political editor Alistair Campbell) in which the man from the *Express* said his information had not come from the Labour Party, but still refused to reveal his source. Meanwhile, Jack Cunningham was pointing the finger at Conservative Central Office. The Tories had admitted receiving a telephone call on the Tuesday night, just before the broadcast went out, from the consultant who had dealt with Jennifer's case, but insisted he had not revealed the child's full name. Cunningham implied that they were lying and had passed the name to the *Express*. Eventually, the Liberal Democrats got a word in. Paddy Ashdown said: 'I reflect on this thought – that we could have, yesterday, been having a serious debate about the Health Service. We've not.'

Trust me. I'm honest. I'm strong.

Grommetgate ground on like background distortion throughout a day of purer, though conflicting, Scottish political signals, many of them emanating from the country's capital city. Untroubled by the health furore, Ashdown would be visiting Edinburgh in the afternoon armed with the confidence that came from the Liberal Democrats, in constituency terms, being the second biggest party in Scotland, though their strength was primarily in rural areas, particularly in the north. But throughout Scotland, their chances depended greatly on benefiting from tactical voting. And they weren't the only party whose fate might be substantially affected by the Scottish electorate's arithmetical calculations. Possibilities existed for many permutations to emerge, and nowhere were the implications more potentially galvanic for the Conservatives than in Edinburgh Pentlands on the city's south-west outskirts.

Pentlands was held by Malcolm Rifkind, a prime example of a Tory politician who looks old enough to be Mick Jagger's dad but is actually his junior. After a difficult spell as Scottish Secretary of State, he had been moved to Transport by John Major, where he became locked into a series of set-tos with Big

John Prescott. Rifkind was reckoned to be more of a one-nation type than rival MPs on the Scottish scene, such as the prickly rightist Michael Forsyth in Stirling. It was ironic, then, that he represented a constituency in which the two nations of Margaret Thatcher's creation were grimly epitomized.

Rifkind's majority in 1987 was a flaky 3745 and his share of the vote just 38.3 per cent. He got away with it because Labour and Alliance support was almost evenly split. The losers were such citizens of Edinburgh Pentlands as those living in the gruelling tenement gulag of Wester Hailes. A pall of depression hung over the place, made more cloying by a spiteful wind which rushed out of the blue Pentland hills, blustered erratically through the stark angles of the tower blocks and released bitter shards of rain on to the forecourt of the local shopping mall. Inside, the concept of consumer sovereignty could be seen to have acquired characteristics its champions had not planned for. Lurking watchfully along ramparts lined with downmarket shops, more mobile dealers in less orthodox merchandise were easily picked out by the practised eye. Two young women, both wrestling with restless children, nodded discreetly towards this youth or that, skulking in dirty trainers, waiting for a punter to pass by. This was a sales point for the heroin trade, an Edinburgh growth industry. The women looked on. The resignation written on their faces found an echo in their speech:

'The Tory government brought the poll tax. In an independent Scotland that wouldn't have happened. But we'll never get independence, will we?'

They would have liked to vote Labour. But since they – like nearly half the population of Scotland – hadn't paid their poll tax, their names had disappeared from the electoral roll. Laughing disparagingly, they considered the impact of right-to-buy legislation in the Colditz they called home. What would be the point of grasping that chance of 'freedom', even if they could afford it?

'The only point of buying would be to help you to move out. And who would want to buy it off you?'

They were, in any case, out of work and such jobs as they might apply for were ruled out anyway because there would be no place to leave their children while they did them; and if there had been, it would have cost them most of the money they could hope to earn. Instead, they stayed home, came to the mall to shop, sit and chat, then went home again, where at least they had the television. Their best bet for a better life was to hope Edinburgh District Council might give them a transfer to some less wretched council estate. That would probably never happen. The council, they said, complained it had no money for improvements. They didn't believe the council. They didn't believe, much, in anything, except that the things they wished to believe in were unattainable. Failing to pay the poll tax had been their one act of political confidence. For them it had been a poke in the eye for Margaret Thatcher, an act from which they derived an unmistakable, vindictive solace. Their gallows' giggles were swallowed up in the ricochetting echoes of the mall.

Outside stood a man with an English Midlands accent, wearing flared polyester trousers, canvas shoes, a drab overcoat, a tweed cap, a red scarf and glasses. He was a representative of the opinion pollsters, MORI. Though forbidden to reveal the details of his findings, he reckoned the result would be 'very close', but suspected that many of the ticks he had gathered for Labour were likely to be worthless because of non-registration. Doing the same job in different parts of the constituency was, he said, like entering another world.

His observation was easily confirmed. A two-minute drive away lay an alternative universe of stern institutional buildings and four-square residential houses with net curtains and pebble-dashed exteriors. The strong arm of the state was conspicuously present. A big, handsome pile housed the headquarters of the 1st Battalion of the Kings Own Scottish Borderers and a signpost advised visitors of the route to Her Majesty's Prison, Saughton. Yet even these apparent bastions of the UK establishment north of the border were the focus of political discontent. Defence cuts announced shortly after the Gulf War's conclusion meant that the Borderers would disappear, merged with another Scottish regiment. The entire cuts package had prompted outrage among hawkish Tory party members. Saughton prison, meanwhile, had become another symbol of Scottish political ferment, thanks to the tenure there of Tommy Sheridan.

A Labour Militant from Glasgow in his late twenties, Sheridan had risen to fame as leader of the All-Britain Anti-Poll Tax

Federation and had been sent down for preventing the execution
of a warrant sale – the forced confiscation and auction of a non-
payer's property to make up the financial shortfall. But incarceration had not humbled him. While inside he had stood for his
home ward, Pollok, as a Militant Labour candidate for Glasgow
District Council and won. Encouraged, he was after a general
election triumph as well, standing under the banner of the Scottish
Militant Labour Party against an established Labour incumbent.
He was conducting his campaign with the help of a mobile
telephone – giving new meaning to the word 'cellphone' – paid
for by footballers from Dunfermline Athletic, St Johnstone and
Rangers of Glasgow. This source of funding says as much about
Scotland's loathing of the poll tax as any other anecdotal titbit:
English professional footballers would never have risked associ-
ating themselves with such a disreputable cause.

But in Scotland, the political goalposts were set up on a very
different field. And the game revolved not around bogus costings
of rival programmes or the nuances of campaign strategy, but
fundamental questions of nationhood, and all the profundities
they implied. It was not only the SNP who were advocating a
constitutional shake-up. The extent of discontent with the existing
arrangement was borne out by the fact that such bold proposals
for devolution were being canvassed by Labour, whose domi-
nance north of the border gave it the status of Scotland's political
establishment. Similarly, the Liberal Democrats were courting
devolutionist sentiment. And by mid-afternoon, Paddy Ashdown
was making his foray into Edinburgh with what had become his
customary energy.

Alighting at the airport from the Liberal Democrats' campaign
plane, with the big yellow slogan 'My Vote' painted on its tail
fin, Ashdown and a bus full of hacks did a chaotic walkabout in
the Tory marginal of Edinburgh West, where Robert Gorrie
hoped to take his party's first Scottish urban scalp. Hosannaed *en
route* by a houseful of supporters who spilled on to the street, he
brought rush-hour traffic to a halt. A troupe of Tory spoilers
sailed up like an affronted blue flotilla, got their mugs in front of
some cameras and made their escape up a side street. Pausing only
to pose, Ashdown then piled back into his charabanc, which
surged on to the city centre and the ancient Parliament House,

now the setting for Scotland's supreme law court, but the seat of an independent Scottish Parliament until 1707. Standing among the historic cobbles, the beautiful dreamer made a brief, typically stratospheric address on the lines of reclaiming a forgotten history as he held before him St Andrew's flag, assisted by Scottish MPs David Steel and Malcolm Bruce, leader of the Scottish Liberal Democrats. The future role of Parliament House lay at the heart of the election in Scotland. A Conservative victory would leave it in the hands of the judges and lawyers. A Labour administration would probably see it reconstituted as the home of a new Scottish Parliament within the United Kingdom. But if the SNP had their way, Ashdown, like Kinnock and Major, would need to carry his passport next time he came to town.

That night Jim Sillars made a speech in Falkirk, a small town with a big tale to tell of the rise of North Sea oil and the decline of Scottish heavy industry. While the oil refineries of Grangemouth had mushroomed, the steel plants had declined, exacting a high toll in unemployment. To the visitor a forbidding maze of roundabouts and ready-mix municipal housing, Falkirk's two constituencies, East and West, were both replete with working-class Labour votes. But the nationalists had won over 15 per cent in both seats last time round. If they were to triumph, they would need to plunder disillusion in these heartlands. And Sillars, with his terse and ready wit, fitted his audience like a fist does a boxing glove.

The meeting was held in the ballroom of the Hotel Cladhan. The low ceiling and matt decor evoked James Last and seventies sideburns. The turnout was good: a couple of hundred at least, mostly men in dowdy casuals, hard-limbed and twisting roll-ups.

'If the Scottish people are concerned about their ability to run their own country,' Sillars began, then inserted a chiding caveat: 'I find it remarkable that anybody should question it, but nevertheless, it's there.' He continued: 'I think there are two things you can do, if you look south of the border. One is [to watch] that bear pit we see on television, called the Westminster Parliament at Question Time, and ask ourselves if we couldn't run a Scottish Parliament in a more civilized and sensible fashion than that. Then, perhaps, we can look at the Labour Party and the Tory Party, yesterday and today. I find it absolutely repulsive that those two are quarrelling over that child. I think it's one of the greatest political scandals that I have seen in my political life . . .'

That political life rewards closer inspection. It tells the tale of a socialist spirit in restless pursuit of its destiny. Sillars first entered Parliament in March 1970, as victor in the South Ayrshire by-election. A left-winger, he had fought strongly against devolution on the grounds that it would split the British working class. Sillars co-wrote a document called 'Don't Butcher Scotland's Future' which set out his case. One of his fellow authors was Harry Ewing, who became the Labour MP for Falkirk East in 1971. By 1973, the pair had changed their minds about devolution. And by 1975, Sillars had moved even further. So dissatisfied was he with the British Labour Party's attitude to Scotland, that he set up his own Scottish Labour Party. The decision was partly prompted by his opposition to the Common Market, as the EC was then usually known. When withdrawal had been rejected in the June 1975 referendum, Sillars argued strongly for separate Scottish representation in Brussels alongside a Scottish Assembly with powers to raise tax. But his old comrade Ewing had been involved in drawing up a white paper on devolution which advised against giving an assembly economic powers. For Sillars, that was the last straw.

The SLP did not last long. Comprised of Labour, SNP and Liberal defectors, it was a fractious and short-lived venture which attracted few votes. But its capitulation, followed by the failure to secure devolution in the 1979 referendum and Sillars's loss of Ayrshire South (to British Labour) in the election of that year, amounted to the final push he required to reach his nationalist destination. He joined the SNP in 1980, and immediately became embroiled in a series of internal rows. By the mid-eighties he had won most of them and married SNP stalwart Margo Macdonald, herself a shock victor in a previous Govan by election. Sillars's intellectual journey from pro-unionist, anti-European Labour MP to nationalist, Euro-federalist MP had earned a bitter tribute from the retiring Harry Ewing at the 1991 Labour conference. He and Neil Kinnock, Ewing said, had taken off their coats to work for a Labour victory. But Sillars 'he turned his'.

In the twilit ballroom, the Govan rebel resumed his denunciation:

'. . . And while they're at that negative name-calling, over that child, who will then be plastered all over the tabloid press tomorrow, for it has now been discovered,' he continued, breaking the latest Grommetgate revelation, 'that the child's parents aren't married. And just you think of the pain that has been inflicted on the personality of that child because those two organizations have got nothing positive to say, except to scratch at each other, like two cats in a bag.'

There is a touch of the old-school moralist about Sillars. His socialist radicalism is spiked with an influence of traditional Catholicism. He opposed abortion and favoured the continuation of Scotland's long history of Catholic state education. His critique of the Grommetgate fiasco seemed coloured by an abhorrence at seeing the sanctity of family life being despoiled. He used this analysis as a springboard for the main theme of his speech:

'Power and responsibility. That's what this election is all about when we boil it all down to its basic, fundamental principles. What is going to determine it is what you, the Scottish people, think of yourselves . . . We are going to decide, as individuals and as a nation collectively, whether [we do] in 1992 just as in 1314 the Scots did as a nation at Bannockburn. This is the modern Bannockburn. We're not talking about crossing swords. We're talking about crossing a ballot paper. But the essential issues are exactly the same. There was no way off the Bannockburn field in 1314. You either stood, or you ran away. And it's exactly the same in 1992.'

These words were delivered with the slow, clipped emphasis of parent spelling out home truths to a wayward child. It was clear and it was compulsive.

'The reason John Major wants to keep Scotland in the union is for English state interests.'

He advanced a litany of widespread Scottish resentments: the dumping of nuclear waste; the placement of American military installations; the waste of North Sea oil revenues. The government, Sillars claimed, intended to 'strip the steel assets in Lanarkshire', and fuel alternative capacity in England with energy produced from gas piped under the sea bed from a huge gas field recently discovered in Scottish North Sea waters. 'So Honest John is not actually telling the truth when he says he wants tae hold on tae us cos he likes us.'

Sillars reeled off the punchline with sardonic relish. The audience liked it. They liked it, too, when Sillars denounced the Labour Party for selling out its socialism to appease Tories in the south. He, by contrast, attacked the prospect of a privatized rump of Scottish steel, which Labour seemed set to accept:

'I was always taught in the socialist movement that when you face that kind of malicious private felon, you mobilized public power and you took [those assets] into public ownership. The only similarity between Neil Kinnock and his policies and Aneurin Bevan and his socialist policies, is a Welsh accent.'

Sillars's accent was tart urban Scottish, complete with vernacular tang. With measured certitude, he extolled his nation's potential:

'We are the twenty-third richest nation in the world in terms of resources to population. We come between Australia and New Zealand. How come the twenty-third richest nation on earth has a third of its people living in poverty? There are 120,000 children who will go to bed tonight in rooms riddled with damp. The reason is that our wealth has been taken from us, and the reason that has happened is that we have given our power away, generation after generation.'

Once that power had been reclaimed, an SNP government would make its first priority work.

'For the working class, that is essential. There's naebody here tonight has two or three million in the bank. All any of us has in here is our ability to work – physically, mentally or intellectually. Our whole lives are determined by whether we can sell ourselves on the labour market. If it is a labour market that has thirty workers chasing one job, you are in a weak position, and you live in a society riddled with anxiety. If you are unemployed, you begin to lose heart. You begin to lose hope. Your personality begins to corrode and your soul begins to erode.

'Now I'm told everywhere I go, and by every newspaper I read, that the idea of socialism is in retreat. I remain an unrepentant socialist. I believe that the philosophy that the community has a right to act to preserve the dignity of the individuals within that community is as sound today as when I heard it for the first time many years ago.'

From socialist principle, to socialist economic practice:

'Let's take the electrification of a railway line, let's say between Edinburgh and Aberdeen. If you think about it, you need steel to make rails; you need to go quarrying to get ballast; you need mile upon mile of electrical wire; you need lots of switch gear; you need new rolling stock; you need new signalling. So you need to take folk off the buroo to manufacture those materials; *off* the buroo to put them in storehouses; *off* the buroo to transport them; folk off the buroo to put it together, to create the electrified railway line. And when you take folk off the buroo, not only do you save the dole money, those folk then, if they're earning a decent wage, they get to pay National Insurance Contributions and tax, and they begin to buy things, and you get your return to the government in VAT, and you take that money and you plough it back into the economy. That's how we can create 200,000 new jobs in Scotland in a four-year period.'

The Falkirk audience listened. Sillars came to his peroration. In it, he returned to the theme of national pride. Independence would be sought in Europe. But socialism would be achieved in one country:

'Think how it will be when we've got other folk off our back . . . all of the arguments, technical and political, won't matter provided we find those intangible qualities that mark out winners from losers. What marks out a winner from a loser? It's pride, self-respect, self-esteem and a sense of national dignity. If we have those qualities within us as a people, we will rise to the occasion on the ninth of April. We will rise to the occasion. And this, at last, will be a nation once again. Thank you.'

CHAPTER NINETEEN

Going for Scotland

(Friday 27 March)

From the forecourt of the industrial estate in Sanquar, Galloway, flew the flag of St Andrew and the flag of the Union. An Austin Montego carried a sticker saying: 'SNP. Yes! Matt Brown.' In the conference room of a carpet factory, the manager told Ian Lang: 'We're struggling.'

So too, according to opinion polls, was Lang, MP for Galloway and Upper Nithsdale and Secretary of State for Scotland. A local swing against him of 4.5 per cent would see the SNP parading his aristocratic head on a pikestaff. Across the country, the Nats were doing better than that. The bad news from the world of textiles brought little comfort to the Conservative.

'It's been pretty flattish, really from January on,' the manager continued. 'Not January this year, but last year.'

In 1990, production had reached a best-ever 68,000 square metres a week. Now they were down to 50,000. The factory was part of 'an American group with strong Dutch connections', which had helped out in the last month, but 'we see that coming to an end next week. And as a result, we've posted a few redundancy notices.'

A secretary earned her keep by taking an order for tea. There were four of us, with Lang's assistant completing the quartet. The secretary was one of eighty-eight employees, part-timers included.

'And when do these redundancies go out?' Lang inquired. His wan face was distinguished by parallel vertical creases. He had this disarming way of looking worried to death.

'We've given them four weeks' notice,' said the manager, a

neat Lancastrian in a sports jacket. 'We've come down in the last few months from 121. So we're talking about less than two thirds the numbers we had two years ago. Which is sad.'

A silence. The tea arrived, super efficiently, in mugs. Lang sipped a little and asked: 'What proportion are you exporting?'

He meant carpet, not employees.

'It's very difficult to gauge,' the manager explained. It seemed the materials came from Ireland, were turned into durable squares which were all sent to Holland where the big warehouse was. Then most came back to the UK again, half of it bought by firms who do export sales. The manager didn't know what they did with it. Weird stuff, global capitalism. But he estimated that his firm satisfied about 20 per cent of the UK market: 'So if there's a decline in UK sales, it hits us pretty badly.'

'Well, you're a consumer product, aren't you?' suggested Lang.

'Not necessarily. I should think 50 per cent of what we do is going to contract.'

'But it's still very recession sensitive?'

'Well, even more so because a lot of what we've done in the last two years has gone into property and that property hasn't been let, so there hasn't been the turnover and an additional requirement for carpet. The people who tend to be at the top end of the contract market and have gone into the more sophisticated office environments, have tended to be the hardest hit. People are downtrading quite a bit, and we've noticed there's been a shift in the product profile.'

A pause. Lang inquired about the workforce: what was its 'quality'?

The manager defined the word in his reply. He said he regretted laying off people whose value he calculated with particular reference to their 'flexibility'. Those best blessed in this regard were the younger ones, many recruited through government initiatives like the Youth Training Scheme, who could be 'trained into your own ways'. The ex-miners – Galloway had been part of the Scottish coalfield – he'd had before were less so. 'We find them pretty motivated and exceptionally cooperative.' For 'quality' read 'flexibility'. For 'flexibility', read what – 'compliance'?

There was a special advantage for employers in having YTS workers: you didn't have to pay them. The government did that, the sums slightly exceeding the unemployment benefit the youngster would otherwise have received. Latterly, if they declined a place on YTS, they forfeited their right to that benefit anyway. And though the manager said he had kept on many of the YTS workers who had come his way, there was never a guarantee of a proper job at the end of their time on the scheme. They had every reason to be 'flexible'. Still, the manager seemed genuinely sad at the laying off he'd had to do and remarked, too, that he had so little time and so few resources to spend on additional training. He was, after all, a slave to the balance sheet which was, in turn, a slave to the recession – the *UK* recession, primarily.

We took a quick tour of the shop floor, Lang's assistant carrying a briefcase and mobile phone, Lang himself walking pigeon-toed, a hand wedged geekishly in the side pocket of his tweedy suit. Awkward conversations with the men at the machines emphasized the chasm between them: Lang, educated at Rugby School and Oxford University, the workers, in thrall to their machines, wondering who'd be next to collect his cards. 'Imagine having to do that all day long,' said Lang's assistant, shaking his head.

Next stop, an aluminium factory next door. The chief engineer filled in some history. The company had once been part of a British group, but was sold to a Norwegian one. The British company had made no investment. The Norwegians had pumped in £5 million straight away. As a result, they were holding their own. It was, the chief engineer felt, the story of British industry since way before Thatcher. He observed, too, that when Matt Brown had visited Sanquar the previous week, he'd had a very good reception.

Out on the forecourt, Lang was intercepted by a camera crew. Belying his meek body language, he firmly told his interviewer that he was 'encouraged' by what he had seen: 'The companies I've been round today have substantially increased their workforce over the years . . . as the country emerges from the recession and . . .' (not forgetting) '. . . other countries emerge from the world recession, orders are going to come back. They've been undertaking new investment, they've been training people up, taking advantage of the schemes and the assistance that we can give them. And they're ready to take advantage of the upturn.'

Funny. That seemed to be the precise opposite of what the carpet factory manager had told him. Perhaps the secretary had put something in the tea.

Bathed in sunshine, the Galloway countryside unfolded like a dream, an idyll only corrupted by a coachload of tourists disembarking to photograph some sheep. Though the far south-west of Scotland is lowland, it boasts hills and glacial valleys, thick, bristly grass and acres of terraced woodland. The Forestry Commission is a leading employer. Farmers are also central to the Galloway economy, though they were feeling the pinch like everyone else.

In such a setting, the latest salvos in the Grommetgate scrap seemed more incongruous than ever. Britain's Next Prime Minister had started the day accusing the Tories of leaking Jennifer's name. Chairman Chris Patten, in his so amusing way, continued to insult, denigrate and demean Neil Kinnock. Paddy Ashdown said: 'I call on Mr Major and Mr Kinnock for the sake of the child, for the sake of the NHS and for the sake of the election, stop it. And stop it now.'

Trust me. I'm honest. I'm strong.

(And I'm not feeling very important.)

In Gatehouse of Fleet, an hour's drive from Sanquar, Matt Brown and a crew of SNP cohorts were plotting Ian Lang's downfall in the car park of a pub at the top end of the High Street. Their intention was to 'create a presence', meaning they'd swarm down the road *en masse* interrupting traders and planting stickers on passers-by. Brown's supporters were a game, motley bunch: a bearded growler uttering unpleasantries about Lang from beneath the brim of a herdsman's hat; a spruce, tidy woman with a crisp document file and a red anorak; a man whose kipper tie flapped defiantly outside his sweatshirt; a fellow in a navy blazer sucking his way through a tube of Refreshers. Brown himself was clearly the professional, a lawyer with the saucy air of the terminally confident.

'Do you have the psephology?' he inquired, intimating with his manner that it might just change my life. Leaning on the boot of his sharp red saloon, he jotted figures on the back of a press release. Since 1987, the SNP poll rating had doubled, the Tories' in Scotland had dropped and the Liberal Democrats' halved. 'They are now in deposit crisis, okay? We need a swing of 4½ per cent, right?' He put on a speaks-for-itself expression, turned and tripped off down the road.

A supporter was quickly discovered behind the counter of a newsagent.

'I think it's time we were a nation again, if you want. I'm fed up with all this shit from England, especially Lang.'

The newsagent's argument with Lang was rooted in a personal tragedy. He had lost his son when a boat capsized off the Isle of Man, and had suspected negligence. He said he'd asked Lang to investigate, and was dissatisfied with the response. But otherwise by 'shit from England' he was referring to matters of style. He didn't think of Lang as a Scotsman.

'Well, what has he done for Scotland? How does he talk, how does he approach people in this, that and the next thing?'

So he had an English manner about him?

'Yes, definitely.'

Lang had addressed that same point briskly when it was put to him in Sanquar. 'I'm an archetypal Scotsman, as it happens,' he countered crisply. 'I haven't got a drop of English blood in me. Would you like to know my family tree? You'll find names like Stewart, Bruce, MacFarlane and others. Perhaps I've been tainted by my education.'

Well, there are those who would think so. But to Lang, such people simply confirmed his explanation for the nationalist allure: 'I put it down to a kind of escapism, a kind of opt-out of the difficult decisions.'

With that in mind, I asked the newsagent where he placed the SNP on the left-right spectrum:

'I've never really thought about that one. Erm. I wouldn't actually say that . . . I'd more or less say that they were going for Scotland . . . going for Scotland. Either left or right or whatever. Going to make Scotland what it should be, and not holding on to the apron strings of down south.'

In different contexts, distaste for dependency was a Conservative rallying call and struck a chord with precisely the people for whom the shopkeeper was most concerned:

'There's one heck of a lot of small businesses going down between here and Stranraer, which I think is wrong. In Maggie Thatcher's years everybody was wanting money, and they got it and now the crunch has come and people can't pay their mortgages.'

So Thatcher was part of the 'shit from England' too?

'Well, to be quite honest with you, her personality, I liked, to a point. Major, I don't. I just don't like him. He's sort of on the same lines as Kinnock. A wimp. He's got no personality, Kinnock. But Maggie Thatcher was strong in her views on this, that and the next thing.'

Hmm.

Outside, two workmen from the local authority were digging up the road. Brown's posse had already given them yellow SNP stickers which clashed loudly with their orange overalls. Why were they for the SNP?

'Cos I've always voted SNP,' said one.

How come?

'I don't know.'

The second workman chipped in: 'It's cos he doesnae like the English!'

Elementary prejudice then, was it?

The first workman just kept digging.

The second offered his own view: 'I think the way the government's going at the moment, they've forgotten Scotland's still here. We're needing somebody shaking them up anyway. I cannae see us getting independence, well, not yet. But the younger generation is coming up, they're all going to be SNP boys. You can see it.'

In another shop, selling candles and craft gifts, Brown was turning on the charm. A Scottish woman, just leaving, remarked: 'The only consolation is it's a beautiful place to be unemployed in.' Brown diverted his attention to the woman behind the till, who turned out to be the proprietress. She was from Rochdale and the thought of Scottish independence made her nervous: 'I wouldn't like to see Scotland and England divided. As I say, "united we stand, divided we fall".' That said, she wasn't crazy for Lang either. 'If only he'd been more like Cyril Smith was to Rochdale.' But it was the huge Cyril's talent for fat-seeking publicity rather than his politics that had impressed her: 'I won't vote Liberal [Democrat].' And yet: 'I don't like Neil Kinnock. Do you know, I was brought up as Labour all me life, and I was so sick of strikes, they drove me round the twist. I just thought, "Well, Margaret Thatcher's coming up, we'll give a woman a chance," and she's been great. I was never a Tory before, but I admire her so much. And I think she cared about the country.' There was no specification of which 'country' she meant.

These snippets of opinion put a different slant on Brown's jotted psephology. Within the space of fifty yards, the motivation of SNP voters had been variously underscored by a mystical sense of lost nationhood, by basic bigotry, and by anti-Westminster umbrage. Only the latter, the view of the second workman, seemed based on any kind of rational assessment of economic and institutional unfairness. No one even alluded to the heady principle of Euro-socialist reconstruction, not even the newsagent who'd said he read Jim Sillars's column in Scotland's edition of the *Sun*. Meanwhile, there was pan-partisan admiration for Thatcher's flag-waving bellicosity. After years of internal division, the SNP itself may have decided where it stood. Some of its supporters didn't seem quite so sure. But then, while socialism draws its faith from the force of logic, nationalism is not such a rational concept.

Having completed his chipper progress to the bottom of the High Street, Brown sent his Refresher-sucking confederate back to fetch the car. As he slid into the driver's seat, the alarm went off, shattering the rural calm. Unable to locate the off switch, but determined to fulfil his task, the Refresher-sucker set off on a kangarooing course, leaving the whining siren to confirm to diehard Tories in Gatehouse of Fleet that there was no real difference between a Nat and a breach of the peace.

Ian Lang's long day was almost at an end. It had begun at seven a.m. with a BBC radio interview and was concluding twelve hours later with the first of two school-hall public meetings, at

the Wallacehall Academy in the little town of Thornhill. About
eighty people turned up to fill the rows of regulation chairs
unstacked on the parquet flooring. The majority advertised themselves as the cream of rural tartan Toryism: the women sat with
their blouse collars turned up and their wool-knit skirts tugged
down; the men wore ancient suits and had their hair arranged in
curious frontal plumes. They were joined by a handful of burghers
with chunky sweaters and beards – they were the ones who would
ask awkward questions later on.

For manners, the Thornhill Tory crew could not be faulted.
Mrs Jeanie Maxwell, the wife of a local farmer and chair of the
meeting, wore an elegant blue two-piece and small-talked with
perfect grace. The young Lord Dalkeith shook hands smartly, his
smile sincere, his grip mild, his body language Woodentop-stiff.
Marshall Douglas introduced himself as a local trader and golfer,
intrigued, it seemed, that a London journalist should be bothered
with such far-flung Scottish parts. (Later, he generously invited
me back to his home for a whisky, where a senior female member
of the family offered the disapproving view that the *Sunday Times*
was getting 'leftish'.)

Lang's address was cogent and confident. He delivered it with
minor assistance from notes written on squares of white card,
keeping one eye on his wristwatch, which he strategically placed
on a tabletop before commencing. He talked about industry and
employment, about education and health, but stressed:

'I believe that constitutional change overrides all these issues.
Because unless we have a stable constitutional base within Scotland, unless we are confident we have the right to full and equal
citizenship in the United Kingdom then, in an atmosphere of
uncertainty, we will undoubtedly suffer and our capacity to
continue with services at the present level will be diminished.'

A bearded questioner asked what was wrong with a federal
structure. Lang replied that there was nothing wrong with it in
the abstract, but in Britain, that wasn't the point. Tradition was
the thing:

'We do not have that system. It hasn't evolved naturally. We
are a unitary state. Power in this country stems from the Crown
in Parliament. The sovereignty of the Parliament is absolute and
has served us extremely well.'

The loyal Tory unionists gave off a burst of machine-gun applause.

Lang dispatched another dissident over the expense of the Trident programme: 'Nuclear deterrence has served to provide us with protection for some fifty years of peace and security, and to defend ourselves and our living standards.'

Applause!

Then back to the isolating impact of constitutional changes: 'Management in the south would say, "There's too much uncertainty in Scotland." How would new companies prosper in an uncertain economic climate, and in a diminishing world market?'

Applause!

But the bearded questioner was still not satisfied. His concern was with the legitimacy of a Tory government re-elected despite the loss of Scottish seats. It had been an impeccably decorous meeting. What followed was the nearest thing to anger.

'I'm sorry,' the questioner apologized, 'for time presses. But with respect, address my point.'

'No,' said Lang abruptly, then elaborated: 'In the words of Queen Victoria, "We are not interested in the possibility of defeat. It does not exist."'

Applause! Applause! Applause!

CHAPTER TWENTY

Local Flavours

(Saturday 28 March)

Banchory is a small town whose personality combines the rural temper of the Grampian farmlands with that of a residential satellite of Aberdeen, the oil capital of Europe. Its weekend began with a khaki SNP jeep coasting down the High Street, broadcasting an indecipherable message through a rooftop tannoy, an act which prompted the proprietor of a shop selling framed prints of local views to say he was imposing a ban on politics from then on. 'We've had them all in here this last week,' he grumbled. 'It's not six months since they were last at it.'

He referred to a by-election in the constituency of Kincardine and Deeside which had produced a crackerjack result. For twenty-three years the seat had been held by the Conservative Alick Buchanan-Smith, a man whose singular spirit did a great deal to secure him in local affections. In 1976, he had resigned as shadow Secretary of State for Scotland over his party's opposition to devolution. It was an act which chimed with a sense of independence in the area which had not yet manifested itself in the ballot box as nationalism. But Buchanan-Smith's death in 1991 was followed by victory for Liberal Democrat Nicol Stephen, who turned a deficit of 2063 into a surplus of 7824. The Tories' defeat was hastened by a recession-driven protest vote, further encouraged by the widespread perception that the new Tory candidate was a plonker. 'He was a politician from forty years ago,' said the print shop proprietor, 'the old school tie, noble laird sort of thing. George Kynoch [the new man] is much more in the Buchanan-Smith mould. The Tories will get back in this time. Mind you, it'll probably be the only seat in Scotland they do win.'

The Tory defeat had been large and humiliating, and Kincardine's True Blues were clearly busting a gut to wipe the memory away. Outside the party's campaign HQ, a supporter in cords and gumboots piled pro-Kynoch billboards mounted on stakes into the back of his Range Rover pick-up. He'd already been hard at work, as you could tell from the predominance of similar favours leaning out over fences and hedges just beyond Banchory's main shopping drag. The supporter sounded confident: 'He's a clever fellow, George. He's on the Milk Marketing Board. He has a wee woollens business. He's a fellow who gets things done.'

Kynoch was off in Stonehaven that day, a seaport, and the biggest settlement in Kincardine and Deeside. Banchory was the only other town of much size. The rest of the constituency comprised a virtual cross-section of north-east Scotland, with some of the country's richest farmland, a stretch of coastal fishing ports to the south of Aberdeen, and a slice of the oil city's western residential fringe. It also contained the stately royal hang-out, Balmoral Castle, where nobody went canvassing unless they were extremely daft. More crucial to the Liberal Democrats were the neat, innocuous private housing estates like the one Nicol Stephen and his team set about sweetening up that afternoon.

The troupe of Liberal Democrat activists gathered in a ward organizer's kitchen on the estate in question. Young men with spots wearing Arran sweaters marked maps with highlighter pens. Stephen organized them with mild courtesy. A lawyer by trade, he has a soft, middle-class Scots accent and an angel face that suggested a man still younger than his thirty-two years. He had had precious few months to annex the local following that had sustained Buchanan-Smith. Setting off through the dank air in his hefty Barbour jacket, he knew it would be difficult to win again.

The estate's residents were an eclectic, unpredictable bunch. A woman out on her porch identified herself as not minding the poll tax. In Scotland, Martians are more common. Equally unusually, given that she commuted to Aberdeen each day to work with the physically handicapped, and 'caring professionals' aren't often Tories, she had been loyal to Buchanan-Smith, but would be voting for Stephen this time. She could not, however, speak for her husband or her two grown-up children. 'You should never assume all people in a household vote the same way,' Stephen observed, 'as Neil Kinnock has just found out.'

He got further encouragement from the middle-aged woman next door: 'You've got to look at the leaders, haven't you?' she said, with the remains of a Shropshire accent, holding back a snuffling terrier. She and her husband had first moved to Banchory so he could improve his lot as a herdsman. Now, like so many others, he worked in the oil trade. The woman continued on the leadership theme: 'There's no way I'd vote for anyone who had Neil Kinnock and I don't think the Conservatives have proved themselves at all. Now Paddy Ashdown speaks a lot of sense. I think he's a person for the people, you know. And it's time the people had a person.' Stephen offered thanks, excused himself, and set off past lollipop shrubs, across a path of ornamental paving slabs sunk into the small but immaculate lawn. 'I don't think that boy's got much opposition,' the woman confided, and added approvingly: 'He speaks well, too.'

A succession of teachers interrupted their gardening or unloading of shopping from cars to give Stephen the nod. So far, very good. But a former Aberdeen harbour authority dignitary, who had voted Liberal Democrat previously, spent ten minutes explaining that he wouldn't do so this time because, while Thatcher had been too abrasive on Europe, anyone other than Major would let Chancellor Kohl and President Mitterrand walk all over them. Then Stephen was temporarily abducted into somebody's sitting room, emerging to explain that he had been told in hideous detail about a woman who'd shot her husband and baby while suffering from post-natal depression. He wasn't expected to *do* anything about it, just listen.

It was gone five o'clock. A canvasser ran over, asking Stephen to spare five minutes to answer a hung Parliament puzzler. These, for Liberal Democrat candidates, were sincerity's acid test. The query came from a woman in jeans and a sweatshirt with a neutral English accent and a coolly appraising demeanour: 'What would your party do if the Conservatives had the largest number of seats, but not enough to form a government?'

She looked the candidate in the eye and waited. Stephen, subtly, fudged. The woman had given no clue to her political affiliation. Until Stephen had gleaned it, he didn't know what the right answer was. Officially, Liberal Democrats would work with either Labour or Conservatives with equal reluctance, as long as a promise was made to introduce legislation for PR. That was fine for Paddy Ashdown to say on television. But at constituency level, even-handedness was not necessarily conducive to wooing the tactical votes on which so many Liberal Democrat candidates depended. Stephen kept fudging. What was the woman more frightened of? A vote for Ashdown helping Kinnock or helping Major? Finally, she relented, revealing herself as a Labour supporter who was willing to trim to the centre, but not if Ashdown was likely to keep Nice John in Number 10. This at least gave Stephen the chance to answer truthfully: the Liberal Democrats were far more likely to be able to work with Labour. That had been clear from day one.

The husband of the house came to the door. He was a Labour activist, and less comfortable than his wife with the idea of giving 'Paddy's Roundabout' a spin, though he was thinking about it. His own energies were concentrated over in Aberdeen South where Labour's Frank Doran was defending a tenuous majority of under 2000. But the main reason for his appearance was to bring word of the first of several opinion polls to be published in the Sunday papers. In the background, television experts were already ruminating on its meaning, the first measure taken since the height of Grommetgate. The findings were not spectacular, but significant enough in that the Liberal Democrats had touched 20 per cent for the first time in the campaign, with both Labour and Conservatives falling back a fraction. If it marked the start of a trend, then Nicol Stephen had a reason to be cheerful and Ashdown could start dreaming of smoke-filled rooms.

As the sky gathered its first tint of dusk, Stephen prepared to call it a day. Three cheeky boys in shell suits with mini mountain bikes and spiky haircuts accosted him for his autograph and me for chewing gum before pedalling off, chortling at their own cheek, leaving Stephen to reflect on the kind of Scotland they might inherit as adults ten years on. A lot depended on how different forces of disillusion gained purchase on the status quo. Scottish Liberal Democrat Malcolm Bruce held Gordon, the next seat north, but beyond that and to Kincardine and Deeside's south, the SNP had three of their four seats. The fact was that Scotland's huge anti-Tory majority expressed itself in many different ways. 'There's a strong feeling here that we're not part of the central belt, we're not inheritors of the Red Clydeside tradition,' said Stephen. 'The SNP's centre-left, Glasgow working man's pub image, Jim Sillars-type message jars with us. But there is this feeling of being neglected and ignored by Westminster, that of a lack of care. It isn't always articulated in terms of constitutional change. Health and education is what they talk about, then if you ask them about it they go on to say, "We need more say over our own affairs, we need a Scottish Parliament, we need to break the control of the Tory Party, of Westminster."'

On the A road out of Banchory, a bumper sticker read: 'I'm A Real Scot from Grampian'. A brazen enough declaration. Yet exactly what a 'real Scot' might be, let alone how he or she might express such an identity in a polling booth appeared, from the evidence of Glasgow Govan and Edinburgh Pentlands, Banchory and Falkirk, Thornhill and Gatehouse of Fleet, to be something of a mystery.

From the car radio, the sound bite simulacra continued unabated. Britain's Next Prime Minister and his wife had celebrated their silver wedding anniversary with a photo-op snog signifying Labour's synonymity with the inviolate traditional family. Nice John had been barracked by demonstrators in Luton. In an unlikely departure from the tattered Tory script, he had stepped up on to a convenient soap box, grabbed a megaphone and talked the hecklers down. As the second full week of campaigning concluded, the Grommetgate saga at last had grown flaccid and faded away. The main events had unfolded as follows:

Tuesday: Labour's broadcast shown.

Wednesday: *The Independent* and the *Daily Express* publish Jennifer Bennett's name. Her mother Margaret Bennett denies that the story depicted was that of her daughter. Her consultant Alan Ardouin claims Jennifer's long wait was due to a bureaucratic error. Her father John Bennett agrees that was an initial reason, but one which in itself was a consequence of under-resourcing. He supports the broadcast. William Waldegrave likens it to propaganda in pre-war Germany. Chris Patten denounces Neil Kinnock. Jack Cunningham denounces Patten. Robin Cook produces letter sent by Ardouin to Bennett, blaming lack of beds,

underfunding and lengthening waiting lists at Kent and Canter-
bury hospital. It effectively confirms Bennett's version of Jennifer's story as told in his letter to Cook. Jennifer and family pose
for the press outside their home in Faversham.

Thursday: Cunningham suggests Jennifer's identity was discovered and leaked by Conservative Central Office. Tories admit
that Ardouin rang them just before the broadcast went out, but
deny he revealed the name. Julie Hall acknowledges revealing
Jennifer's first name during a pre-broadcast briefing on the
Tuesday afternoon, but denies anyone could have worked out the
rest of the details from what she said. David Felton, deputy news
editor of *The Independent*, denies their information came from any
political party or from the hospital. Peter Hitchens of the *Express*
denies his came from Labour or was stolen from *The Independent*.
Cunningham releases list of names of other long-wait grommet
cases. The 'Bennetts' turn out to be unmarried.

Waldegrave is ambushed at an afternoon press conference. He
admits receiving a fax from Jennifer's grandfather – the ex-Tory
mayor – giving many details about the broadcast, and further
admitted suggesting to Ardouin that he get in touch with a
newspaper. The *Express*, of course. 'Nothing wrong with that,'
Waldegrave protests, apparently believing it. 'Nothing wrong
with that at all.'

Friday: Cunningham apologizes to those on his list who never
gave permission for their names to be released.

What was left was a stink of incompetence and corruption.
Labour had shown astonishing failures of foresight. They should
have known that the Tories would seek to exploit any gap
between 'the facts' and their factional depiction, and should have
taken every precaution to prevent it. If you are going to claim
that a piece of propaganda is *based on* the experiences of 'real
people', the first thing you do is make sure that *all* those people
are absolutely watertight: that they do not have potentially
embarrassing sympathies and connections with political
opponents; that their anonymity is totally assured. In the event,
Labour took no such steps. Nothing emerged during the saga to
suggest that they even bothered to find out Jennifer's mother's
opinion about her daughter's treatment, let alone her political
views. So much for the new woman-consciousness. As for the

Conservatives, self-appointed guardians of family life, they had been revealed, thanks to Waldegrave, as actively encouraging the exposure of the Bennetts in collusion with their collaborators in the 'free' press. What a grubby little shambles it had been.

CHAPTER TWENTY-ONE

Alternative Networks

(Sunday 29 March)

P addy Ashdown lounged serenely on David Frost's flesh-pink telly couch. He was wearing that soft, dun suit again and trying not to look too pleased about the two polls out of five published in the morning's papers that gave his party 20 per cent. There was a glow about him, a glow of importance, a post-Grommetgate glow.

'Our strategy was quite simple,' he told Frost, his matter-of-factness just about concealing his delight. 'It was to try and meet as many people as we could, the old style of things that elections are supposed to be about.'

His right arm hung casually on the back of the sofa. He couldn't resist a quick I-told-you-so:

'I do find it pretty depressing that this whole election so far has been about a sort of long-range artillery barrage of insults from inside £300,000 television studio sets between the leaders, and it just seems to me that this is an election from which the British people so far have been excluded.'

This was a very different encounter from that between Frost and Britain's Next Prime Minister a fortnight before. Where Kinnock ended up stuffed and filleted, Ashdown settled in to a gentle marination, coolly sipping orange juice between answering questions. Frost asked him his opinion of his two rival leaders. Ashdown said, as he always said, that they were fine and able men, but lacked any vision for the future. Frost pressed him to confirm that legislation for PR was his one non-negotiable condition for a pact in a hung Parliament, and Ashdown comfortably complied, adding that it would have to be enacted within eighteen months and repeating that, if necessary, he would work to that end with either main party.

Then Frost quoted from a campaign leaflet distributed by one of the many Liberal Democrat candidates fighting a seat from second place behind a Tory: '"Only the Liberal Democrats can beat the Conservative. Labour cannot win here. So make your vote count." You've just said,' charged Frost, 'you may co-operate in keeping the Tories in, in which case all these people have been misled.'

Ashdown waved this aside, as if dismissing an unreasonable fly: 'But David, I want the Tories out. I am determined to get this wretched government out! But what I want as a politician, and what I must *do* in order to honour the judgement of the ballot box are two totally different things. The first [question] is "Will you honour the judgement of the ballot box?" As a democrat I say, "Yes". Mr Major and Mr Kinnock say "No" . . . if it isn't in accordance with what they want.'

Trust me. I'm honest. I'm strong.

Ashdown breezed through the interview, frowning, smiling, laughing, chiding, feeling those floating voters begin to melt into his soldierly arms. Later that day he and his entourage caught a ferry to Boulogne where Ashdown made a Euro-fraternal speech partly in French. He was coasting, cruising, becoming more important by the day. But the flowering prospect of hung-Parliament power was producing signs of nervousness among his lieutenants. It was all very well to stick out your chin and draw in your bottom line, but in reality there was no obligation on a minority government to concede Ashdown's central demand. It could, as Ashdown told Frost he suspected would happen, try and limp on without him. And if a spurned Ashdown carried out his threat to vote such a government down, it would force another election and might destroy his claim to be the people's noble knight – the last thing the voters would want was another campaign grind. That wouldn't be friendly at all.

By lunchtime, countervailing Liberal Democrat forces were being assessed in another television studio on the west side of London in Shepherd's Bush. BBC 1's *On the Record* is a Sunday fix for political junkies, comprising in-depth analysis and forensic interviews conducted by Jonathan Dimbleby. For its penultimate broadcast before election day, the programme inspected the entrails of Grommetgate week to divine what message they contained for Paddy Ashdown.

On a gantry at Television Centre, a gaggle of producers, assistant producers, editors, researchers and technicians tweaked an edifice of technology or gazed down on to the studio floor as transmission time approached. Jonathan Dimbleby was already at his slate-grey interview desk, neat and dapper with a rather racy, silky green tie. On strolled Charles Kennedy, the Liberal Democrats' President.

'Hello Charles!' chimed Dimbleby with bright familiarity, his voice funnelled up through a gantry monitor.

'Hello Jonathan, how are you?' returned Kennedy, every bit as cheery.

He sat down opposite Dimbleby and small-talked chirpily as a sound engineer clipped a microphone to his tie. A former SDP member, the MP for the Scottish Highlands-and-Islands seat of Ross, Cromarty and Skye, Kennedy was a bright spark in the party firmament. Still only thirty, his face retained an adolescent plumpness and his red hair was cut in the style of Herman's Hermits. He was already hot favourite to succeed Ashdown as leader whenever the beautiful dreamer was jerked from his slumber. Witty and gregarious, Kennedy is a dinner-party politician, and, for all the Liberal Democrats' pretensions to mould-breaking, an establishment man, totally at home among the BBC bourgeoisie.

The *On the Record* set signalled its insider orientation. The interview desk was set against a background which parodied the view from inside the clockface of Big Ben. Just before the *One O'Clock News*, which preceded *On the Record*, Dimbleby straightened his shoulders into his on-camera posture, turned away from the mock-clock face and delivered a quick programme trailer, its purpose being to persuade the dithering viewer not to switch over to watch Brian Walden grilling Britain's Next Prime Minister on ITV. On a screen in the control room, I watched Moira Stewart present the day's campaign events so far. Nice John Major had done a photo-call outside his local church to mark his forty-ninth birthday, but declined to oblige the cameramen by giving Norma a kiss. Down in the studio, Kennedy and Dimbleby continued to trade badinage until Ms Stewart disappeared and the opening credits rolled.

Dimbleby began by introducing the main item, a report on what the Liberal Democrats' tactics should be if they held the balance of power on 10 April. It included David Steel mildly repudiating Ashdown's PR-first-or-nothing line. As he did so, down on the studio floor, Dimbleby laughed as Kennedy made elaborate fanning motions at his forehead as if to cool a fever. Then, as the item came to a close, the pair composed themselves into different people. Their smiles gave way to straight-faced sobriety as they aligned themselves eye-to-eye from opposite sides of the desktop. Chumminess gave way to professionalism. They became men adapted for television.

Kennedy knew what he had to do and Dimbleby knew it too. Kennedy knew that Dimbleby knew. Dimbleby knew Kennedy knew. None of this, though, was made overt as they set about their business, the interviewer politely probing, the interviewee respectfully insisting. Yes, Kennedy confirmed, the Liberal Democrats would *rather* vote out a minority government than compromise on PR, but the most important thing was that 'before we could get into any discussions about a programme for government over a four-year Parliament', there would have to be 'a clear understanding' that the next election 'would be fought on the basis of a reformed voting system'. He said nothing which precisely contradicted Ashdown's line, but neither did he make a similar demand that PR legislation would have to occur within the first eighteen months. In this way, Kennedy constructed a plank-and-twine bridge across the Steel–Ashdown ravine at a speed the MGM cartoon character Roadrunner would have envied, while Dimbleby stood at the precipice filing courteously at the stanchions. When the interview ended, the frame froze, leaving the viewer to assess whether the bridge would hold up under stress. 'Well, I thought that was quite interesting,' said an assistant producer over my shoulder. Quite interesting, yes. But not as interesting as the bits the electorate didn't see.

With the programme completed, everyone wove their way through the labyrinth of Television Centre to a small hospitality suite, where the sandwiches were fresh and dainty, and the red wine rich and good. Dimbleby, still wearing his make-up, stood tucking in and drinking demurely. Three sides of a quad of couches in the centre of the room were occupied by programme editor Glenwyn Benson, BBC political editor John Cole (who contributed an endpiece sketch to *On the Record* every week), a couple of in-house researchers and Kennedy. The chatter of common career interest bubbled out of them like hot spring water. Meanwhile, Dimbleby discussed his campaign workload with equal enthusiasm. *On the Record* was his regular weekly slot, but the daily *Election Call* was a welcome, invigorating bonus. The public, he confirmed, could take liberties with etiquette where politicians were concerned which he as a professional could not.

There was no need for Dimbleby to explain any further, to elucidate the unwritten rules and intangible conventions which govern Westminster circles and enable the maintenance of the symbiotic relationship between insider intimacy and 'serving the public', so essential to the successful conduct of a broadcast journalist's career. Politicians feel a greater obligation to appear on television during general elections, but under routine conditions they often require persuasion. If they think they are heading for a hiding, they may decline to give up their time. Conversely, there is no more pervasive medium for winning hearts and minds. Consequently, all concerned settle for a negotiated give-and-take which manifests itself on camera in the form of debates within parameters predetermined by the concerns and common decencies of the Westminster world.

So as the United Kingdom entered the last full week of the closest and most bitterly fought general election since the war, *On the Record* had enlightened the public to the extent that we now knew that *if* there was a hung Parliament, and *if* the Liberal Democrats had firm hold of the balance of power, and *if* they were invited to negotiate the creation of a parliamentary pact with one of the two main parties, then Charles Kennedy might be content to agree a slower pace for the introduction of PR legislation than Paddy Ashdown would, *if* a such a principle was agreed before further negotiations ensued. This enlightened the viewer to the extent of knowing that *maybe* Kennedy and Ashdown would argue about it *if* all the preconditions were fulfilled, and maybe, if it came to it, they would not.

'Are you going, Charles?' Dimbleby asked Kennedy, after bidding a charming farewell.

'Yes, I'm going, Jonathan,' Kennedy replied.

And together they headed off to the car park, all pals again.

CHAPTER TWENTY-TWO

No Nasty Tories

(Monday 30 March)

'Who's on yellow? Who's on yellow?'

Election Call producer Nick Utechin, blundered into the continuity studio, a slip of white paper, eight inches by six, flapping in his hand.

'Who's on yellow?' he threw himself, curly hair quivering, into his pivoting office seat and eyeballed a glowing screen filled with horizontal bars of colour. Electronic digits ranged along each bar formed the name of a contending caller and the gist of his or her question. Utechin barked maniacally into a microphone: 'Right, next up on yellow. Dalbin fellow on interest rates.'

From a nearby monitor came the Humberside blunderbuss tones of Big John Prescott reaching the end of a sentence, then the more manicured inflexions of Jonathan Dimbleby: 'And now, Tony Dalbin from Surrey. Good morning.'

Mr Dalbin from Surrey was through to *Election Call*. Utechin turned from his screen and laser-scanned the slip of paper. It was a phone-in *pro forma* with spaces for name, occupation, location and telephone number. In the top right-hand corner a box marked 'party' invited the telephonist taking the call to write 'Lib', 'Lab', 'Con', or whatever. Down the same side of the page, the caller's potential qualities as a programme participant were assessed in boxes ticked where appropriate alongside the following: 'Articulate?' 'Passionate?' 'Boring?' 'Listening to You?' Then underneath was scribbled the intended question.

'No. Boring, boring, boring,' grumbled Utechin, discarding the slip. He was loving it, every minute of this complete and utter chaos.

Through the monitor, Prescott rattled monotonally away to a

sceptical Mr Dalbin: '. . . The importance of the interest rates, basically, is to get a stable economy. We have now got a real mess in the economy. This is the second in the thirteen-year-period, and it always starts off with tax cuts, set the market free. It ends up with balance of payments crisis, less investment for the manufacturing, less people being trained and that's effectively the market system . . .'

Utechin yelled to a runner on her way out to the switchboard: 'Very, very quickly!'

Some suit had rung in on a car phone and Utechin wanted to get him back.

Prescott concluded his stream of consciousness: '. . . with the stability of the currency in the ERM, I don't think your fears will be realized.'

'Thank you, Mr Dalbin,' said Dimbleby. 'And next on *Election Call* we have . . .'

Another caller went through. From inside the studio, out of Utechin's sight, editor Ann Carragher piped up: 'What we really need is some nasty Tory . . .'

Utechin turned to me with a pretended air of panic: 'There are no nasty Tories! Remember? There are no nasty Tories!'

Balance, balance, balance! It was a joke, but getting past one.

The car phone caller could not be retrieved since no one had jotted down his number. Still, it had been a lively show. Prescott had kept calling Jonathan Dimbleby 'David' and at one point Dimbleby called Prescott 'John Smith'. An earlier caller had rubbed Prescott's nose in a gaffe he had made on BSkyB near the start of the campaign when he had said the minimum wage would cause 'some shake out of jobs'. This time Prescott was ready, denying that unemployment would result, but saying: 'A dynamic economy does have adjustments and changes, I can't ignore that.' There had also been a hideous American on the line, spouting star-spangled homilies. 'It's going to be very good under the next Labour government,' countered Prescott, as northern bluff as the caller was apple-pie evangelical. You don't get many like Big John to the pound.

In the studio afterwards, Dimbleby recalled a couple of replies the Tories might try to make him suffer for. Prescott, mopping off his make-up, reckoned he could live with it. Just getting on the programme had been a good crack, and one in the eye for the Walworth Road smoothies who thought he frightened the middle classes. 'I know they didn't want me on, that's half the reason I accepted. Would you believe it, I got off the train coming down last night and there's two of them on the platform waiting to rehearse me through this list of questions! We went through 'em and I said, "I don't know the answers to 'alf these."'

Negative reactions to Prescott's plebeian persona among Authority's Experts were essentially fuelled by snobbery. Tories snickered at it, 'electable' Labourites winced. All agreed that Prescott went against the grain of standard telly-texture without, apparently, considering what a relief he might be to viewers fed an unbroken diet of sanitized slicksters. With Prescott, what you saw was what you got, a cliché Britain's Next Prime Minister was never likely to attract. He and Prescott's polar-opposite attitudes to mass media politicking partly explained the recurrent antipathy between them. This had first come to a head when Prescott challenged Roy Hattersley for the Deputy Leadership in 1988, threatening to undermine Kinnock's claim to mastery of the party. Prescott's contention was that the Deputy Leader's role should be redefined as primarily a campaigning one, concentrating on cultivating Labour's grass roots. It suited the Kinnock regime better, though, for grass roots to be dormant. Looking good on television was far more important.

The day before Prescott's *Election Call* appearance, Britain's Next Prime Minister had turned in one of his better interview performances, head-to-head with Brian Walden in the same time slot as *On the Record*. Around mid-morning, at the instant-tech White City building just up the road from TV Centre, *Panorama* staffers were mulling over the Walden show in their open-plan office.

'I thought Walden won by half a point,' offered one, leafing louchely through the *Daily Telegraph* with his feet up on a coffee table.

'Oh, I thought Kinnock won,' said a chic young woman, looking up from a copy of *The Times*.

It was apt to discuss the interview as if it had been a punch-up. Walden is a pugnacious interrogator, a bit theatrical, a deliberate pain in the arse. His strategy is to pick out one or two fine policy details, worry away at them like a mog at a rodent's corpse, expose a weakness in his subject's defences and extrapolate from it some broader policy indictment. For Kinnock, Walden focused on the effect of higher taxation levels on work effort and the relationship between public sector and private sector pay. In the first case, his charge was that higher taxes were a disincentive, in the second, that Labour's commitment to 'end the deterioration' of public sector pay in relation to the private sector meant a commitment to the public wage bill defined by developments beyond a Labour government's control. Walden's sub-text was: here's how you're going to screw up the economy.

The Labour leader had coped well on the incentives question and tolerably on public sector pay, but what most viewers take away from a television interview is an impression of a personality rather than a count-up of points scored over specifics. From that perspective, the Walden interview may have benefited Labour because Neil Kinnock, rather than Britain's Next Prime Minister, seemed to be sitting in the opposite chair. It was not the Neil Kinnock who likes his ale and dirty jokes, but Neil Kinnock the Labour machine man, the grafter, the tough. The confrontational character of a Walden interview, with its spartan studio set, seemed to suit him better than the prefabricated informality devised for David Frost. At one point, towards the end, he even essayed a sneer at Walden in acknowledgement of being permitted to elaborate on a point: 'Oh I know, you're *endlessly* tolerant.' There was a hint of meanness about that riposte. It wasn't pretty, but it contradicted public perceptions of Kinnock as 'weak' or 'soft'. A little more honest nastiness might have done him a power of good.

In the *Panorama* office, the staffers fell silent over their papers. That evening, their show's own star interviewer, David Dimbleby, would have his crack at the Labour leader. Maybe his cultured urbanity would pierce Kinnock's armour more effectively. A few feet away, behind a smoked glass office wall, a small Asian man was engaged in conversation with someone else, seated out of sight. The Asian man was Samir Shah, the News and Current Affairs department's head of weekly programmes. Just a few weeks before, Shah had been at the centre of a controversial decision to withdraw a *Panorama* programme about the causes of the recession. Written and presented by BBC Economics Editor Peter Jay, it had taken a close look at the role of government policy in its precipitation. Scripts of the spiked programme had been leaked to the press. They showed that Jay had obtained an interview with Nigel Lawson in which he accepted that errors had been made. The explanations offered for the recession by the Major administration were analysed, and the broad conclusion reached that the execution of economic policy had been faulty and the Thatcher–Lawson 'miracle' had been originally a mirage. 'Sliding into Slump', as it was provocatively called, was due to go out the night before Norman Lamont's big denial budget, but was pulled at short notice on Shah's orders. It had all the hallmarks of a bottle job, and the fear that motivated it was, almost certainly, of Conservative Party displeasure.

The 'Sliding into Slump' débâcle was the latest twist in the relationship between the BBC and the government which had been tense for years. *Panorama* itself had been the subject of rows and legal actions, among whose fallout had been damages payments and apologies[1] and regular browbeatings by a succession of Tory chairmen, notably Norman Tebbit, Kenneth Baker[2] and even that *so* refined and amusing Chris Patten. While the Tories made hay with lunatic allegations that the BBC was out to get them, many in the media feared that the Corporation was capitulating too readily. Samir Shah's heave-ho of 'Sliding into Slump' confirmed their worst fears for the BBC in general and *Panorama* in particular. Since the mid-fifties, it had been the BBC's flagship current affairs programme, an emblem of the Corporation's commitment to public service – as opposed to government service – broadcasting. There now seemed legitimate grounds to question whether that service was losing its edge.

For the general election period, *Panorama* had opted to stick

1. These followed an edition of *Panorama* called 'Maggie's Militant Tendency', which investigated links between Conservatives and ultra-right wing organizations. Just after the opening of the libel case (heard in 1986, more than two years after transmission) brought by two Tory MPs, the BBC backed down, handing out damages of £20,000 to both, paying their costs and apologizing in full.
2. Author of a repulsive speech to the 1990 Conservative conference, following a *Panorama* investigation into the secretive processes by which the Tories garner funds.

with convention and devote itself to set-piece sit downs with the three main party leaders. Ashdown had been first, Kinnock was second, John Major would complete the run on the final Monday of the campaign. These interviews, explained *Panorama* editor David Jordan, perched behind a desk just round the corner from Shah's, had been organized months in advance and involved considerable negotiation. Ideally, the BBC would have liked to bring the leaders into a Shepherd's Bush studio – it was cheaper and easier that way. Unfortunately, there was precedent for the Prime Minister to be interviewed in Downing Street (not at Number 10, incidentally, there were rules about that, but actually at Number 12) and, because the other parties thought that made him look more grave and statesmanlike, they wanted to pick their own grave and statesmanlike outside broadcast setting too. Jordan had conceded the argument. Hence, Ashdown had looked grave and statesmanlike in a room at the National Liberal Club and Neil Kinnock would look Britain's Next Prime Ministerial in a grave and statesmanlike room at the Institution of Civil Engineers: wooden panels, polished desktop, dour ranks of heavy tomes, that kind of thing.

Jordan conceived the leaders' interviews as being in keeping with the best *Panorama* traditions. Their aim was to 'test the propositions that the leaders are putting forward more exhaustively than most people will ever get an opportunity to do'. This service was a 'duty' performed by Dimbleby 'on behalf of the general public' and required forensic skill. Politicians, Jordan explained, 'have standard answers for most questions'; it took 'the art and skill of a great interviewer' to find ways past them.

But it was no joke doing that or even 'getting politicians off their chosen territory'. Preparations involved comprehensive war-gaming on both sides. For *Panorama*, a team of researchers would fine-comb all the politicians' recent interviews for weak points or stock responses and plan accordingly. The politicians themselves rehearsed interviews assiduously, knowing, said Jordan, that these intense TV encounters were among 'the more taxing things they have to do during the campaign'. As for the public: 'You hope that they learn something, in the sense that the questions are ones they would like to know the answers to, and that the politician has been under the pressure he might be if you were in a pub full of people arguing the toss. Or you hope the impression that is generated adds to how well they feel they know the person concerned.'

As to whether the entire palaver, the advance scheduling and venue-negotiations, the researching, second-guessing and war-gaming produced television which made any real difference to how people placed their crosses on a ballot paper, Jordan shrugged: 'who knows?'

CHAPTER TWENTY-THREE

Labour Calling

(Monday 30 March)

Three hours before the Kinnock–Dimbleby encounter, Chris Smith, MP for Islington South and Finsbury, approached the Market Estate, a local council block, with a little gang of canvassers. They were a varied bunch, almost as catholic as the north inner London polyglot's electorate itself: Edna, a middle-aged woman with a candy-striped tunic top and a walking stick; Jim, wearing jeans and an anorak, talking generous north London; Eric, a chartered surveyor with a Doctor Who-length scarf; Robin, Smith's assistant, in a crisp suit, sporting a pomade of handsome curls; and Smith himself, a faintly clerical figure with his steel rims, neat demeanour and reassuring listening style.

'This is the cream of local authority rehabilitations,' he explained, heading towards a security guard in a glass-fronted booth, bashful beneath his uniform cap. Smith had beautiful manners and a big red rosette. The guard beamed and buzzed us through the main ground level security door. In so doing, we passed the first of a series of initiative tests. Somewhere beyond the maze of security electronics, lay a packed warren of people.

Smith examined a panel of numbered silver buttons on a wall beside a clamped corridor entrance door, and turned to his confederates.

'The idea is just knock on the door, "We're from the Labour Party. Chris Smith your MP is here, would you like to speak with him?"'

Eric stepped up, pressed a button at random and awaited a reply. It came crackling quizzically through an intercom grille:

'Hello?'

'Hello, I'm from the Labour Party,' said Eric, talking back to the intercom with necessary ingratiation. 'Chris Smith your candidate is here. Would you like to talk to him?'

Buzz. Like bank robbers penetrating a vault, we were in. Before us stretched fifty yards of enclosed concrete corridor, with artexed walls, thick blue industrial flooring and screaming strip lights, punctuated down both sides with numbered apartment doors. As the canvassers crowded in, one of the doors eased ajar. Smith scuttled towards it, tilting his head like a sympathetic sparrow.

'Hello, nice to meet you. Are you going to be supporting us?'

It was an old man in a vest, unshaven, toothlessly smiling.

'Oh definitely, definitely.'

'Would you like a poster?'

Smith produced a red-and-yellow flier, bearing his and his party's name.

'I've got one already,' said the old man, 'in the front room.'

'I'll give you another one. Just peel off at the corners,' said Smith, flipping the flier over to demonstrate.

'Thanks very much.'

'Thank *you* very much.'

Down the way, bells were ringing and heads appearing from other doors.

Eric's voice: 'Hello, I'm from the Labour Party. I've got Chris Smith, the candidate, here.'

Smith dashed twenty yards. 'Hello. Are you going to be supporting us?'

This time an old lady, really grateful. 'Oh yes, oh yes.'

Jim's ring yielded a pair of slightly shabby children, a girl and a boy, roughly eight and ten. Their dad was out. Smith smiled. 'If you can just tell him that I called, and if he'd like to stick that poster up we'll be very grateful. Thank you.'

Heads were popping out like organ stops. The canvassers' patter floated up the corridor from left and right:

'If you want to put it in the window, those just come off and it goes straight on.'

'I won't come in because I've got to get round to as many doors as possible.'

'Hello, we've got Chris Smith here, if you'd like to have a word with him?'

'Those just peel off at the corners.'

We infiltrated the next corridor up. Dogs began to bark.

'Labour Party, mum.'

Smith: 'If you don't vote, you've got no right to complain. Why don't you do it just this once, because we can change the government this time.'

Eric: 'No? Right, okay, thank you, 'bye.'

Some little kids spilled out, one on a scooter, another gripping the crust of a bread doorstep, dripping with raspberry jam.

'Sorry, no English.'

'Chris! Someone else for you to say hello to.'

A woman gave Smith a kiss

'Hello . . . oh, thank you.'

On to a third corridor, a fourth, a fifth:

'I'm half-way. I'm half-way. It definitely won't be Tory.'

'Hello, Chris, I've met you before. You won't remember me.'

'Oh, the face *is* familiar.'

Buzz, clang, ring. Black people, white people, poor people, proud people. A Chinese adolescent boy in day-glo joggers. The clack-clacking of roller skates worn by a wan little girl.

'Hello-ah, sorry to have kept you waiting.'

'So all this poll tax will be demolished?'

'I'm sixty now and I'm wondering if I'll ever get any work again.'

'I'm wondering what you can do for me, cos I've just been made redundant . . .'

'Alfie, get in 'ere, you got no feet on!'

Within ninety minutes we had, in Eric's expression, 'blitzed' both sides of the estate. It could have been done still quicker, but for Smith's willingness to stop and talk. 'The problem with Chris,' said Jim, making ready to head off, 'is he's too nice a person.'

A nice person and a brave one, the first MP to come out as gay, despite the damage homophobic voters might have inflicted on the tiny margin of 363 by which he first won his seat in 1983. His courage was rewarded by an increase in that majority to 805 four years later, followed by promotion to John Smith's shadow Treasury team. The fiscal expertise this appointment required him to obtain had come in useful on an earlier canvass: 'This man said, "How am I going to cope? I'm going to be £7620 a year worse off under a Labour government." I worked out he must be earning about ninety grand. I said "Well, I can't really appeal to your self-interest, can I?" '

South Islington demonstrates precisely the cheek-by-jowl proximity of haves and have nots in many parts of the metropolis. Nearly half the voters are white-collar middle class, but only 12 per cent of the housing is owner-occupied. There is huge ethnic diversity – Caribbeans, Asians, Africans, Mediterraneans, Latin-Americans, Irish – and high unemployment. The professionals are often pinkish, which partly accounts for Smith's main challenge being from the Liberal Democrats and, previously, the SDP, which won mass defectors from Islington's Labour council when it was first formed. In the middle-class parts of the constituency, you never knew who you might unearth. 'Another man I met that night said, "Yes, I'll vote for you, um, what are you going to do about London Transport?" So I launched into the line about more investment, seeking funds from the private sector, blah, blah, blah. "Well," he said, "I'm a member of the London Transport Board. How exactly are you going to do this?" '

On the whole, Smith's canvassing had been encouraging, 'much better than last time'. There had been little creeping homophobia, but some Fear of Kinnock: 'Mmmm. I talk about "the team".'

Smith and Robin dashed off to another appointment. Edna, Eric and I retired to Eric's house in Barnsbury, with its rugs, ethnic sculptures and shelves of books, the regular paraphernalia of the north London post-bohemian intelligentsia. Oliver, a big, genial youth with a rockabilly quiff, did battle with the local dial-a-pizza. Three more Labour activists turned up, a young woman, a guy in a hat, a younger man called Simon. All were well-dressed, clean and smart, and spoke in classless accents. We settled into an elegant upstairs lounge and tuned into *Panorama*.

'Mr Kinnock,' began David Dimbleby, 'in what way would you define the difference between Labour's plans for speeding us out of recession and the Tories' plans?'

Kinnock's hands pressed on the polished tabletop before him like laced raw sausages. He was Britain's Next Prime Minister. He looked incredibly tense.

'This is an investment-led recovery that will lead to a sustain-able recovery, not just to that surge and then slump which has been the Conservative pattern.'

Dimbleby proceeded to dissect John Smith's shadow fiscal programme. How could Labour accuse Norman Lamont of borrowing £2 billion for a tax bribe, he inquired, when they were doing the same thing in a different way? Ah, responded Britain's Next Prime Minister, but Labour were being more helpful to the less affluent. Eight out of ten families, remember, would be better off. Dimbleby pointed out that six million of that eight-out-of-ten would gain just tuppence a week. But the point was, said Britain's Next Prime Minister, that the overall package was geared to facilitate recovery. Dimbleby suggested that Labour's promises would depend hugely on obtaining higher growth than the Treasury projected. That would happen, Labour's leader insisted, but he would put no figure on it.

Towards the end Dimbleby asked if a Labour government would consider devaluation to kick-start recovery. With the ensuing disavowal came, for the first time, a truly plausible response. Since 1945, the big issues about Britain's decline had been dodged, claimed Britain's Next Prime Minister. Successive governments had believed them solved by the fifties boom, by the sixties devaluation, by entering the EC or by the discovery of North Sea oil, 'in each decade, a means of avoiding the basic questions about the British economy, the need to improve invest-ment, the need to embrace long-termism, the need to raise the level of skills, the need to compete more effectively'.

Dimbleby concluded by asking if Labour would deal with the Liberal Democrats in the event of a hung Parliament. Britain's Next Prime Minister said what he always said, which was that there wasn't going to be a hung Parliament. And with that, after the hours of researching, the weeks of negotiations and the heads-down rehearsal sessions, the closing credits rolled.

In Eric's lounge, the audience-jury considered its verdict.

'That wasn't interesting television,' said the man in the hat. 'Most people would have turned off after ten minutes.'

'If you think of the people you met with us on the doorstep tonight,' observed Eric, 'how many would have been likely to have watched that programme from beginning to end? How

many people are really interested in the finer details of the Public
Sector Borrowing Requirement and whether we're going to
devalue? You're actually interested in how much is going to go in
or out of your wage packet a month or week. They know they're
not going to get those answers from David Dimbleby asking set-
piece questions. It's like ping-pong.'

The young woman considered that *Panorama* was often an
interesting programme. But, 'I think set-piece interviews are
boring.'

Edna simply felt we hadn't seen the real Neil Kinnock. 'I
think they've ironed out too many of the creases. I think it's a
shame to do that because he's got such real feelings. It's a shame
to try and make him different.'

These were intelligent and politically-literate people. Yet a
primetime cross-examination of their own party's leader on the
BBC's standard-bearer current affairs programme had left them
yawning, and sceptical of its value to others. Something was
obviously wrong. It wasn't that the *Panorama* exercise had been
worthless. Dimbleby had, if you really listened hard, managed to
expose Labour's eight-out-of-ten families line for the public
relations claptrap it was. More generally – and perhaps half-
consciously – he had teased out the true cautiousness of Labour's
economic proposals. None of Kinnock's war-gamed verbiage had
actually repulsed Dimbleby's painstaking offensives.

And yet, the Islington activists were right: it had all seemed
rather sterile, repetitive, dull, a chess match played to stalemate in
some generic gentleman's club far from the everyday whirl. There
was a gap between substance and impact where excitement should
have been, the excitement generated by visions extolled, by great
issues passionately declaimed, by clashing values expounded and
explored. Election '92 had come at a point in Britain's history
when the economy was capsizing, when the world was turning
upside down and when the social convulsions brought about by
the most iconoclastic government since the war would either be
challenged at the last gasp or flagged through into the next
century. Those were the themes the British people should have
had served up for their evening viewing. What we got were two
establishment professionals disputing with perfect etiquette how
to define the value of tuppence. Somehow it just wasn't enough.

CHAPTER TWENTY-FOUR

Credibility Gaps

(Tuesday 31 March)

Filmed amid Monday night's darkness somewhere in central London, Chris Smith appeared on BBC *Breakfast News*, responding to the latest economic report suggesting that everything everyone was arguing about was based on complete fantasy. He made a decent fist of interpreting the news as being bad only for the Conservatives: 'It gives the big lie to John Major's claim yesterday that he would reduce tax every year for the next five years.'

Another day, another big lie, another big denial coming up. The report at issue had been produced for *The Independent* by the City accountants Coopers and Lybrand Deloitte. It calculated that the Treasury's predictions for growth over the coming five years were seriously over-optimistic and that whoever formed the next government might have to raise the basic rate of income tax by at least four pence in the pound. It confirmed the essence of the *Guardian*'s post-budget report of Monday 23 and heightened the mildly hysterical feeling that the election was a farce.

By five past nine, on *Election Call* Norman Lamont was being invited by a gent from Derby to admit the game was up. He declined. The thing was, he explained blandly, that when he had said yesterday that there was 'very little room for manoeuvre', it didn't contradict Prime Minister Major's promise of annual tax cuts. Small extensions of the spanking new 20 pence band *were* possible, he insisted, the corners of his mouth resolutely refusing to curl upwards into a smile. So we could all relax. By 1997, all those people on Family Credit and Housing Benefit would have a whole extra pound to spend every week. You could buy two and a half copies of the *Financial Times* for that.

Tax, tax, tax, tax, tax, tax, tax. The Tories had launched their third week's campaigning with another 'costing' of the 'credibility gap' in Labour's plans. In his shadow budget, John Smith had calculated Labour's planned spending increase as £7 billion. Lamont used a different brand of abacus. He made the figure £38 billion. At their morning press conference, the Conservatives had produced a little slide show to show every one of Britain's 25 million tax payers – not just the 'middle-income' or 'middle-class' ones – how those socialists would run off with their money: a car assembly worker, married with two children (and with a personal allowance, a marriage allowance, mortgage relief and child benefit entitlement) earning £12,000 a year would pay £359 more under Labour; a clinical nurse working in London in the same circumstances, on £23,875 would pay £2010 more; a 'middle manager' on £32,000 would pay £3361 more. This was 'How Labour's Tax Bombshell Would Hit You', it said on xeroxed sheets handed out to all the journalists. The message boiled down to this: you'd have to move to a smaller house; you'd have to go without your summer holiday; you'd have to sell your car! And the only reason those socialists want to do it is because they are spiteful! They are envious! They are vicious!

The horrors depicted in this 'costing' mirage were intended to disturb the peace in John Major's Model World, and a transformation was occurring in the temper of its archetypal citizen. The faulty toaster had been returned to Woolworths, but the angry nerd's fury had not been assuaged. Nice John had displayed his nasty streak to an audience in Birmingham only the night before, armed with the miserable Chancellor's astonishing new sums: 'A Labour government would mean £38 billion of extra spending. That's the equivalent of £1250 a year on average for everyone who pays income tax, on top of Mr Smith's mock budget tax attack. What price then the new car, the holiday, the mortgage?'

The television pictures showed him looking deathly against the luxuriant blue backdrop of the half-a-million pound stage set. '. . . In other words, a Nightmare on Kinnock Street . . . So don't be fooled. Here's the Labour leader, nodding and winking and grinning, a foot-in-the-door salesman, trying to sell you a gentle, harmless semi-demi-socialism.'

And the fairy lights had clicked on again in the Glorious Past theme park: 'Ladies and gentlemen, the world is moving fast. Shifting under our feet. We have won the Cold War . . . So under whose leadership do we go from here? Let us remind people who won back for Britain the respect in which we are now held abroad. We did.

'Who came to the defence of the Falklands and again in Kuwait? We did.

'Who stood firm beside the United States in leading the NATO alliance? We did.

'Who safeguards Britain's security by keeping our nuclear deterrent up to date? We do.

'But what of Mr Kinnock, with Mr Kaufman walking half a step behind? What of him?

'Who campaigned for CND when the Cold War was at its height and then let his membership "lapse" when others had won it? He did.

'Who fought NATO's policy of standing up to the Soviet Union and opposed putting in Cruise missiles when they had nuclear weapons targeted on us? He did.

'Who called our closest ally – the United States, the bastion of the free world – a threat equal to the Soviet Union? He did.'

This section of the Monday night speech was designed to complement the theme of Tuesday's assault on Labour over defence. There was no doubt that Labour's commitment to unilateral nuclear disarmament had cost them votes in the previous two elections. With the collapse of the Soviet Union and Labour's gradual shift to a multilateral position, much of the heat seemed to have gone out of the issue. But the Conservatives knew that parades of bombs and missiles still caused hats to be thrown in the air in the Glorious Past theme park. The trick was to frighten people with stories about swarthy, demented foreigners with big red buttons to push, and to imply that spineless socialists, like that idiot Neil Kinnock, would sit back and let them do it.

That was the angle taken in the evening's Conservative party election broadcast. Swallowing their distaste, so pronounced the previous week, for the use of children in emotive commercials, the Tory film depicted a doe-eyed youngster playing a video war game whose images became those of real conflict. 'The Cold War may be over,' intoned a coolly grim voice, 'but just how safe is the world in 1992?' It went on to state that the last three Labour Party conferences had voted for cuts in defence spending of 27 per cent, conveniently neglecting to add that Britain's Next Prime Minister had said straight after the last one that he wouldn't take the blindest bit of notice, thus proving how 'electable' he was. It showed a Trident nuclear submarine dematerializing at the mention of Labour's failure to pledge funding for a fourth such craft. It produced old footage of Neil Kinnock making a speech on a CND platform and alleged (echoing Defence Secretary Tom King's claim in a press conference earlier that day) that all references to CND membership among Labour parliamentary candidates had been erased from the final version of their Candidates' Directory. The broadcast concluded with the camera panning away from the child's bedroom window, to show a street full of mock-Tudor houses otherwise at peace in the dead of night.

The contention that Labour was not fit to secure Britain's interests was also made by Michael Heseltine in a crisp little sound bite on an evening news bulletin. 'Can you imagine Neil Kinnock speaking for Britain abroad? Neil Kinnock arguing for Britain in Europe? Can you imagine Neil Kinnock toughing it out in the interests of Britain's defence?' But defence only took up a fraction of the day's television coverage. And only a fragment of John Major's Monday night speech (its full text pumped out from the Central Office engine room for inclusion in the journalists' press packs), slipped on to the news bulletins – the bit about the 'Nightmare on Kinnock Street'. And yet that, for the Tories, was probably the crucial part, for it spoke to the portion of the voting public's soul that John Major understood. They're after your mortgage! They're after your holidays! They're after your car!

This message was delivered while disquiet continued to seep from Conservative circles about the style of the national campaign. Initially, the complaint was that Nice John was being *too* nice. Now it was said that Nasty John just didn't look plausibly savage. There was unease about the soap-box. Since ad-libbing an open-air showdown from this makeshift platform in Luton on Saturday, Major had repeated the exercise in Cheltenham (doing his bit for poor John Taylor) on Monday. Now the nation's viewers saw him at it again in Chester, commencing his oration with one of the campaign's less exotic pledges: 'I promise you this: wherever I go between now and 9 April, this soap-box is coming with me. There's no way they're going to keep the Conservative message from getting right out on to the streets . . .'

It was a tactic Saatchi and Saatchi would not have devised in a million years. Directly invoking hustings techniques from an almost forgotten era could not have jarred more violently with standard wisdoms about modern political communication. Authority's Experts seemed thrown by its apparently spontaneous advent. What about gravitas? What about a statesmanlike bearing? When newsreaders reported that 'John Major was out on his soap-box today', it sounded as if they were describing a small boy's adventure in a pedal car. They conveyed the information in tones of exaggerated casualness, as if to disguise their incredulity.

Yet the message Chinese-whispered from the Conservative camp was that Major's devotion to his soap-box was both genuine and, for the man himself, intoxicating, as if for the first time since calling the election he had taken a piece of his fate into his own hands. It was, too, part of the Boy from Brixton hagiography that Major used to stand on south London street corners spreading the Tory word. In that respect, the soap-box ploy harmonized perfectly with the Major myth. And there was something else, less gift-wrapped, about the sight of the British premier in the thick of the electorate, frightening armed, plain-clothes police guards half to death. To call the new Major 'nasty' did not do justice to his approach. Snuggled in his Barbour, with his sensible parting and windscreen specs, there was no air of menace. The Nice John smile remained intact. When anger showed, it suggested common decency rudely affronted, a basic civility stung into self-defence against an alien contagion. Cars and holidays and mortgages meant a lot to the private citizens of John Major's Model World. They were tangible rewards that hadn't come easy and no one was going to be allowed to waltz down the garden path and help themselves.

There were two other items of election coverage on television during the evening which suggested the soap-box ploy might not be as daft as, to some, it looked. The first was a clip of Margaret

Thatcher heading off to an appointment in America to negotiate some bloated consultancy fee. Buttonholed by a reporter, she looked wild-eyed and sour-mouthed: 'We *fight* to keep all of those things which we did in the last twelve years, like trade union reform, like wealth creation, like property-owning democracy, which Labour fought tooth and nail while we were doing them. And we *fight* . . .'

The reporter tried to intervene, but Herself ploughed rudely on: '. . . and we *fight* to keep the standing of Britain in the world.'

Loony tunes, loony tunes. But for all that, her lecture encapsulated key elements of changes fostered under her leadership, whose souring legacy her successor, with his different style and preoccupations, was better suited than she to defend. The lasting achievement of the Thatcher reign had been to convert a decisive proportion of the affluent working-class to her cause. But the relationship which fuelled those conversions was not straightforwardly that of benefactor to beneficiary. It was also that of monopoly supplier to dependent client. The sacred C2s and others who had derived short-term benefit from 'trade union reform', from 'wealth creation' and from owning property were now paying the price in job insecurity and debt. Yet where were they to turn for relief? To Labour?

The second telling item of election coverage was a cross-examination of John Smith on BBC 2's *Newsnight*. Like (to a lesser extent) that of *Channel 4 News*, *Newsnight*'s approach was less dully collaborative with the party managers. Its presenter, Jeremy Paxman, exuded a pleasing scepticism towards whichever political specimen he was charged with dissecting. In concert with two economists, he challenged Smith on his plans to refloat the economy. Smith persistently ducked out. He wouldn't set a target for reduced unemployment. He wouldn't admit that a run on sterling would oblige him to put interest rates up. He wriggled on the point that the minimum wage might lead to higher inflation and people being sacked.

Of course, he was in no position to do much else, because Labour had no serious commitment to cutting unemployment, to containing an outflow of investment or to much improving of workers' rights should employers prefer to fire them rather than abandon poverty pay. To have done so would not have been thought 'electable'. At best, he offered a fraction less unemployment, a minor reduction in government borrowing and a tiny bit more growth. At worst, he offered none of those, and only the prospect of higher interest rates and inflation – in other words, a direct threat to the very client citizens Thatcherism had supplied, now menaced by the demons of repossession and bills landing on doormats. And what might happen to their share dividends, their pay packets, their private pensions? No matter how much they felt betrayed by the mayhem of market forces, they still had, thanks to Thatcher, a vested interest in sustaining the administration that had unleashed them – an interest against which Labour offered only the mildest arguments. And meanwhile siren voices, like Coopers and Lybrand Deloitte, were wailing that the best-laid plans would come to nothing.

John Smith was offering floating sceptics not very much that might not happen at all. John Major, on his soap-box was offering them empathy, and a pledge to protect what was left. In their creeping fear of losing it lay his greatest hope.

CHAPTER TWENTY-FIVE

Meadow Well

(Wednesday 1, Thursday 2 April)

James Naughtie rounded up the hot news on *The World at One*: 'The City has reacted nervously to the latest opinion polls which suggest that Labour is on course to win the election. The Footsie[1] index opened well down and is now showing a loss of more than 40 points.'

Here was the break Labour had been praying for, and here was the predictable response from the Conservatives' irregular army. Three polls had been published that morning. They showed Labour seven, six and four points in front. The cause was not a rise in Labour's own support, but a slide by Conservative voters towards the Liberal Democrats. In response, the Tories had started the day attacking Paddy Ashdown's gang, and the stock exchange dealers had assumed the role of undermining Neil Kinnock's.

Market analysts spoke of the city's fear of taxes, fear of sterling seepage, fear of higher interest rates. Taped earlier in Bristol, Nice John was heard on his soap-box getting nasty amid raucous cheers and jeering: 'Let me tell you why we're going to win this general election with a clear majority for the next five years, despite Mr Kinnock's Trojan Horse with the yellow posters . . .' But in Hertford, responding to this and some tart remarks by Chairman Chris, Paddy Ashdown relished his latest fix of importance: 'Neither Mr Patten's insults, nor Mr Patten's scares, are going to in any way deflect us from what we continue to do. For the last seven days of this campaign we will do what we have resolutely done for the last three weeks – put forward *our* ideas.'

Trust me. I'm honest. I'm strong.

1. Acronym for Financial Times Share Exchange 500 index (FTSE).

Meanwhile, in Leeds, Britain's Next Prime Minister was basking. 'Things are going very well indeed. The sun is out, the daffodils are up, and things are standing us in good stead.'

Not much sun and daffodils two hours further north. By mid-afternoon, the A1 artery into the Newcastle conurbation was oppressed by a smothering rainstorm, turning an already (to the unschooled) complex eastwards shuttle to the city's one Tory constituency into an endurance test. Tynemouth's name is self-descriptive, wedged as it is in the armpit of the River Tyne and the rocky coast of the North Sea. Relationships with water define much of the constituency's split character. For years, the estuary banks sustained some of Britain's most famous shipyards and other, related heavy industries. They nurtured the Labour vote. But upcoast, the seaside dwellers and their suburban neighbours outnumbered it. As a result, Tynemouth has been Conservative since before the war. Yet while the traditional industries have shrivelled, so too has the Tory majority, a process hastened by boundary changes. In 1987, right-winger Neville Trotter only held on by 2500. This time his team were working long hours to prevent Labour turfing him out.

'Good evening, Conservative office.'

The emphasis was on the 'Con', but only because Perry Wilson, Trotter's agent, spoke with the local accent. He sat behind the former counter of a converted corner shop fielding calls, with two blue balloons dangling like Disney testicles over his head. Above them, its placement inviting disrespectful comparisons, a poster of Nice John Major had been pinned. A plaque commemor-ated the opening of the office by Viscount William Whitelaw. 'It's probably the only Conservative constituency office with an outside toilet,' remarked Wilson cheerfully. He recalled the poor Willie being a touch embarrassed by having to use it.

Wilson stepped over a red tombola to brew up a cuppa. Slim and good looking, with limpid brown eyes, the knowledge that he had served for twelve years in the navy recalled that song about what all the nice girls like. He had decided to become a Conservative agent while watching Prime Minister's Questions on television and forsaken a job he'd lined up in Aberdeen, making charts of the sea bed for an oil company. Acquiring his position had initially entailed attending a weekend course in St

Albans with written tests, a mock cocktail party with the examiners, followed by a dinner 'to make sure you don't eat with your fingers', and initiative games (thirty minutes in a team of six to devise a charity fundraising event), all designed to test leadership qualities and social skills. Then there was a year's training. It wasn't a bad job. 'The worst part, having been in the forces, is having to rely on the goodwill of volunteers.' He'd reached the rank of petty officer. In the navy, people had to do what they were told.

Wilson came from Gateshead across the city, home to the mighty Metro shopping centre, a monument to the entrepreneurship of ex-miner and Thatcher knight, Sir John Hall. His father is a self-employed panel-beater, his mother a retired nurse and social worker. He supposed he was a Conservative because 'I'm independent, I like hard work, I like to see hard work rewarded, I suppose I admire strong leadership. I believe you mustn't carry those who won't try. I think it's basically common sense. Common sense politics.' He shrugged, as if being so proximate to urban Labour sentiment had made him used to being challenged. 'Perhaps it's my warped sense of logic.'

Devotees of 'common sense' had had a bewildering time of it in the Tynemouth area the previous late summer. They, like millions of others who saw the fire bombs flying on the news, could see no 'common sense' in what happened on the Meadow Well estate in North Shields, just a mile down the road from Wilson's office. What was the point of those kids burning out their own community centre and little local shops? Why did they get such a kick from raising hell in hotted cars? Why did they so hate the police? Why had the trouble spread further across the district with such terrible haste? As ever, the post-mortem debate revolved around two mutually-repulsing polarities: one, the theory of social deprivation; two, the attribution of individual wickedness. Wilson, being a Conservative, tended to the latter.

'The police tell me there are about ten, fifteen families who are real thugs, real scum, who terrorize the rest of the people on the Meadow Well. There are, I suppose, a hundred feckless kids, who just follow anyone who gives them a lead. What's required,' he continued, switching to juvenile crime in general, 'is a very big change in attitudes. Though I don't myself believe in God, and I don't believe that if I steal a car I'm going to go to hell

because of it, I don't do it, because from a very early age I got a
clip round the ear if I took something that wasn't mine.'

Unemployment in the Newcastle area had been chronic. But
Wilson couldn't comprehend the idea that it is the seedbed of
disorder.

'There's never been a sense of despair. Perhaps it's because the
only time I'm in [central] Newcastle is to go drinking, and very
few people despair when they're drinking. They despair when the
bar closes. But I've never been aware, and I still live on a council
estate now, of a great lack of jobs or money.' With no real
rancour he embarked on a familiar litany: unmarried or single-
parent families lead to indiscipline; violent television encourages
copycat conduct; teachers are apathetic; young women who get
pregnant have only themselves to blame and would learn to be
more careful if they didn't know they'd get bailed out by the
state. He didn't believe the Thatcher years had encouraged a
culture of greed. 'You can still get something, if you're prepared
to work hard at it,' he concluded amiably.

Rummaging through wads of raffle tickets and piles of election
fliers, he came up with a piece of a map. This he photocopied and
meticulously marked in the Meadow Well with a yellow highlighter pen. 'My friends in the Labour Party, they say they're
very, very apathetic down here, they blame any government
that's in power, whoever's in power.'

I left him to his telephone and his tombola. He would be there
till well after nine, then go home to his wife and baby and eat his
microwaved dinner. As to Neville Trotter's movements, he
wasn't entirely sure, though he thought the MP would be opening
a fish factory at ten thirty the next morning. My planned
excursion to the danger estate would have to be undertaken alone.

'We don't canvass on the Meadow Well,' Wilson grinned.

Next morning, the polls were back to normal. One showed
Labour two points ahead, another put the Tories in the lead by
one half. The Liberal Democrats were on 19 and 20. Kenneth
Baker opened the Conservatives' press conference account,
defending their record on crime: they supported the police; they
believed in tough punishments; Labour was 'soft'. As this poured

from the car radio speakers, a slow prowl round the Meadow Well revealed almost no signs of life, only of torpor and yesterday's rage. It was early, wet and windy, but even so . . . The rain, slow and filthy, made the windscreen wipers squeak.

'If you exclude car crime,' Baker was saying, 'Britain is one of the safest countries in Europe.'

The estate is not of the tower-block type. Its dwellings are mainly detached, two-storey buildings in red brick. A pair of front doors serves each one. They are arranged on streets of concentric circles, making meaningless progress simple. Periodically, graffiti appeared: 'Free Willie Hunter.'

Round a corner, and there again! 'Free Willie Hunter Now.'

In so far as buildings can, the Meadow Well's looked despondent. Most of the doors were regulation council issue, though a few had been done up. A man in overalls was ferreting under the bonnet of his car, the first sign of human activity. Net curtains flailed from an open window. Eventually, the residential curves opened on to an arc of shops in front of which the car thieves had performed displays of handbrake turns. They had dug a trench in the road and poured in petrol to create walls of flame to stoke up the delinquent thrill. The Goliath Fish Bar, a newsagent and several other premises were completely sealed up, their walls still bearing the smut of arson. Incongruously, a light was on in a butcher's shop. It was still before nine in the morning.

'According to the polls, you are in serious danger of becoming Prime Minister, though you may yet be spared.'

The *Today* programme presenter, Brian Redhead, was interviewing you-know-who.

'There's no danger to the country,' said Britain's Next Prime Minister, his 'electable' baritone rolling, 'that's the important thing, because it'll give us the chance to get on with building recovery and making the commitments to the health, and the education services and paying the pensions and the families; in implementing the policies. So that's no danger, that's a great help.'

Outside, in that weather, even the grass looked sad. There were a few posters for Labour's candidate, Paddy Cosgrove, but if predominance of names on buildings was any measure of support, Willie Hunter enjoyed more of it.

'But even the hint in the polls that you might win put the City in a flurry,' said Redhead. 'Now if you win in a hung Parliament, the City, which fears uncertainty more than anything else, will be a), worried because you're in and b), even more worried because you haven't got power.'

'I would hope that the City would be more clinical,' Britain's Next Prime Minister replied, 'because what they know is that under Labour governments the City does very well. So does profitability in industry generally, and if they look at the last year under the Conservatives, in both the manufacturing sector and the services sector . . .'

Beneath a satellite dish, a woman stared out of a window.

'But you've moved from left to centre,' observed Redhead. 'Was that pragmatism or opportunism?'

'I think that the opportunities that existed, because of the movement in world affairs for instance, and also the requirements of the country because of the very great unsteadiness of the economy throughout most of this last thirteen years, has produced the need from any responsible political party to address itself to the current realities . . .'

Moderate plus professional equals electable. Time to visit the butcher.

It was bright and busy inside, with three women scuttling about. They didn't just sell bacon and pies. You wanted milk, they'd got milk, full cream or semi-skimmed. You wanted crisps, they'd got them, cheese and onion, salt and vinegar, plain. You wanted sweets, they'd got them too. Some little kids did. A tiny shoal of them scurried in and reached up to the counter, holding hot handfuls of change:

'Shut the door,' said one of the women gently. She went over to a shelf containing a row of boxes full of day-glo gums and chews: 'Right, you can have one of them, one of them, one of them . . .'

The second woman, younger and chatty, said she'd had enough of politics: 'I switch it off, it bores me to tears, they go on and on and on. They're all telling lies to get in, every single one of them. The country's in such a state it's gonna take years and years, isn't it? They should all get together and compromise.'

The reason for all the crisps and sweets being sold was 'to try to help people out'. All the other traders in the promenade had got burned out, brassed off or both. The next nearest shop was a fifteen-minute walk, except, bizarrely, for another butcher's premises which carried the same family name: E. Hoult, Pork Butcher. The third woman, older, wearing a nylon overall, seemed to be the boss. She lived over the shop in the grand English tradition, and had been in on the night the riots began. Shuttling through a doorway, carrying trays of pies, she remained dauntless, movingly so: 'I've been here forty years and this estate . . . it's just a few, just a handful, the minority that's caused all this trouble. They've all got chips on their shoulder. It's just some of the young ones. I've seen the bairns get married and bring their bairns in. I wouldn't change. I wouldn't, honestly. I'm staying here.'

The shoal of little kids flitted excitedly back out into the rain. A man bought two mince pies and two sausage rolls. Though appreciative of Neville Trotter's occasional visits to the shop, the older woman scoffed lightly at the relevance to Meadow Well of the ongoing democratic process for which we were meant to be so grateful. 'You cannot blame the government. They cannot do anything much. It's the parents.'

You could only listen and nod and marvel again at the infinity of cynicism dividing what the politicians were saying, and what people's experience told them were the harsh realities of life. The women's objectivity had been routed by repulsive experiences (in the first case, well before the riots) of brats in balaclavas storming in and smashing up a set of scales, or the tale of another shop where some kids had pinched a charity box from the counter, the same type the butchers themselves had defiantly planted on their own front counter. 'Frightened?' said the second woman. 'No, you get used to it. I'm sitting in the shop and I think, "You're not gonna frighten me."'

Mr Kinnock believed in addressing current realities. Mr Baker believed in getting tough. The pork butchers of the Meadow Well estate didn't believe in either of them, but as representatives of the nation of shopkeepers they believed in not being defeated by the nation of 'nasty little petty thieves and thugs'. Their determination was expressed in variations on Perry Wilson's 'common sense'. The blame lay with parents, with a few bad apples, with people who just didn't try. In this, they spoke for millions, for those who were worlds away from Meadow Well and the like. To them, it was nothing to do with 'politics'. But from such bitter sentiments grow Conservative votes.

CHAPTER TWENTY-SIX

Unforgettable

(Thursday 2 April)

Above the growl of traffic in Birmingham's Soho Road came the sound of Madonna urging exultation to a bounding house backbeat: 'Come on, vogue . . .' It was impossible to locate the source with certainty. Perhaps a tape player lugged by one of the gang of schoolchildren piling on to a bus: black, Asian and white teenagers with sharp haircuts and killer trainers. An elderly man in traditional Muslim dress picked his way through them, passing the Shalimar Sweet Centre, the Wonderful World Of Wallpaper and the B–Trendy Bazaar, with its 'fashionable clothes at rock bottom prices'. A fly poster for a magazine called *Tan* inquired: 'Do Asians Have Sex?' At Number 210, a notice on the doorway of a dreary office block announced the Birmingham Ladywood Labour Party campaign office. Several dark flights up, a tatty, rectangular office contained a long, wooden table around which a group of women volunteers staffed an envelope-stuffing sweatshop. Piles of slippery Labour leaflets carried the name and photograph of the Ladywood candidate: Clare Short, dark-haired, with an attractive, crinkly smile. Within a few minutes she was there in person, gasping under the weight of another box of literature. 'I've just been to this school round where I live,' she enthused, a trace of a Birmingham accent intruding at the end of her sentence. 'They're so lovely, aren't they, little kids, especially when they're all black and white and Asian and Vietnamese.'

Short had been Ladywood's MP since 1983. She inherited a constituency with 40 per cent unemployment, up from 9 per cent in 1979, thanks to Margaret Thatcher setting everybody free. The seat includes Birmingham city centre, with its famous Bull Ring, but the heart of it is the Soho ward and its cosmopolitan, sometimes-working-class population. The West Midlands took the full force of manufacturing industry's massacre, 'but people here have got great heart,' said Short as we headed off into the rush hour for her next appointment.

Resilience is something Short and her constituents have in common. In conventional parliamentary shorthand she is usually described as 'soft left' but there is not much that is soft about her, in the sense of pliancy or weakness. The saga that made her famous stands as proof. In 1986 she introduced a private members' bill 'to make illegal the display of pictures of naked or partially naked women in sexually provocative poses in newspapers'. Her intention, entirely noble, was to purge pornography from mass-circulation publications. The endeavour brought upon her head a sustained and unprecedented campaign of hatred.

All but one of the newspapers whose content she had in mind were in the forefront of the assaults upon her. The exception was the *Daily Mirror* which supports Labour (as long as it is not too socialist) and whose pin-ups are neither as crudely presented nor celebrated with the same sweaty-palmed relish. The remainder set about trying to wreck Clare Short's life. They were led by the *Sun* — to whom Page Three girls are a precious institution – and the *News of the World*, the two most profitable titles in the Tory-worshipping stable of Rupert Murdoch. First, Short was portrayed as an envious, sexually inadequate killjoy. Then her private life was raked over and denigrated. Just to trick out the exercise with novelty value, five Conservative MPs agreed to pose gloatingly alongside Page Three girls. It all amounted to a punishment consistent with the liberty her bill sought to curtail: the 'freedom' to treat women as dirt.

Well, Clare Short survived. And what seems to be the essence of her survival is what might best be called morality.

'I don't really have to do this,' she remarked, in reference to her 10,028 majority, as we walked through the entrance of a geriatric nursing home. 'I just think it's a kind of duty.'

We made our way to a dining hall, bland and open, sixties-style. About twenty people were arranged, in some cases literally, around formica-topped tables. Most were in wheelchairs. Almost all showed what, to the inexperienced, are the disturbing symptoms of senility and motor neurone disorders. They gazed at plastic water jugs and beakers, set out with a military orderliness.

Short sauntered into the middle of the room, wearing an expression of presumptive complicity.

'Well, you know why I've come, don't you?'

Till that point, there had been utter silence. But a few residents offered noises of affirmative inflexion.

'I always come at this time, don't I? At the election?'

A few confirming sounds.

'Are you all gonna vote? I've brought you some leaflets. And some stickers. You don't have to have them if you don't want.'

She began moving among the tables, distributing the glossy literature. A man called Cecil said that he couldn't read.

'You can't read? You'll have to look at the pictures.' She did a quick *Crimewatch* parody: 'Have you seen this woman before?'

In the far corner, a man made sporadic howling noises, his head rolling, his left arm rammed straight out.

'I've got a programme for our commitment on the disabled. I should have brought it with me, shouldn't I?'

Someone close by seemed to have cheekily agreed.

'I could send you a copy. Are you the shop steward?'

There was a ripple of laughter at this. The man in the far corner howled again.

'So what else? Tell me what you think about the world. Or the election.'

This brought a clearly intelligible response from one resident: 'I'd like to have a Labour government.'

'I agree with you. Anything else? How's the food? Pork pie and salad? You're learning to swim? Very good. Can you do a few strokes? I went last night, in Handsworth. It's open till half past ten. It's instead of going to the pub.'

More laughter. The air of complicity was beginning to be shared. By this time Short had got round to the noisy one in the corner. The fingers on his ramrod arm groped agitatedly towards her. She bent down to hear him speak. Another howl.

'Do I remember you? Absolutely I do. Who could forget you?'

Canvassing is a whistle-stop business. After ten minutes it was time to go.

'Well, cheerio then. I've got to get on.'

The noisy one flapped and howled again.

'Cheerio . . . *unforgettable.*'

Back at the media election, the obsession of the day was style. The previous evening had seen Labour's government-in-waiting parade explode into full-tilt triumphalism at a massive rally in Sheffield. Before 40,000 red-rose revellers, Neil Kinnock had been given the complete, conquering hero build-up: 'And now it's time! Time for the Next Prime Minister!' And Kinnock had strutted onto the stage, punching the air and whooping: 'Well, all right! All right!' He was the rock'n'roll reformist, the evangelist of 'electability', the pink pretender preparing to claim his crown. It was the side of the real Neil Kinnock who reduced sensitive people to quivering embarrassment. Another side compensated in his speech: 'What's at issue in this election is not the soap-boxes that the Prime Minister stands on,' he raged. 'It's the cardboard boxes that people have to live in.' There were no half measures with the real Neil Kinnock. The righteous and the ridiculous were equally integral.

At his morning press conference the morning after, a still-bubbling Neil Kinnock had been asked about John Major's soap-box ploy. He spoke disparagingly of 'a second-rate Barbour', then began to backtrack, chuckling. 'Oh I don't know if it's a second-rate one, it just looks second rate on the telly, I don't know . . . Oh personal attacks, I take it all back, I take it all back!' Someone asked if he didn't look rather remote by comparison, swanning about in a Daimler: 'I don't think I'm in the least bit remote,' he objected. But as long as he played the part of Britain's Next Prime Minister, he was, remoteness personified. The question was, did remoteness assist 'electability'?

The answer would be provided in eight days' time by half a million voters in ninety-four seats. But Ladywood was not one of them. There, remoteness was the last thing a politician required.

Short's last local appointment of the day, before racing off to Channel 4 in London, was a public meeting held at the Summerfield Park community centre, a bleary old building with exotic pipework that used to be a school. This, too, was 'a duty', happily discharged. Making herself available to be challenged or chided was a matter of propriety.

Around 200 people came, an encouraging cross-section of the Ladywood polyglot, plus a few committed spoilers. One of the first questions concerned education:

'Okay, to the young man from the Liberal Party, who's got his yellow poster rolled inwards,' began Short observantly, very combative in her red jacket and trousers. 'I think it's very fine to promise two billion pounds for education *and* they're gonna transform the world on it. But the Liberal Party opposes the proposals we've made to cut taxation for the poorest. They're opposed to the proposals we have to tax the well off. So I think the Liberals are promising different things to different people. I think they're playing a lot of games. Then it pretends to be the only *clean* party . . .'

This distaste for self-misrepresentation had underpinned a series of differences Short had had with her own party in the recent past. These ranged from minor matters of presentation to major questions of policy. She recoiled – rather splendidly – from the idea that she might be improved by image advisors. More seriously, she had resigned from Labour's front-bench team over the party's Gulf War posture. Her reasons for this and the alternative line she proposed say much more about her politics than the mere application of a 'soft-left' tag.

The unequivocal support for the Allies' saturation bombing offered – with apparent gusto – by Britain's Next Prime Minister, was something she could not share. But equally, she did not join with the Campaign Group in opposing the entire enterprise. It was a matter of practicality, of principle and of care. She wanted no share in bloodshed's reflected glory, and believed more effort should have been made with sanctions and negotiations. Equally, ordinary British people were candidates for coffins. So though it was true that the Allies' motives were far from purely altruistic, and true that Britain's imperial history had sown the seeds for Saddam's rise and his claims on Kuwait, invocations of historical abstracts amounted, in those circumstances, to little more than gestures. But any deviation from the front-bench ranks was thought bad for 'electability'. Presented with the choice of shutting up or being fired, Short stepped down and kept talking. It was, she says, all very civilized. Short's singularity has earned respect, even from the chronically obedient in Labour's upper echelons.

Another question from the audience, this time about the minimum wage.

'A national minimum wage is both about decency, and, look at these Tory scare stories about destroying millions of jobs! That's simply a lie, and it's also about having a more efficient economy. And it *will* affect some people in small enterprises, but some jobs are so badly paid that they *should* go.'

It was a far more truthful account of the minimum wage's virtues than the leadership was presenting. By acknowledging that the few jobs – and only the Tories contended that it would be more – that might be lost were remunerated disgracefully, it gave the moral and practical virtues of the policy greater force.

More questions came, fielded three at a time. One concerned the Asylum Bill, a contentious proposal designed to keep out refugees and which Labour, it was remarked, had considered compromising its opposition to if a few clauses could be traded first prior to Parliament's dissolution. The young white man who raised the point said the bill was racist and on no account negotiable.

Short suspected an ulterior motive. 'Listen, I *know* more about it than *you* do,' she scowled with awesome distaste. 'I've got no *respect* for the Trotskyist groups. You're only interested in your own *selfish* projects.'

As a member of the NEC, Short had voted for Dave Nellist and Terry Fields's expulsion. On the way in to the crucial meeting, she fumed to a reporter: 'Militant have a bloody cheek. They're running candidates against *our party*! They have *no honour*.'

As well as prickly, the Ladywood public meeting was heartening and funny. A fellow in the front row wearing baggy khaki shorts and yachting pumps kept butting in. He had a gripe about the state of the roads. 'He's a cyclist, you see,' explained Short. 'He's worried about holes.' A question on defence policy prompted her to comment on the latest Conservative poster, which represented the difference between the parties in hedgehog form: a bristling, virile Tory specimen stood proud next to a cringing, spineless Labour one. 'I like ours much better,' said Short. 'I'd like to take it home and give it a blanket.'

There's a lot to be said for a politician prepared to do the decent thing.

CHAPTER TWENTY-SEVEN

Fear of Kinnock

(Friday 3 April)

'Well, good morning, ladies and gentlemen,' began the chair of the Liberal Democrats' regional press conference on education. He addressed this greeting to a single television camera. There were no 'ladies' whatsoever in the room. If you excluded the characters who came with the camera, there were no gentlemen either, except for me. I controlled myself with difficulty.

'With me in Sheffield this morning are, on my left, the Earl Russell, Professor of History at King's College, London, who is the party's spokesman in the House of Lords on social security. And on my right Dr Peter Gold, who is the parliamentary candidate for Sheffield Hallam.'

Quite a guy, this Earl Russell, son of Bertrand. Before the start of the daft charade, as a technician adjusted appropriate stick-on slogans ('My Vote!' 'Changing Britain for Good!') on the self-assembly backdrop, his Lordship puffed effetely at a cigarette. In the great tradition of toff intellectuals, his clothes fitted him insecurely, like the cardboard garments children used to snip from the backs of cereal packets and attach to cut-out people using fold-over tabs. When the TV producer deferentially put it to him that he might tighten the knot of his tie ('Can I just make a suggestion to you, sir?'), he responded with the pursed-lipped affectation of an Elizabethan court wit:

'Ah yes, this is the one matter on which I am in agreement with Kenneth Clarke, who, further, for all his manifest faults, at least has the good taste to be a fellow smoker.'

At this point, there should have been a peal of flattering laughter. Instead, there was a slightly bewildered silence. Peter

Gold, a neat, pleasant fellow, cleared his throat. It was then that the 'conference' commenced.

'You will have seen in this morning's papers,' Russell commenced, 'a letter from 900 academics, complaining of the decline in standards under thirteen years of Conservative government. I agree with every word of it. It's a bit understated, as a letter for mass signature . . .' ('signature' became 'sig-nee-ah-tu-er') '. . . must be. I wasn't asked to sign it. Peter Gold wasn't asked to sign it. The list of signatories . . .' ('sig-nee-ah-tu-eries') '. . . looks like a Labour front. The whole of the letter carries the suggestion . . . ('sugg-ess-tee-on') '. . . that Labour would be better for higher education than the Conservatives. I agree with General Booth. I don't see why the devil should have all the best tunes.'

He then embarked on a detailed breakdown of precisely where the Liberal Democrats' £2 billion would be spent, drawing contrasts at several points with Labour's 'not a penny'. At the end, the chair asked the 'ladies and gentlemen' if there were any questions. I asked where the Liberal Democrats stood on the specious trad-versus-trendy argument about teaching methods. Earl Russell produced a detailed reply about undue executive interference.

Then the camera crew's frontman, who had arrived a little late, threw in a wild card about 'the markets' not liking the idea of a penny rise in the basic rate of income tax. 'The City trusts Beith,' Lord Russell replied, 'they don't see him as hostile to the creation of wealth.'

The frontman had been tuning in to the morning press conference. From them, he would have known that the Tories were turning the spotlight on the share-price falls of what they had dubbed 'Red Wednesday' as evidence of catastrophes to come under a socialist reign of terror. Chief Secretary to the Treasury David Mellor had discovered a new minority in fear of persecution: 'The financial community,' poor loves, who had 'no confidence in Labour'. It looked suspiciously like the onset of panic, and followed a day of strategic electoral sky-writing by Britain's Next Prime Minister in an effort to seduce soft centrist votes. On Thursday morning, all sober and statesmanlike, he had spoken of the need for 'consensus' government, and promised to form a commission of inquiry into constitutional reform if Labour won. Representatives of other parties would be invited to sit on this commission, which showed what a 'moderate', 'professional', 'electable' fellow he was. And had he not already shown his willingness to countenance – though not, of course, actually advocate – change by appointing Professor Raymond Plant to produce a report into the pros and cons of alternative voting systems? Paddy Ashdown had rebuffed this crafty come-on with reference to Kinnock's buttocks, saying, 'He has shifted his bottom along the fence, but he's still sitting on it.'

What it all revealed was the calculation by both Labour and the Conservatives that Britain's Next Prime Minister really looked as if he was. The burning question was whether he would preside over a Labour majority, or just have the largest number of seats. Kinnock's commission flirt was a bid to make the difference. The Tories had resorted to calling up the spectre of apocalypse. The consequences for Liberal Democrat candidates like Sheffield Hallam's Peter Gold were still anybody's guess.

The Hallam constituency was Sheffield's one Conservative seat out of six. The other five were all held by Labour, four of them with sledgehammer majorities. Long famous for its steelworks and more recently acknowledged as a model of leftish local government (led till his election as MP for Sheffield Brightside by shadow Social Security spokesman David Blunkett), Sheffield looked set to stay red even in Hillsborough, where the Labour majority (over a Liberal Democrat) was slim. But Hallam too was just about a marginal. In 1987, Gold had come second, trailing by 7637 votes. Labour were third with 11,290. If a good chunk of those went for the pragmatic option and enough former Tories broke faith, then Gold was in with a shout.

His first campaign appointment was at a Roman Catholic primary school. As he parked his car, the air was filled with a truly terrific stench as if something had gone horribly wrong in a chemistry class. 'Oh that's my catalytic converter,' said Gold unconcernedly, as a thousand Sheffield sparrows fell, stunned, from surrounding trees. 'I checked with my garage. They said it was perfectly all right.'

We walked to the door past a glorious display of daffodils and under a hand-coloured banner which said 'Ballot Station'. The pupils had conducted their own mock election. Gold had come to congratulate them on their experiment in democracy and, hopefully, have his picture taken by the *Sheffield Star*.

In the foyer, a suffering Jesus gazed down from a cross on the wall. The head teacher, a middle-aged woman with set hair, wearing flat shoes and a floral scarf, invited him into the staff room for tea and asked which party the Liberal Democrats would support if there was a hung Parliament. Gold, perhaps symbolically, balancing cup and saucer, repeated the standard text: we're not taking sides; it's up to them. He had a biscuit. I thought about the message on Gold's own campaign fliers: 'Labour cannot win. So if your priority is to defeat the Conservative then vote Peter Gold, Liberal Democrat!'

Ten minutes later, down in the assembly hall, a little lad called Thomas in a neat blue uniform clutched his right elbow with his left hand and shuffled nervously. On his chest was pinned a slightly floppy yellow rosette, constructed from crêpe paper. Gold congratulated him on his triumph. Thomas blushed and made a succinct acceptance speech: 'Erm . . . Thank you very much.' Gold led the applause and commenced a brief address on the grown-up exercise the children had charmingly aped:

'The election is terribly important. For thirteen years we've had a Conservative government. After Thursday, it's quite possible we'll have a different sort of government . . .'

The head teacher had made a point of insisting that Gold's talk was non-partisan. Mindful of this, his description of the Hallam contenders was exhaustive:

'. . . and there's a candidate from the Revolutionary Communist Party. I don't know what they stand for. Perhaps for getting rid of elections altogether.'

He went on to explain why he thought proportional representation was a fairer system, carefully making it clear that not everyone agreed, before head teacher wound things up with a remark of ultimate diplomacy: 'We hope that whoever wins, it will be for the best.'

That was supposed to be that, but there was a query from a boy called Jack: 'If there's a hung Parliament, what will happen?'

'Could we have a quick and *neutral* answer to that, please,' said head teacher, quickly.

Jack refined his question: 'Whose side will you be on?'
On a table by the doorway another anguished Jesus looked on.
Gold thought for a moment. 'See if you can guess.'
The children held their counsel. They were learning fast.

On the west side of the city, historically upwind from the smog
of heavy industry, Hallam contains more people with university
degrees than any other seat in the country. At its border with the
fringes of the Peak District lies a large acreage of residential
territory occupied by that strand of the middle class whose
trelliswork is matured by mildew and whose toy shrubs have deep
roots. Comfortably cultured behind bay windows and pebbledash,
they are the kinds of green-tinged traditionalists whose dislike of
vulgarity offers hope to Liberal Democrats. But how much?

Gold canvassed gamely, his raincoat collar turned up against
a gathering squall. The ivy-framed door at the end of the first
garden path opened to reveal a large, blue-rinsed woman in a
wool-polyester skirt, who all but had the word 'Tory' tattooed
on her forehead. An ingrained sense of what is proper, however,
restrained her from directly admitting to loyalties that were
screamingly obvious. Needing to at least fill in the appropriate
space on his canvass sheet, Gold employed all his verbal dexterity
to make it easy for her to snub him.

'Would it be reasonable to assume you might have voted
Conservative before?'

The woman turned this over carefully in her mind, weighing
the implications of such a sacrifice of privacy. Finally, unwillingly:
'You could probably assume so, yes.'

Five minutes to flush out a dud. Things could only get better,
and they did, though not decisively. What soon became crystal
clear was that the mathematics of a hung Parliament were
exercising many of Hallam's higher-educated minds, hardly discouraged by the headline in that day's *Yorkshire Post*: 'Kinnock
Offers Talks on Vote Deal.' The next house yielded a mad-haired
man who was solidly Liberal Democrat, but made known his
great misgiving: Fear of Kinnock. Up a long drive, to meet a
Laura Ashley woman with lashings of face-saving foundation,
who normally voted Labour but would 'make her vote count',

just as Paddy Ashdown asked. But two big muddy boys, fresh back from a wholesome hike, said they liked the idea of Gold's crew staking out the middle ground, yet they *did* have this Fear of Kinnock.

At the next house, a small dog intervened. Gold said to it: 'There, there.' It was about as profound a remark as anyone could have managed in the circumstances, but it had precisely no effect on the animal, which yap-yapped at the candidate's heels all the way to its owner's bow-fronted door. It was opened by a dishevelled academic. Bundling the dog into the kitchen, he declared himself a Tory-Lib Dem floater. He knew enough about Gold, who taught at the local business school, to appraise his educational pedigree:

'Difficult for a Cambridge man to vote for an Oxford man with the boat race coming up,' he chuckled soothingly.

Gold, impeccably courteous, agreed that it was indeed, and was rewarded for his tolerance by the academic's opinion of his rival, the vigorously Thatcherite Irving Patnick.

'He's obviously a fool.'

Patnick rose to local prominence during the Blunkett administration. He used to wear a gold chain bracelet and call the Labour councillors 'communists'.

But the academic had some thoughts on the Labour Party too: 'Neil Kinnock I regard as an intellectual pygmy.'

Fear of Kinnock, Fear of Kinnock, Fear of Kinnock. Your heart had to go out to the optimistic Gold. No matter how many Hallamites might agree with the dishevelled academic about the incumbent Patnick, his fate seemed inextricably linked to perceptions of Britain's Next Prime Minister. And on the evidence of that afternoon with Sheffield's middle class, they could spot Neil Kinnock lurking a mile off.

CHAPTER TWENTY-EIGHT

Guns And Primroses

(Saturday 4, Sunday 5 April)

'We were just admiring your garden,' said Dennis Donaldson to a woman in her fifties, standing proudly on her doorstep.

'Well, thank you,' replied the woman, tilting her head with faint embarrassment at the compliment. 'The hard thing is keeping it nice once you've got it how you want it.'

It was a tiny front garden, just a couple of staggered flower-beds arranged below a narrow terrace. A pair of miniature plaster gnomes, the sort Nice John Major's father might have made, grinned fixedly over the wall. Some of the bedding plants were beginning to bloom.

'Where did you get those primroses?' inquired Donaldson, a short, stocky man with his brown hair blown slickly back behind his ears.

'Andersonstown,' said the woman, and turned quickly to her right to reach a hand across her fence. 'Hello, Gerry! Good luck!'

Gerry Adams offered his hand in return. It was received with greater warmth than that of any other politician I had witnessed in the election campaign so far. That warmth was evidence of the deliberate omission, amid all the teases and pieties about proportional representation, parliaments for Scotland and Assemblies for Wales, of the desperate constitutional issue no British political party had the guts to tackle – the war in Northern Ireland.

Merely to describe the blood-letting which torments that land as 'a war' is, of course, to sin against the fearful cross-party consensus which insists it is something else: 'The Troubles', a contest between 'peace-keeping' and 'terrorism', between 'democracy' and 'the gunmen'. But war is what it is, a civil war which, by that very definition, renders absurd the idea of the 'United

Kingdom' of which 'the province' of Northern Ireland is officially a part. So much is painfully self-evident, or would be if it was not for the fact that anyone pointing it out – such as Ken Livingstone – risks bringing upon themselves the full force of establishment loathing, fuelled by what? Guilt? Embarrassment? Fear? What exactly *are* the British Army doing there?

The glib answer to that question hits you, with the same heart-stopping recognition familiar to all first-time visitors to Belfast, within minutes of entering the city: what the army is doing is avoiding getting killed. You've seen the photos in the papers, you've seen the documentary films. From them you know about the surreal, city-centre juxtapositions of soldiers in full combat gear and women with carrier bags. But when you see one for the first time, peering through your taxi window, the shopper stepping brightly along the pavement, the trio of servicemen shuttling warily across the street, throwing their backs against some office block wall and scanning the windows opposite, machine-guns poised, there is still the sense of the unbelievable becoming real before your popping eyes. The soldiers seem to be acting out a scene from a parallel world they've yet to realize they've departed.

But these (you quickly remind yourself) are the routine incongruities of urban guerrilla conflict. And as you begin to feel your way around Belfast's half-visible sectarian walls, the full panoply of big city warfare quickly reveals itself, the regular inventory of frontlines and bloodlines, bunkered rage and propaganda.

Dennis Donaldson provided a tour. It started out from the Sinn Fein Advice Centre at the top end of the Falls Road, where a metal security door gives way to a wooden one with a peephole, and your bag is checked ('if you don't mind, mate') by a half-tough party worker in a T-shirt and jeans. The Advice Centre had been attacked that February by a deranged Royal Ulster Constabulary officer, who tricked his way in with a shotgun and shot three men dead. Reception is a small, square converted bedroom with second-hand armchairs, an electric fire and its one window plugged with blockboard. The press officer, apologizing for the wait, had had his right arm reduced to a stump surely betraying – it was hard, in this setting, to presume anything else

– the ill-fortunes of war. Donaldson had endured reverses too, though the five years he spent from 1972 in the old Long Kesh prison camp (later renamed Maze) had less permanent effects: 'Oh, it was all right,' he said, remembering, then added, just to save me the embarrassment of asking, 'I was a convicted bomber.'

By then we were in a car park outside a shopping centre, looking out for Sinn Fein canvassers. Donaldson was confident, but the Sinn Fein President could not be sure of retaining his Belfast West seat, the most angry, deprived and ravaged of the whole 650. He first took it in 1983 and commenced a boycott of Westminster which he had sustained ever since. His closest challenger was Joe Hendron, a medical doctor representing the centre-left and nationalist Social Democratic and Labour Party, which takes most of Northern Ireland's Roman Catholic minority vote. Belfast West is 70 per cent Catholic, but its fierce Republican-ism had tilted the normal balance of Catholic voting Sinn Fein's way. The big question was whether the 18.7 per cent of the electorate who supported the Unionist candidate at the last election would switch to Hendron in order to get Adams out. To Unionists and to the British, Adams is the IRA with a shark's smile and a rosette. To Republicans, he is a man of courage and truth.

We finally tracked Adams to the Turf Lodge housing estate, where the conversation about the primroses took place. It is a heartland of what has been described as 'the terrorist community',[1] a place backbench Tory troglodytes dream of having cleansed by the SAS. For the moment, they have to make do with occupation and surveillance. On a ridge overlooking 'the Turf' stands an army fortress with high metallic walls behind which a camera pivots on a high spindle. The fortress is located directly in front of a primary school. Donaldson said 'the Brits' use it as a human shield.

Adams was accompanied on his canvass by an informal entourage: a few larky lads, a couple of women clutching leaflets and a shower of little kids. Crop-bearded and bespectacled, he strolled with steady steps from garden gate to garden gate, soaking up gratitude and admiring the sprays of plastic flowers that decor-ated front-room windowsills. Adams's Republican past is long and varied. A former barman, he had been involved in the civil rights

[1]. By Peter Brooke, Secretary of State for Northern Ireland.

campaigns of the late sixties, particularly in the field of housing where discrimination was rife. The suppression of the movement, first by the legal, Protestant para-military Ulster Defence Association[2] and then by British troops (sent in as 'saviours' in 1969, ostensibly to prevent loyalist extremists from slaughtering the residents of the Falls), was the crucial catalyst for the revival of armed Republicanism, which had become virtually dormant. 'It is hardly an over-simplification to say that the Catholics were forced off the streets into the arms of the IRA,' wrote one of Ireland's most respected journalist-historians. It was, he concluded, 'hard to over-estimate' the benefit to the guerrillas of British policy.[3]

In 1972, Adams was one of an IRA delegation who met William Whitelaw the then Secretary of State for Ireland, responsible for the newly-imposed, direct Whitehall rule. By then he was a senior officer in the IRA's Belfast command structure. The meeting took place in the Chelsea home of a millionaire junior minister from Whitelaw's department, and achieved next to nothing. Another of the Republican party recalled the Secretary of State's attitude to his own forces with rancour: 'Whitelaw is a callous bastard. "We can accept the casualties," he said, "we probably lose as many soldiers in accidents in Germany."'[4] Confirmed in his conviction that no Irish settlement can ever be achieved without a wholesale British withdrawal, Adams went on to personify the Republican mantra that the British would only depart if the power of both the Armalite and the ballot box were brought to bear. For his pains he has been shot (in 1984) by loyalist gunmen and silenced by a government ban on the reproduction of his voice (and all Sinn Fein members') through the broadcast media. The stricture was lifted at election time. So too was Adams's general profile as TV covered the launch of their manifesto and hacks parachuted in to gaze at Britannia's bogeyman. Matthew Parris of *The Times* picked up the tastiest quote of the day as Adams exchanged pleasantries with yet another Turf Lodge family.

'Who'd be a politician?' sighed Donaldson to one of the canvassing crew, adding, wickedly: 'It was easier when we were just bombing and shooting, wasn't it, Joe?'

2. Now banned, since August 1992.
3. Tim Pat Coogan, *The IRA*, Fontana, 1980, p. 434.
4. Ibid, p. 492.

Bingo. Parris scribbled gleefully. So did I.

Joe panicked and said, 'Speak for yourself.'

Twenty-five years after its renewal, the war that isn't a war looked certain to grind on. The most recent initiative by the British had been the 1985 Anglo-Irish Agreement with the government of the Irish Republic, which set up a limited platform for bilateral discussions about border security. Unionist politicians denounced it as treachery, led by the great ululator of Protestant fundamentalism, the Reverend Ian Paisley. The Republican analysis was that Thatcher realized she needed, in Donaldson's words, 'new allies in Ireland – the Irish government and the SDLP. That's why the Unionists were made to swallow it.'

(Paisley had called Margaret Thatcher a 'Jezebel').

'The British were basically saying to them, "If we give you what you want, and we defeat the IRA, you people will only re-create the conditions which gave rise to the IRA in the first place."' Implicit in the analysis was what British military leaders have themselves quietly acknowledged: that the IRA cannot be militarily beaten, only opposed – for as long, perhaps, as 'we can accept the casualties'.

Donaldson was broadly agnostic about the election in Britain. If anything, he preferred a Conservative win. They were more likely, he felt, 'to take a bold decision' than Labour, who would 'think they had to prove themselves to be tough, stand up to terrorism and all that'. He probably had a point. Roy Mason, a Labour Irish Secretary during their last administration, had been the most bloody-mindedly authoritarian of all, during a period when Republican prisoners were tortured in Irish jails.[5] And when in 1981 Thatcher reacted to the death by hunger strike of ten Republican prisoners (led by Bobby Sands MP) in the Maze prison as if she had a nasty smell under her nose, Michael Foot supported her.

The martyrdom of the hunger strikers is now as much part of the Republican grievance as the regular cullings of Catholics which have punctuated British policy in Ireland for four centuries. At one point, Adams was joined by one of the hunger strikers' brothers, a resident of Turf Lodge. One of the women with him spoke of two relatives presently in jail: 'It's *our* country,' she said, simply.

5. As revealed by Amnesty International and an inquiry under Judge Harry Bennett, QC. See Coogan, op cit, p. 547–8.

A little boy of eight or nine came over to stare at me.

'Are you from England?'

'Yes.'

He said nothing for a bit, then remarked, 'My daddy's in England.'

'What is he doing there?'

This time the little boy just stared at the ground.

Donaldson provided the answer for him: 'He's in prison, isn't he?'

The little boy nodded. The conversation we would both have liked to engage in died.

His gladhanding stint completed, Adams gave a quick interview as a black London-type taxi rumbled at the kerbside and the sound of Fenian rebel songs struggled from a cheap loudspeaker on its roof. 'I can't see any significant progress being made while loyalism still has the prop of the Union to sustain it,' he said, leaning against a fence. By 'progress' Adams meant the defusing of sectarian hatreds and an end to the 'armed struggle' of the IRA. He defined his objectives in socialist terms, explaining religious rivalries as the tool of British colonial domination, and professing a desire to be 'past all of that, and into the cut and thrust of dealing with poverty and people's right to a decent job. I worked in and near the [Protestant] Shankill Road when I was in my teens. The air is the same, the water's the same, the poverty's the same. I don't pretend to represent the political allegiance of the people there, though I certainly do my best to represent what I see as their class interest.' But: 'The history of class politics in this state is that to be radical, you have to be anti-imperialist.'

To be anti-imperialist, in Adams's terms, still meant the use of guns and bombs. He mused on the question of how closely support for Sinn Fein and support for the IRA coincided. The last few years had seen some grotesque IRA operations, most notoriously the bombing of a funeral cortège in Enniskillen which had resulted, not in the deaths of British soldiers, but of eleven mourning civilians. Further, their activities in Britain itself had resulted in deaths and injuries which looked, at best, the result of gross military misjudgements, at worst, gratuitously vicious. 'If the IRA does something the people don't agree with,' Adams concluded, 'their tolerance goes down. But the IRA is still here and it certainly has popular support.' And despite rumours to the contrary, he insisted, Sinn Fein's vote closely reflected it. Meanwhile, he led the only significant Irish political party not invited by the government to the latest round of inter-party talks. 'Britain is supposed to be this great mother of democracy. Are these people's votes not valid?'

The Martyrs' Memorial Free Presbyterian Church in Belfast stands on the opposite side of the road from a golf course. On the front of it is a clock and beside that, a stern message for passing sinners: Time Is Short. Not so short, though, that the lady worshippers who had gathered to hear the Reverend Ian Paisley preach had been unable to spend the early part of the morning brushing-up their Sunday best. Most striking of all were the hats: Spanish hats, broad-brimmed hats, little pill-box numbers, each a milliner's monument to the absence of perversion. Beside them, their husbands' garb was as subdued as their wives' was resplendent. And all the while, up in his mighty pulpit, the Big Fella from Ballymena did his sin-and-redemption thing.

It may have been election time, but there was no overt political message from the king of militant Unionism. That said, it was scarcely necessary. For one thing, the majority of 23,234 by which he held his North Antrim constituency for the Democractic Unionist Party could take pretty good care of itself. For another, the emblems which surrounded him resonated with unmissable political symbolism. To his right hung the flag of the Union. To his left, a glimmering crest bearing the legend: For God and Ulster. Their synonymity for the Reverend Paisley and his congregation required no explanation. Together, they drank from the clear waters of celestial certainty. The goodness of Jesus, the Reverend urged, has always been constant. It was the same yesterday. It was the same today. It would be there tomorrow also, he concluded with heavy reflection, bouncing lightly on his heels: 'It will never change.' A male voice from the back cried: 'Amen!'

Outside in the voting domain, the line between right and

wrong was not drawn quite so clearly. The electoral pact between the DUP and James Molyneaux's less strident Official Ulster Unionists looked as if it had broken down. Instead of endorsing the DUP's Denny Vitty for the Belfast seat of North Down, Molyneaux had pledged support for the independent Ulster Popular Unionist incumbent James Kilfedder. The disagreement had found its way into the local papers. Paisley was quoted describing Vitty as 'the only traditional Unionist in the field', whereas 'Jim Kilfedder has stated in Westminster that he is a liberal Unionist'. For Paisley, that self-description would almost amount to a contradiction in terms.

For those concerned with blueprints for an eventual British withdrawal, such splits within the Unionist ranks suggest that fears of an inevitable sectarian bloodbath are overstated. In other words, that no single Unionist grouping would be able to focus mass loyalist wrath. Yet Paisley retains his totemic power, despite the Anglo-Irish Agreement and any other tiny tremors from the political ground beneath his feet. The merest whiff of British backsliding will always bring from him stentorian accusations of incipient surrender. Many and varied may be the reasons for Britain's continuing claims on Northern Ireland. Perhaps the stigma of loss of face is the most potent of them all.

First donning his overcoat to facilitate a swift exit, Paisley led us through a final, purifying hymn. Then, swiftly, he made for the exit to shake hands with his departing flock.

'Hello. Are you from England?'

'Er, yes.'

Was it really that obvious?

'Are you a press man?'

'Um, sort of.'

'I hope it won't be the last time we see you,' he beamed.

Time may be short, but hope springs eternal, even in Belfast.

CHAPTER TWENTY-NINE

Not Where I'm Sitting

(Monday 6 April)

Five out of the six Sunday newspaper opinion polls still showed Labour leading the Conservatives, in one case by six points. The BBC Poll of Polls put them ahead by three, and the Liberal Democrats up by four since the start of the campaign. After three weeks, the advance of Ashdown, the beautiful dreamer, was the only significant change and that was more of a problem for Nice John Major than for Britain's Next Prime Minister. Surely, not even Fear of Kinnock could stop Labour winning on Thursday.

It was a day for Labour's leader to be suave and sober. By mid-morning in the cool, clean atrium of Number 4, Millbank, Labour were preparing a photo-*femme* offensive to woo the nation's doubting women. Nearly all the party's female candidates with a realistic chance of winning had been assembled for a deluxe press call with their tough-but-tender leader. Everyone gathered on the top flight of a sweeping marble staircase, the women an informal I-mean-business chorus line checking each other's shoulder pads, Britain's Next Prime Minister, the Prop Forwards' Union's answer to Mr Fred Astaire. From the floor below, the Busby Berkeleys of the paparazzi called 'action', and down the steps rolled Britain's Next Prime Minister, not too heavy on the no-necked, iron-shouldered, splay-footed swagger, not too quick with the gleam of gratitude under the sweltering arc lights. The new Labour ladies were supposed to signify modern thinking and moderation. It wouldn't do for people to think he looked like Jack the Lad.

Come mid-afternoon, the government-in-waiting scam resumed again back at the Institution of Civil Engineers. It provided both the most substantial and the most ludicrous set-piece of the entire Labour campaign.

'Neil Kinnock Lecture' it said grandly, at the head of the press office guest list. The names beneath were an inventory of tame pink brainboxes and caring enterprise culture folk. Not a trade unionist in sight. Britain's Next Prime Minister threw the Electable Baritone switch and embarked on the long trek through his eleven-page prepared text:

'Britain is now gripped in the twenty-first month of the longest recession since the 1930s . . . It is a recession which in north and south, and in the High Street and the boardroom, has seriously eroded the confidence on which a strong economy depends . . . unemployment – and the fear of unemployment – is undermining the confidence of consumers and home-buyers . . .'

The tone was set, the contours defined. Prosperity was about endlessly buying houses and new cars, about ensuring business and consumer 'confidence' – consensus territory with the Tories. The difference lay in the degree of government tinkering proposed for achieving it.

'Once consumers start spending again and steady demand growth gets going again, it is argued, all will be well. That is all, it is said, that is needed. [But] it neglects the simple fact that the growth of demand was excessive *relative to the growth of supply* and that the growth of the productive capacity of the British economy has, for the past thirteen years, been slower than that in any other major economy . . .'

He talked on about his 'supply-side' measures: the education, health, infrastructure and training provisions. Labour's policies, he said, were: '. . . designed to break the British habit of taking the soft option of consumption-led growth and to replace it with the sustainable power of investment-led growth – the sort of growth which means that the ability to produce in Britain increases with demand in Britain. A recovery, in short, made in Britain.'

But:

'That will obviously not preclude encouragement for inward investment in any way. On the contrary, capital and employers from overseas will play an essential role in building world market success, and improved supply-side provision will increase the attractiveness of Britain.'

Furthermore:

'With an active and sustained supply-side policy, the ERM becomes the foundation upon which long-term decisions can dependably be taken.'

The 'lecture' ended to loyal applause which gave way to an extraordinary question from a woman at the front. It wasn't so much an inquiry as a cue to take a lap of honour:

'Isn't it the case that the biggest boom and bust has been experienced in the eighties, and isn't it the case that the Tories' only means of reducing inflation is by increasing unemployment and driving small businesses to the wall? Isn't it the case that Tory policies aggravate business, and isn't it true that Labour in partnership with industry, in the government that you would be leading in four day's time, will mitigate the business cycle and prevent future recessions from becoming anything like the current Tory nightmare?'

The place errupted with laughter. Given no choice but to face up to the absurdity of the entire, ghastly love-in, a joshing Neil Kinnock briefly emerged.

'Oh, I'm not sure I'd agree with that question . . .'

Later, in an attempt at disruption, a journalist shouted from the back: 'Mr Kinnock, would you consider answering a question for readers of the *Daily Mail*?'

Well, of course he bloody wouldn't. What would be the point? But then what had been the point of the 'lecture' in the first place?

On the way out, I stopped to talk to Meghnad Desai, a Professor of Economics at the London School of Economics, recently made a Lord and becoming in the process Britain's first Asian peer of modern times. On budget day, prior to joining Ms Walsall and Mr Affable in the drizzle-drenched Commons queue, I'd had a drink with him in one of the Upper House's bars. Sipping sparingly at the poshest tipple known to all humanity as the grey swathe of the Thames slipped imperceptibly by outside, I had listened to him correctly predicting the miserable Chancellor's 20 pence tax band gambit. Since Lord Desai had been one of the few economic experts to get anything right for a while, I asked him his opinion of what we had just heard. He said that it was probably the clearest and most comprehensive exposition of Labour's economic policy to emerge during the campaign so far. And looking back over the text, free of the ridiculous public relations context in which it had been delivered, it seemed he was probably right.

It was a recipe for managing capitalism in a more humane, less chaotic way than the Conservatives had achieved. It proposed that John Smith's 'fair tax system' would provide the cash for the government to improve the general population's learning, health, railways and skills, and encourage businessmen from home and abroad to build new factories. These would generate wealth and, in turn, more taxes with which to help keep a 'virtuous circle' rotating. And there was no need for those folk in the boardrooms to be frightened. Indeed, they were to be carefully catered for. Yes, they would have to pay higher taxes, but not *that* much higher (and still less than they had to pay up until Nigel Lawson's 'miracle' budget in spring 1988), and their taxes too would go to oil the virtuous circle. Trade union powers would be almost as tightly policed as under the Tories. ERM membership was an insurance against a nightmare sterling crisis. A Labour government, in short, would cater to *almost* their every desire, while doing its best to reconcile this with its historic mission to improve the condition of the poor and old, by emphasizing that Smith's mashed Bible and porridge oats would itself generate more spending and more government income.

So there it was, Labour's economic policy, intoned to a hand-picked audience containing many academics and a few entrepreneurs, but, oddly enough, no bankers or major industrialists at all. Most of the journalists, meanwhile, would either ignore the event or distort it as their proprietors and editors would require. The best publicity that could be hoped for was a few frames of Britain's Next Prime Minister looking statesmanlike in front of the dark wood power-panelling on television later on. The *full* argument for an economy led by investment rather than consumption would not be properly placed before the British people. And as for the City of London, those institutions whom John Smith hoped so much would not be beastly to him if he won, they, of course, remained in Neil Kinnock's words of 1976, 'sworn ideological enemies'. But it was far more Prime Ministerial to act as if they weren't.

Eight thirty in the evening and 5.8 million viewers got themselves comfortable in front of ITV's *World in Action* with referee/ presenter Sue Lawley, the three main party leaders and the Granada 500 – a studio full of voters from the super-marginal constituencies of Bolton West and Bolton North East. Paddy Ashdown went on first, and was bombarded with the usual stuff about hung Parliaments and deals on Proportional Representation. He provided his regular, sparkling repertoire of cake-and-eat-it answers: we want stable government; PR legislation is a prerequisite; demanding that prerequisite is not inflexible, because stability depends on it; voting down a minority government is not causing instability, because it is unstable anyway. There was a bit of booing and cheering and then a commercial break.

Second in line was Britain's Next Prime Minister. He was immediately challenged over the inflation, unemployment and industrial relations disasters of the last Labour government. Cornered, he delivered what all subsequent Labour leaders had been so reluctant to do, a short but firm defence of that administration along with a reassurance that mass and flying pickets would not be permitted to return. Then a nursing sister put it to him: 'Given your record for changing your mind, how do we know that what you say today is what you'll believe tomorrow?'

This was greeted with huge, mocking, applause.

He replied: 'I think it might be fair to point out that I'm not alone in changing my mind . . .'

Groans!

'. . . It appears that the whole Tory Cabinet has changed its mind on poll tax . . .'

Cheers!

He concluded with his standard spiel about the duty to attend to 'realities'. It wasn't painless, but he survived.

Then, the last question, from Alec Dunn aged twenty, a first-time voter: 'I'm in favour of PR. I want to know where you personally stand on the subject.'

Kinnock: 'Yes, well, I'd be delighted to be able to tell you . . .'

Lawley: 'Now?'

Kinnock: '. . . but not at this juncture.'

Laughter!

Kinnock: 'Oh, I'd be delighted to. But what I do . . .'

Dunn: 'It's either yes or no, isn't it?'

Kinnock: 'Yeah, sure. Well, as you may know, Mr Dunn . . .'

Dunn: 'Well, either you do agree with it or you don't agree with it.'

Kinnock: 'Well, fine. Ah, no, it isn't quite as simple as that, not where I'm sitting.'

Groans!

Kinnock: 'Can I just say . . .'

Lawley: 'You've got thirty seconds to tell them, Mr Kinnock, why you won't say where you stand on this.'

Kinnock: 'I'll be glad to explain, as I have many times in public, exactly what my approach has been. It is that two, two-and-a-quarter years ago, I established a procedure in the Labour Party, because it's important that we get the analysis and the recommendations on the proportional representation and electoral reform, and . . .'

More groans!

Lawley: 'You've got fifteen seconds, Mr Kinnock. They want to know where you stand on PR . . .'

Kinnock: '. . . that is what we will do. And that is what we will do, and I find it extraordinary that the current government believes that our system is incapable of improvement. I refuse to take that view.'

Yells! Cat calls!

Lawley: 'You refuse to give them an answer on where you stand on PR?'

Kinnock: 'I've given them an answer.'

Wind sock? Billowing wind sock?

CHAPTER THIRTY

Party Popper

(Tuesday 7 April)

On every seat in the curtained-off area of the Wembley Conference Centre there was a large brown envelope containing a typewritten message:

DEAR AUDIENCE MEMBER

TONIGHT'S RALLY IS THE LAST BEFORE ELECTION DAY AND WE NEED YOUR HELP TO ENSURE IT'S SUCCESS.

The placement of the apostrophe in the word 'it's' betrayed the need for certain persons at Conservative Central Office to 'get back' to the three Rs.

THIS ENVELOPE CONTAINS A SKIP HAT, UNION JACK AND PARTY POPPER.

PLEASE KEEP THIS WITH YOU AND *DO NOT* USE ANY OF THE CONTENTS UNTIL THE END OF THE RALLY.

IMMEDIATELY AFTER THE PRIME MINISTER'S SPEECH HE WILL BE JOINED ON STAGE BY MRS MAJOR. BY THIS TIME YOU WILL VERY LIKELY BE ON YOUR FEET APPLAUDING AND *AT THIS STAGE* PLEASE PUT ON YOUR HAT, WAVE YOUR FLAG AND EXPLODE YOUR PARTY POPPER.

THANK YOU FOR YOUR HELP.

An evening of wild spontaneity was ensured. It commenced with an appearance by Cilla Black. The former Priscilla White is the archetypal professional Liverpudlian. That is to say she has built her career on corrupting her native city's most attractive characteristics into a caricature of Merseyside working-class bon-homie, a Scouse parody upholstered for television. Her act portrays everything smug southern Tories want a northern prole to be: quaintly demotic, chirpily deferential, glutinously cuddly. That brown envelope looked like coming in handy.

'The phone rang an' our Bobby, me 'oosband, came in. 'E said: "There's a phone call for yer. There's a Mr Archer on the telephone." I said, "It can't be Dan . . ."'

The stooge audience enjoyed that. It was the measure of Conservatism's talent for electoral survival that they had co-opted the culture of Our Cilla to their cause. So complete was the process that, in this company, cross-references to Radio 4's middle-class soap opera could be accomplished with a complete absence of stress.

'. . .'E said, "No, it's Jeffrey." I said, "Oh, Jeffrey Archer. No, tell him 'e can't go on *Blind Date*, 'e can't!"'

Oh, how they laughed! Then Our Cilla got all confidential, like, knoworramean?

'Why am I voting for John Major? I'll tell you why: I'm voting for John Major because 'e is, ladies and gentleman, a great Prime Minister. I'm voting for John Major because 'e doesn't *poonish* success, 'e promotes it. Oh, yes.'

Oh, how they roared!

'I'm voting for John Major because I don't wanna go back to *all* those strikes, and *all* those pickets. Can you face *tharragain*?'

No, they couldn't!

'Did you see the telly last night, with Sue Lawley? I mean, what a simple question to Neil Kinnock. Can you give us a simple yes or no, and 'e said, "oh, er, it's *norraseezee* as that."'

The Tories were crucifying Kinnock for that one. At the morn-ing press conference the amusing Chairman Chris and the gorgeous Michael Heseltine had re-enacted the Granada 500 exchange in all its agony. Respectable Swansea boy Heseltine even put on a South Wales working-class accent for his part. Look at that Neil Kinnock: he's a windbag!; he's stupid!; he's two-faced!; he's *Welsh*!

Our Cilla completed her turn:

'I'm voting for John Major, ladies and gentlemen, because I don't wanna be your comrade. I'd much rather be your friend.'

Applause!

Large brown envelope!

Finally, Cilla introduced a 'lirrel' film collage of people saying lovely things about Nice John. More telly celebs and some sporting ones were interspersed with 'ordinary' people, relating meaningfully to the Boy from Brixton: 'I fink 'e's probably got more understanding of a bricklayer or a builder, or a council worker than probably most prime ministers ever 'ave.' After that, a Tory dignitary announced that four members of the audience were going to profess their devotion to Nice John in words they had composed themselves. It was a bit like the class creeps getting to show off in assembly, but also drew on the Conservative conference tradition of showcasing defectors from the ranks of enemy interests. Naturally, then, the first speaker was a nurse.

'Sheila Scott,' asked the dignitary innocently, 'why is it important to you that we have a Conservative victory on Thursday?'

Like a mum in a Fairy Liquid commercial, Sheila Scott replied:

'Because I'm concerned about the elderly. And I think for the elderly, there are three key issues: the first one is that inflation is kept low so that their pensions and savings are protected; secondly, they must be assured that if they are no longer able to care for themselves, the country is able to create enough wealth to continue effective health schemes; and thirdly, above all else, that their dignity is maintained. Only a Conservative government can achieve those things. Older people know that they can trust John Major, and they know that his word is his bond.'

Applause!

Large brown envelope!

After the nurse came the head of a grant-maintained (i.e. opted out of local education authority) comprehensive school in Surrey, a fund-holding (i.e. opted out of local Family Health Services funding authority) general practitioner and an ethnic-minority retailer. Then there was a speech by Alan Sugar, the Chairman of Amstrad, the man who had risen from being a north London market stall-holder to create the most successful computer and satellite dish company in Britain. He had thrown in a few bob with Rupert Murdoch to help create BSkyB, and so given the the British public the incomparable freedom to watch even more dating shows like Our Cilla's. Amstrad dishes were strong on the European market. But things were pretty tight. And if the socialist threat came to fruition, Sugar explained sadly, everything would be ruined:

'If Labour's statutory minimum wage forces up wages, my dishes will become uncompetitive, and before you can say "say-onara", the Japanese will take away yet another market. The Birmingham [Amstrad] workers, for whom the minimum wage was supposed to bring better living standards, well, they'll probably be out of a job.'

Poor man, he'd have no choice. It would either be that or no dating games with Rupert.

'I've personally made a lot of money in my time,' Sugar said, 'despite coming from a working-class background.' Then he slipped in a little crowd-pleaser: 'By the way – there's nothing wrong in making money.'

Jackpot!

Applause!

Large brown envelope!

After Sugar had finished speaking, it began to become apparent that things were running late. Eight o'clock was fast approaching, and Nice John hadn't started his speech. At this rate, the BBC wouldn't have time to edit the best bits for the *Nine O'Clock News*. And then who should walk out on to the apron of the half-a-million-pound stage set, but the amusing Chairman Chris to give what looked suspiciously like an off-the-cuff pep talk. There was an air of mild derangement about him as he stalked up and down. He had spent the whole campaign commuting by helicopter between London and Bath where his own majority was only 1412 and threatened by the Liberal Democrats. He looked decidedly haggard as he inquired, menacingly:

'Who doubts now, that recovery is within our grasp? Taxes down, inflation down, interest rates down, strikes down, confidence rising. All that is needed in order to trigger an economic recovery, giving us the same sort of sustainable increase in our living standards that we enjoyed in the 1980s, all that is required, is a decisive Conservative victory on Thursday.'

Almost all the scientific evidence still suggested this was not going to happen. Already that evening the results of by far the biggest opinion poll yet taken[1] showed Labour on 38½, the Conservatives on 36½ and the Liberal Democrats on 20. The latest BBC Poll of Polls came up with 39, 37 and 20. Meanwhile, Authority's Experts – and a continuing, muted chorus of Tory moaners – still thought the campaign was incoherent. And there were two clear signs of deep Conservative panic. One was the front page of the *Daily Mail* that morning, which had – despite, astonishingly, having voiced some prior criticism of the Tory strategy – given its front page over to a frenzied editorial comment. Its headline hollered: 'WARNING – a Labour government will lead to higher mortgage payments.' Below it Sir David English spelled out the truth as he and the ghost of Thatcher were desperate for the electorate to see it: 'The mood of voters is heavy with resentment . . . Only one thing is certain: if Labour forms the next Government, Mr Smith's budget would at a stroke turn recession into slump.' It went on to launch a splenetic personal attack: 'What the Shadow Chancellor lacks in financial acumen, he more than compensates for by an excess of self-righteousness . . . This man, who is such a cosmetic asset to his party, would be an unmitigated disaster for Britain.' The editorial concluded: 'You have been warned.'

The second sign of panic had been a new emphasis in Major's speeches on the constitutional issues. On the previous Sunday, again at Wembley, he had made the future of the Union his keynote:

'To imperil the tried and successful Union of our four nations for party benefit, as our opponents do, is unforgivable. To toss aside the Union through which, over three hundred years, this country has moulded the history of the world. That is unbelievable.'

Click, click, click! The fairy lights in the Glorious Past theme park suddenly burned at a billion watts.

'Can you, dare you, conceive of it? Consider the outcome. The walls of this island fortress that appear so strong, undermined from within, the United Kingdom untied, the bonds that generations of our enemies have fought and failed to break, loosened

---

1. Compiled for the Press Association by ICM.

by us ourselves . . . If I could summon up all the authority of this office I would put it in this single warning – the United Kingdom is in danger. Wake up, my fellow countrymen. Wake up *now*, before it is too late!'

Paranoid patriotism, the last refuge of the modern Conservative Party, was now being whipped up with unfamiliar fervour in John Major's Model World. And when, finally, too late for the *Nine O'Clock News* and probably too late for the *News At Ten*, he stepped on to the podium before his latest audience of five-star fawners, he warmed, once again, to this desperate theme:

'On Thursday, Britain is going to return a Conservative government. It's going to vote with us for the right to own. The power to choose. The will to win. And the future of Britain . . . There's no road back with socialism. There *must* be no road back for socialism. Not here. Not anywhere. Not the Lib road. Not the Lab road. Not the Lib-Lab road . . . Once before this century Britain stood alone. We stood then against tyranny and oppression. We are not going to stand alone in the nineties, ignominiously defending state socialism and state control when the rest of the world is rejecting it. That's not the way for Britain. Not now. Not ever. Never.'

Off we went on a fantasy ride in the chariot of blue-rinsed Britannia, through the treacherous straits of the Maastricht agreement, the opulent freedoms of Kuwait, the cringing back streets of CND and onwards, ever onwards, into the garden of free-market paradise, the fertile composts of reduced taxation, the dead wood forests of trade unionism and the verdant flatlands of inflation. 'I know that we have in our grasp a truly glorious future . . . Let us go out together on Thursday. Let us seize that opportunity. And make that golden future ours!'

The Prime Minister was joined on stage by Mrs Major. The audience was on its feet applauding. They put on their hats, some red, some white, some blue. They waved their Union Jack flags. They exploded their party poppers. And perhaps they took their large brown envelopes home for future, alternative use in the small hours of Friday morning.

CHAPTER THIRTY-ONE

Badinage and Beacons

(Wednesday 8 April)

'We're going to move the table,' said the woman primary school teacher, firmly. 'And we need two chairs.'

From within the ruck of press personnel, the necessary seating appeared.

'Two chairs, lovely.'

The photographers, journalists and reporters were squashed into the classroom about five deep. The teacher chivvied the children into their positions.

'Are you in the doctor scene? No. You are. Are you in the doctor scene? You're first. Right, where's Anna?'

Anna was located, wearing a long white coat and a stethoscope, and sat down on one of the chairs. In the corner stood Nice John Major. It was almost his last photo opportunity of the campaign he seemed set to lose, but he looked remarkably calm. A little bell rang close beside him.

'*Entre*,' piped Anna, efficiently, and a junior mock-patient trotted across the floor, sat on the second seat on the other side of the table and made with the theatrical *malaise*.

'*Bonjour. Comment as-tu? Tu as mal?*'

A bit familiar, this doctor, but no slouch. The stethoscope was wielded, '*au revoir*'s exchanged, and five more poorly students of elementary French treated at equal, lightning speed. At the end, the press corps clapped and Nice John declared: 'Now you know why they are treating more people in the National Health Service!'

Throughout the performance his body language had been characteristically inelegant, one arm held horizontally across his solar plexus, the other dangling redundantly down. But he had conferred with the teacher without any air of grandeur. And, with the children's performance complete, he turned his attention to them.

'Well done. Now how many of you speak more than two languages? Do you know, in this area, there are ninety-two different languages?'

The area in question was part of the City of London and Westminster South constituency, held by Northern Ireland Secretary Peter Brooke and containing Whitehall, the Houses of Parliament and Buckingham Palace. Its cosmopolitanism was as much attributable to the internationalism of modern business than a product of the inner-city melting pot. Here, primary school children sit still long enough to be educated in French. Gathered around the crouching Prime Minister they looked on, bewildered, as the camera shutters clattered.

'Which of you speak three languages?' asked Nice John. 'Which of you, with all these talents, are going to grow up to be photographers?'

The Pentax posse enjoyed that. For the entire campaign entourage, it was end-of-term time. Even the little flock of chinless Tory volunteers, on whom the official party sweatshirts looked so shapeless, seemed ready to share a joke. Perhaps, given all the internal carping, it was purely out of relief. As for Major himself, he really did seem, as the commentators kept remarking, thoroughly unperturbed. His last few television appearances had all been stamped with that anachronistic, but oddly engaging blend of benignly mannered politeness and filing cabinet detachment. He had been unflappable on Granada 500, moderately contrite about the recession in his *Panorama* interview less than an hour later, and entirely serene this Wednesday morning on *Election Call*, when he had even acknowledged the possibility that he might soon be required to study a Labour government's Queen's Speech.

It all made the hideous Wembley flag-waving seem still more incongruous. The Major vision of consensus individualism really had been better conveyed from the soap-box than by hi tech. In a previous campaign interview, he had talked about his first public speaking experiences: 'When I was in my early teens, I used to occasionally erect a soap-box. I had two soap-boxes. One that I used to erect in Brixton Market and the other in Brixton Road, and I used to talk about political matters of the day. And everyone was very tolerant. Some people used to listen. Some used to engage in badinage. Lots of other people smiled cheerfully and moved on . . .'

What a curious, quaint Model World he lived in: a world where soap boxes are 'erected', people 'engage in badinage', 'smile cheerfully' and are always tolerant; a world whose essential temper is one of contentment, and any kind of disturbance is regarded much like a disease. The day before, someone had thrown an egg at him in the street. It had hit him in the face and cut his cheek. 'Not to worry,' had been his impossibly homely response to those around him, before indignation took over: 'I'm not going to be moved off the street by that, not now, not ever!' There spoke the determinedly respectable citizen of modest, but independent means. There spoke the quiet everyman of English suburbia. Now, he spoke again, more softly, to the striving primary French students: 'I hear that this one drank fifteen lemonades the other day! Right, hands up those who've drunk more than fifteen . . . Good gracious me!'

Mid-evening in a hotel conference room in Tory Taunton (majority 10,380), and Paddy Ashdown was making a speech, deploying those short. Sharp. Sentences. Full of. Heroic visions. And crusading zeal:

'I want to put. It on record tonight. We owe him a great deal. Through you. But in his absence. I'm sure you will want me. To say this – thank you, Des Wilson, for all you've done, to help us with this campaign.'

The hall was packed and scores more Paddy partisans were standing outside in the dusk, listening to an outdoor PA. 'He's a marvellous chap! *Marvellous* chap,' said a man who had come all the way from Cornwall to find every seat had gone: 'He'd make a great Prime Minister.' Ashdown's tribute to Wilson seemed well enough deserved. True, sending out what Wilson had been relentlessly promoting as 'our *positive* message' may have been the privilege of a party that could not win. True, the Wilson–Ashdown idealism was exceedingly hard-boiled. But idealism it had been, certainly by comparison with the others. And, true again, they had stuck to their own agenda, they had promoted a broader range of issues and it did seem to have paid dividends. Most impressive of all, Ashdown had not blown a gasket. Up there on the stage, wagging his finger and shaking his head, he looked even more disgustingly fit than when he had started out. Now, on the eve of polling day, euphoria was in his veins.

'Two things stand out. About the Liberal Democrats. First. Where the others have been so evasive. The Liberal Democrats have all. *All*. Been *positive*. And second. Where others have thought. Only about the past. We. Liberal Democrats. Have always had our eyes firmly fixed on this country's future. I believe that the success. Of our campaign. May even have altered the nature. Of British general elections. Both of the other two, you see, were determined that this election would concentrate on their negative attacks. They have been forced to adopt our style. To imitate our approach. At the start of this campaign, Britain was. I believe. In great danger of descending into a form of negative politics like that. In the United States. In which the party which bribed the voters most. And attacked the opposition most. Was always going to win. It was the Liberal Democrats. Who had the courage. To stand up. And be counted.'

A drunk in the audience wanted to be counted, too, but he didn't seem able to stand up. He just muttered loudly: 'What are you gonna do about Ireland?'

Ashdown, soaring, ignored him. 'The decision we make tomorrow. Is a decision made today . . .'

That was the problem with so much flying. Time has lost all meaning.

'. . . but which will shape our country as it passes into the new century. Into. The new millennium . . .'

'What are you gonna do about Ireland?' burbled the drunk again. Men wearing yellow laminated passes began pushing through the seats towards him.

'To every voter, I say this,' continued Ashdown, every sentence now block-built into an endless spiral of peroration: 'Pause. Pause for a moment before you vote. Pause at the door of the polling station. And ask yourself this simple question: what is this election really about. Is it really just a vote for me? Or is it also a vote about. Our children's future?'

Fingers were being wagged at the drunk. He got up with difficulty, and left. What *he* wanted done about Ireland remained anybody's guess.

'You know, in the old days,' Ashdown said, his eyes lifted once more to that now familiar far horizon, 'they used to send. Signals of great events. Across many miles. By beacons, lit. Upon the hills. And the mountains. And the tors. Of Britain. Often, those beacons were a warning. But often they told of good news. And that's how it shall be at this election tomorrow night. There will be beacons. Lit. Across the West Country, Liberal Democrat breakthroughs every one. From the furthest tip of Cornwall. To Devon, north and south. On into Somerset, *this* Somerset . . .'

It was there, in his bones, 'this Somerset', ancient province of Liberal ley lines!

'. . . across Dorset, through Avon and Gloucester, up the Marches to Hereford, where they'll meet the bright glow from Wales, from Brecon and Montgomery and Ceredigion across the border . . .'

The itinerary stopped at that point. Perhaps things were not looking so good in the Ribble Valley. And Scotsmen were being prissy about negotiations for PR.

'. . . and from the lands of conscience of the West. From the lands of conscience and reform. From these ancient bastions of hope. The flames will fan out in all directions. Consuming the shabby campaigns of the old parties' out of date policies, visionless futures. They are the flames which. I hope. Will tomorrow. Power the source to break the cycle of Britain's decline, unlock the potential of our people, pave the way for future success . . .'

They were roaring now, those outsider under-managers and organic farmers, those wholefood retailers and barn-dance instructors.

'This time the Liberal Democrats are on the march! Join with us and we will win!'

Two theatrical spark bombs exploded at the front of the stage amid a mighty cloud of dry ice. From the loudspeakers, Paddy's Theme struck up, an 'Eye of the Tiger' pastiche, all disco-thump and synthi-fanfares. Ashdown strode forward through the throng and disappeared through the exit. At that point, ideally, a disembodied bass voice would have boomed: 'Mr Ashdown has left the building,' but instead someone said apologetically: 'If you would be so good as to take your seats . . .' Buckets were appearing. There was going to be a whip round.

Within minutes a crowd had gathered in the street, looking up hopefully at the balcony on the front of the hotel. The police had stopped the traffic and television arc lights were glaring. The crowd began to chant: 'We want Paddy! We want Paddy!'

Some of them were holding flares, specially provided for the occasion. An old man in an overcoat said: 'He might do an SAS job, mightn't he? Storm down over the roof on a rope.'

It took a while, but at last Ashdown emerged to stand, triumphantly important, behind the parapet. The old man was right; if someone had placed a bucket of water on the pavement below, Ashdown would have dived right into it.

'Let it begin now, let it begin at this election!'

The pagan gods of Olde Wessex were gathering in the night sky. A platoon of Euro-yeomen were making ready for the march, yea, even unto the credit manager of the independent Central Bank.

'I spoke to you a moment ago about the beacons. The beacons that will light across the West Country. We have now lit the torches . . .'

They had! They had!

'. . . so go out into Somerset. And into every village and every hamlet and every community . . . I have one message for you. One alone. Here in Somerset, we once again raise the flag of rebellion against the Tory Party in Westminster!'

Hurrah!

'No Battle of Sedgemoor this! No Battle of Sedgemoor this! We are determined to win!'

Hurrah!

'Good luck. Good campaigning. It's in your hands. Thanks very much . . . And don't forget the good morning leaflets. Goodbye, good luck!'

Trust me. I'm Superham.

CHAPTER THIRTY-TWO

England's Glory

(Thursday 9 April)

Steamer Street, Schooner Street, Ship Street. The names, like the matchboxes with a clipper on the front, spoke of England's Glory. As the sun came up on Barrow Island, every inch of the place seemed to vibrate with images of yesterday: the cobbled walkways; the red stone, turn-of-the-century tenements; the lines of washing that hung between them; the men on pushbikes rushing to the early shift at Vickers Shipbuilding and Engineering Limited; even the old-fashioned lettering of the street signs themselves. To a romantic eye – or, perhaps, to an eye too used to seduction by designer-nostalgia commercials – the place might be existing in a time warp. Except for one thing: the sleek, black creature moored in the harbour dock as you crossed the bridge connecting the Island to Barrow itself. That was no cosy retro-signifier. That was *Vanguard*, the first of the Trident nuclear submarines, an emblem of the future, though whose future it guaranteed, and how completely, was open to debate.

'I'll be voting for Labour,' said one young man from the swarm of blue overalls passing through the factory gates. But was he worried about losing his job? There were two further Tridents, *Victorious* and *Vigilant*, at earlier stages of construction at Vickers. The Tories had proudly ordered a fourth. Labour intended to cancel it.

'Not really worried, no,' said the young man. 'The Conservatives have lost all the jobs in Vickers as it is. I don't think Labour'll make it any worse.'

In 1990, the Vickers workforce had peaked, thanks to the Trident commissions, at around 14,000. Since then it had been reduced to under 8500 and was certain to fall further. The fortunes of the shipyard, together with the company's other armament manufacturing capacity – or, more specifically, the workforce's anticipation of those fortunes – had lately swung in tandem with the political complexion of the Barrow and Furness constituency.

From the Second World War till 1983, a preponderance of manual and skilled blue-collar workers had ensured that the seat went Labour's way. That changed alarmingly when Labour's non-nuclear defence aspirations frightened thousands into the arms of Mancunian Conservative Cecil Franks. They stayed there, for the same reasons, four years later. But the Defence Ministry's 'Options for Change' provisions meant government spending cuts. VSEL job losses followed accordingly, Trident notwith-standing. When defence spending goes down, Barrow goes down with it. Suddenly, the potential existed for old political loyalties to be renewed.

A polling station, set up at a primary school, was doing steady business. Outside, a woman pensioner with a dog called Poppy ('she's half Border Collie, half Sheltie'), described the job-loss devastation as it had hit her family:

'I'm a bit browned off with Cecil Franks, one way or another. And Vickers especially.'

Poor Cecil and the factory were, it seemed, synonymous in her mind.

'My younger son was made redundant from Vickers nearly a year ago. His children are five, four and a year old, and it come as a hell of a shock to him. It upset him to such an extent he damn near cried. He went in on the Tuesday dinner time, they told him he was finished, just like that. Nothing he can do about it, is there?'

Her eldest son lived in fear of a similar fate.

'He's got a managerial job there, but even he's not safe.'

The younger son, a crane-driver, had been offered a position in Kent. But he didn't want to leave the family behind. And what were his chances of buying a house, his Mum wanted to know? 'So what the 'eck are you going to do? He hasn't got a cat in hell's chance, and he's only twenty-six. His wife's got relatives in Canada and Australia. Maybe he'll try there . . .'

She had just been and voted Labour, always did. But she wasn't too impressed with Britain's Next Prime Minister:

'Well, he's a bit of a loud-mouth. Now if John Major could take Kinnock's place, it'd be a different matter. But sometimes loud-mouths get somewhere, don't they? Maybe if Labour gets in it'll help. I doubt if they'll change in Vickers, though. They're too far gone now.'

Barrow's increasing reliance on VSEL over the decades makes it inherently vulnerable to sudden redundancies. Wedged into the west Cumbrian hillside, the town's original development was based on its proximity to iron-ore deposits. Shipbuilding followed naturally, but the iron and steel smokestacks were all but smouldering stubble by the sixties. Vickers, though, still thrived. Founded in 1871 as the Barrow Shipbuilding Company, it was bought twenty-six years later by the Vickers brothers, steel entrepreneurs who crossed the Pennines from Sheffield. It became a central cog in the British war machine and, almost by definition, its story now stands as a virtual parable of Britain's rise and fall as an industrial and military power.

For over a century, defence has been a key sector of British industry, the one area where research, skills and investment have kept up with the rest of the world. Vickers has been a lynchpin, though in different incarnations. It remained a private company until 1977 when it, with the rest of the indigenous shipbuilding industry, was pooled and nationalized to become part of British Shipbuilders. In 1986 it was denationalized, but despite co-opting its original name for reasons of prestige and sentiment, it is now a quite separate concern from those still owned by the original Vickers company, such as Rolls Royce. Among the recent products of its expertise have been *Dreadnaught*, the country's first nuclear-powered submarine, and two of the craft that went with the Falklands task force: the aircraft carrier *Invincible*, which came back; and the destroyer *Sheffield*, which did not. Throughout, the high standard of Vickers workers had been recognized worldwide. But Barrow is now paying the price for an industrial over-emphasis which once expressed the ambitions of an imperial power, but now begins to look like lack of foresight fuelled by neurosis.

The long-term future of the shipyard had been debated by local Labour people before. Cumbria County Councillor Nan Tate, collecting polling cards, remembered the views of Albert

Booth, the Labour MP (and one-time Cabinet minister) whom Cecil Franks replaced. 'Albert wasn't against what they were doing. He just thought they should diversify, but they didn't. I think eventually he was proved right.'

A real Labour stalwart, Nan was sitting at a child's desk in the cloakroom-cum-entrance, surrounded by coatpegs and paintings in vivid colours, as the voters filed through.

'Hello, can I have your number please? 793, thank you very much. You're in the first polling booth, just through there.'

The booths were set out in the dining hall, the traditional stubs of pencil hanging on bits of string.

'Hello, are you all right, love? Can I have your number, please? It won't cost you anything, honestly.'

Nan was born on the Island. She seemed to know almost everyone who came in. I told her that if I used my imagination, the lines of washing became strings of bunting, circa Coronation Day. She tutted: 'The media always show all that when they come here.'

Another Labour woman joined us. She seemed to know everyone too. 'It's all extended families here,' she explained. 'You'll see them as they come in. Mums with daughters, grandads. I can walk the streets at night here in perfect safety and not even feel frightened. There aren't many places in this country where you could say that.'

For all Nan's chiding about the washing lines, it was still difficult not to take in the sights of Barrow Island without a sepia-tinted filter forming before your eyes. Little playbacks of a post-war optimism which more and more of us only know about from movies, kept running through your head: tight communities of extended families, where people felt safe; skilled manual labour for thousands strengthening the nation; summer sunshine and the wheels of democracy smoothly turning. Maybe by the morning there would be a Labour government too, firm in its commitment to working folk and the welfare state. And maybe the nation would rise as one to sing 'We'll Meet Again'.

At around twelve-thirty, when their lunch break began, the VSEL workers started coming in. One was accompanied by his wife of eighteen months. They proudly pushed a newborn baby in a pram. He was an electrician. She was a nurse. They'd both voted Tory last time, because the Trident programme looked like being a long-term job insurance, but now they felt 'betrayed', the husband clocking on each day, wondering if it might be his last. He harboured other awkward feelings, too: 'a bit of guilt'. He told of a couple of lads working there who wore 'No To Trident' T-shirts and sent donations off to CND. He was stuck with the guilt for as long as he had the job. And when that had gone he would be stuck with nothing. His wife would keep on working. He would become a house husband, content enough, but with his skills on the scrapheap. Changing the occasional lightbulb just wouldn't be the same.

'Hello,' murmured Nan, 'here's Cecil.'

Franks was all decked out in a pseudo-nautical rig: navy double-breasted blazer with polished buttons; pale grey casual slacks; appalling, thin-soled slip-ons à la Heseltine. To complete the rakish effect, a pair of tinted glasses and a cravat. What a dish.

'Hello, Nan, how are you?'

Franks – according, it should be said, to unfriendly Labour gossip – had been getting controversial. In response to complaints by students that they couldn't live off their grants, he had suggested in the local paper that they got on their bikes to Blackpool and sold a few sticks of rock. He and Nan conversed, a little warily, on matters of local interest. Franks then bade farewell with immaculate cross-party etiquette.

'Anything I can do for you, Nan. Any time.'

It was the promise of a politician anticipating re-election. Off he cruised, a man with everything except, possibly, a yacht.

Nan looked on, shaking her head.

'He's crackers,' she said.

CHAPTER THIRTY-THREE

The Count

(Thursday 9, Friday 10 April)

At ten o'clock the polling stations closed after fifteen hours of voting, and the BBC revealed the results of their exit poll, conducted as the punters actually left the polling stations. Its conclusion came as a shock: the most likely result was that the *Conservatives* would have the largest number of seats, though short of an overall majority by twenty-five.

Driving into Islwyn something over an hour later, the first result came through to the studio of Radio 4. Labour's Chris Mullin had held Sunderland South with an increased majority. However, the swing towards him at the expense of the Conservative was just 2 per cent. It was only one seat, which Labour had no chance of losing. But if Britain's Next Prime Minister was going to make a speech of triumph later on that night, his party would have to do a great deal better than that.

Blackwood itself was silent and unwelcoming. None of the High Street pubs had their televisions tuned to the results programmes. But there was certainly some action in one nearby boozer that night. A Radio 4 reporter had found it in the form of a lad called Shane. He was buzzing. The joint was rocking. Downing Street, here we come. But was the optimism in the beer? A second result had come through. The Tories had held Torbay, suffering a negative swing of less than 1 per cent. And then, just before midnight, came the totemic Essex marginal of Basildon, live and nervous:

'I, being the returning officer for the Basildon constituency, hereby give notice that the total number of votes given for each candidate at the election was as follows: David Anthony Andrew Amess, Conservative – 24,159 . . .'

A mighty cheer went up in the background.

'John Russell Potter, Labour – 22,679.'

An even bigger cheer went up.

Labour had hoped to win by four or five thousand. Instead they lost and achieved only a swing of 1.3 per cent when what they needed across the country was 8.

Was there some malfunction? Were even the exit pollsters' findings falling apart in the face of reality? The fourth result, was Guildford, a prim Surrey commuter town. The Tories retained it, as expected, and again the swing against them barely existed. Then came Cheltenham at a quarter past midnight, and with it confirmation of the pessimism expressed with such eloquent sadness by the old lady with the pushbike and the café proprietor. John Taylor had gone down by 1668 votes, the first Tory seat of the night to be lost. Several plausible explanations could, and would, be advanced: tactical, anti-Tory voting; the 'local' factor; the Liberal Democrats' records as councillors. Any and all but the one no one wished to mention. The most insidious form of racism is that which denies its own existence. No facility services it better than a secret ballot. And who knows how many white Tory voters had actually swallowed their prejudices in the name of party loyalty? John Taylor would never know. The victorious Nigel Jones would not much care.

The counts were rolling in now, and it was clear that Labour were struggling, even though Big John Prescott had sauntered home in Hull East. Paddy Ashdown improved his majority in Yeovil by 3133. A more intriguing denouement happened in Coventry South-East. Dave Nellist had come third, but with 10,551 votes he was only 1351 behind the winner, Hattersley's choice, Jim Cunningham. The split in the Labour vote had enabled the Conservatives to come a close second. Yet for Nellist, his performance was still a personal triumph – outlawed independents are not supposed to do that well.

The Coventry cliff-hanger was followed ten minutes later by another Labour vindication in Glasgow Govan. To Jim Sillars's switchback *curriculum vitae* could now be added another plunge, submerging him to a depth of 4125 votes. A mandate for Scottish independence was becoming a mirage. So too was the expected

Labour government. Brian Redhead and his guest psephologist David Butler grappled with ever bluer projections.

It was one o'clock and a crowd of Kinnock supporters were pressing against the crash barriers outside the local leisure centre's entrance where the Islwyn count was taking place. From a transistor came news of more Labour reverses: John Butcher, favoured with the Heseltine manifestation, retained Coventry South-West. Teresa Gorman improved her majority in Billericay (though Alison Miller closed the gap on the Liberal Democrat). David Alton, the anti-abortion Liberal Democrat, held off Neville Bann in Liverpool's Mossley Hill.

'How can people do it?' implored a young man with wiry hair. 'How can they be so *selfish*?' The mood of the Islwyn Labourites hovered half way between head and heart: in the first, they knew – even said so – that all their hopes were turning to dust; in the second, every impulse told them they had dreamed too hard to deny themselves some celebration.

'We want Neil! We want Neil!'

At one fifteen, their calls were answered. Out of his car he bounded, Neil Kinnock, miner's boy, nurse's son, and headed straight for his clamouring people, winking and joshing, both arms pumping, a pair of great, tactile tentacles. Like the faithful, he must have known the game was nearly up. Like them too, perhaps, he had stored up too much exultation to succumb to depression. Yet.

Everything was upside down in Scotland. Michael Forsyth clung on in Stirling. George Kynoch turned over Nicol Stephen. The Conservatives even gained a seat, as quietly threatened, in Aberdeen South. Then came the high-tensile announcement of Bath. It sounded rowdy across the Bristol Channel as the returning officer spoke:

'Donald Michael Ellison Foster [Liberal Democrat]. Twenty-five thousand . . .'

He was interrupted by near hysteria.

'. . . seven hundred and eighteen. Duncan McCanlis [Green Party], four hundred and thirty-three. Christopher Francis Patten [Conservative] twenty-one thousand . . .'

At this, the howls from Bath were drowned by those in Blackwood.

'The bastard lost!'

'Patten, good riddance!'

There could be no more telling comment on the temper of the night, than that the greatest joy for Labour's Islwyn activists had come with a Liberal Democrat gain. And by the time John Major stepped forward, some twenty minutes later, to make his acceptance speech in Huntingdon, he already knew he also had a parliamentary majority falling into his hands as well.

It was nearly two before the police let us into the gymnasium. On the stage with the returning officer and their agents stood the Liberal Democrat's Andrew Symonds, the intrepid Tory Peter Bone and Helen Jones of Plaid Cymru whose president Dafydd Wigley had already held his seat handsomely up in Caernarfon. There was also the statutory exhibitionist from the Monster Raving Loony Party. A woman to the right remarked: 'He probably got quite a few votes, cos he promised a drink at the Red Lion for everyone who voted for him.'

In the event, the Loon got 547. Peter Bone's score was drowned by cries of 'Wanker' and 'Out, out, out!' But Kinnock, Neil Gordon, received 'thirty thousand . . .' The remaining numerals were engulfed in a tidal wave of cheers and a chant of 'Kinnock! Kinnock! Kinnock!' followed by exhortations to 'shhhh!' as he stepped forward to speak.

'I should like to thank the returning officer, and fellow candidates. And can I also thank all the people who've worked so hard today in the polling stations and with the count . . .'

With the stage being high and a ruck of people at the front, it was impossible to see him. But despite the rubber acoustics, the re-elected member sounded conciliatory and calm.

'. . . It's never an easy task, and they've performed with maximum speed, given some of the difficulties encountered with getting all the votes together. May I also thank the other candidates in this contest who have conducted themselves, as I've had to witness from some slight distance on this occasion, with great good humour and, as we expect, in the good spirit of democracy in this constituency. We know the result here, as you may not know, is the biggest Labour majority in this constituency ever . . .'

'Yeah!!!' roared the audience, high on defiance.

The speech continued, with thanks to both the local party and the constituency agent, Doreen Moore, and then 'to the other special woman, my wife Glenys . . .'

'Yeah!!!' the audience howled again. This touched a tender nerve.

'. . . Incomparable Glenys. In this campaign, and I think this is the place to say it, she has been the target of such spite that it disgraces those who offer it . . .'

'Yeah!!!'

'. . . and she bears it with dignity that makes me proud of her as well as love her dearly . . .'

'Yeah, well done, Neil!'

Who could fault him at that moment? Glenys Kinnock had, indeed, been set about by the lowlife newspapers, not just during the campaign but for years before it. In that tribute, her husband revealed values that were at the core not just of his domestic life but of his politics as well. Values which had only emerged with real passion during the past four weeks when he made his platform speeches. They were, at heart, patriarchal, sentimental, philanthropic. But they were warm values, none the less. Would that they had been enough.

'And so to this election,' he resumed, and there was a heavy hush. 'Even now, as recounts are going on in a very large number of seats, the result of this election is not decided . . . What we do know is that we have made gains from Plymouth to Cambridge, through London and some places in the south-east, into the Midlands and into the north-west, including Barrow . . .'

Where sea-dog Cecil had been sunk.

'. . . and into Scotland. And naturally, of course, we have made gains, here in Wales. The battle is not yet over . . .'

But these were the first reluctant offerings of consolation. He concluded with a solemn declaration:

'That battle goes on. We will know tomorrow how it has been resolved. But I take this opportunity to dedicate myself to the service of my constituents and in any capacity whatsoever to the people of my country. I'm proud to come from this area, and proud to be British, and I've always been proud to serve this democracy. Thank you.'

And with that Britain's Next Prime Minister tacitly acknowledged that he was no longer any such thing.

Before heading back to London, I located the buzz-bomb Shane, a dark-haired, friendly soul in a black bomber jacket. 'At that time it was still in the marginals,' he said, recalling his radio interview just three hours before. 'But it's so disappointing now, cos it's just going higher and higher as we go on . . .' He'd been campaigning far and wide – Cardiff Central, Monmouth, 'all over the place to be honest. And for the future of this country, I don't know. Some people just look after the money in their pocket and see the rest of the country fall down. There you go. It's frightening.'

During the journey up the M4 almost all the remaining pieces of Election '92 fell into place. In Liverpool, Angela Eagle had taken Wallasey and Jane Kennedy, Broad Green. The Tories had held Sheffield Hallam in spite of Peter Gold, Taunton in spite of Paddy Ashdown's beacons, Edinburgh West in spite of Paddy Ashdown's walkabout, Edinburgh Pentlands in spite of Wester Hailes and Neville Trotter had held Tynemouth in spite of – or maybe because of – the Meadow Well Estate. The incarcerated Tommy Sheriden secured 6287 votes, coming second to official Labour. Ken Livingstone and Chris Smith had both strengthened their majorities in London and Clare Short had done the same in Birmingham Ladywood. Gentleman Ian Lang had made it a depressing night for chipper Matt Brown and the rest of the SNP.

Instead of the 37 seats they'd dreamed of winning, with Galloway the crowning glory, they had ended up losing one to Labour. And everyone's hopes of wiping the Conservative Party off the face of Scotland were brusquely disappointed. The Tories actually increased their yield from nine to eleven. The news was brighter for the SNP's Welsh counterparts. Plaid Cymru ended up retaining its three incumbencies and coming from fourth place to take Ceredigion and North Pembroke from the Liberal Democrats. The new member, Cynog Dafis, had shared a platform with the Greens, so providing the environmentalist party with its first input into parliament. The big news from Belfast was that Dennis Donaldson had been wrong: Joe Hendron took West

Belfast from Gerry Adams, almost certainly thanks to Shankill
Unionists voting tactically.

As for Paddy Ashdown; his crusade had failed and all those
hung parliament speculations had been rendered academic. The
Liberal Democrats gained four seats but lost six, leaving them
with 20 in all. Labour lost five but gained 44, giving them a total
of 271. But while the Tories relinquished 44, they still picked up
ten. And their final, reduced, balance of 336 and slashed majority
of 21 concealed the fact that their share of the overall UK vote, at
41.9 per cent, had barely been eroded at all compared with 1987.
Labour's had gone up by just 3.6 per cent mainly at the expense
of the Liberal Democrats.

Election '92 was supposed to turn the UK inside out. Instead,
the Empire had struck back.

At a deserted motorway service station, the last one before the
capital, a corner-mounted television showed John Major, complete with Nice John smile, arriving at Conservative Central
Office in Smith Square with Norma and a not-all-that amusing
Chairman Chris Patten in tow. The staff were hanging out of the
windows. They were singing in the street. The cameras followed
Nice John inside where he mounted some stairs to gushing delight
and delivered a few precise words. The cut on his cheek was not
visible. His perfect parting remained in place.

'We've won, tonight, a magnificent victory,' he said, 'that
people thought was beyond our grasp. But one that the Conservative Party always believed was there for the taking.'

The motorway service station café was staffed by two young
Asian women. They were not paying any attention to the Prime
Minister's little speech. The average hourly rate of pay for service
station café assistants is £2.80. Their lives had not been improved
by the events of 9 April 1992.

At 9.25 a.m. on the night of Friday, 10 April, the IRA exploded a car bomb containing 100 pounds of explosive in the heart of the City of London. Many of the Square Mile's workers were still toasting the Conservative victory. Eighty people were injured. Two were killed. The following Monday morning Sir Patrick Mayhew, the newly-appointed Northern Ireland Secretary, said that the entire government was committed to the defeat of terrorism.

In the afternoon, Neil Kinnock resigned as leader of the Labour Party. Even before he'd done it, Labour MPs were complaining that John Smith had been anointed his successor even before they'd had a chance to discuss why the party had plunged to its fourth successive defeat. Clare Short was not alone in resenting the feeling of 'being bounced', and spoke of a 'stitch up with a couple of trade union leaders and a few leader writers telling us who we've got to elect'.

The eventual leadership contest produced three candidates: Smith, Bryan Gould the Shadow Environment Secretary and Ken Livingstone. Livingstone did not receive enough nominations from fellow MPs to advance to the contest proper. When the final results were announced in July, Gould, a soft-left ideas man, was trounced by Smith who received 91 per cent of the votes of Labour's electoral college. He was also defeated for the Deputy Leadership, as was John Prescott, who again advocated a vigorous regeneration of the party's grass roots. The victor was Margaret Beckett, number two in Smith's Shadow Treasury team. For Labour, it looked like business as usual.

In the meantime, there have been riots on housing estates in Blackburn, Burnley, Coventry, Huddersfield, Bristol and Salford. In Willenhall, a little boy has been abducted and murdered. Family man David Mellor has been exposed as having an extra-marital affair with an actress. Commuters on Network SouthEast continue to be worried about their jobs, their businesses and their mortgages. Unemployment has kept on rising. Cuts in public spending are on the agenda. John Major and Norman Lamont have carried on forecasting an imminent economic recovery. It has yet to occur.

Not very much has changed.

I live in the London Borough of Hackney. It is officially the poorest place in Britain. We have 20 per cent unemployment and thousands of us have not paid our poll tax. The local Labour council is currently imposing cuts on local education services in the name of 'efficiency'. However, the council are delighted to have won a grant under the City Challenge scheme introduced by Michael Heseltine to help improve the urban environment. I gather this will enable the expansion of a shopping mall and the creation of an ambient waterside market place. Those of us who have some disposable income will be able to go and spend it there. Pretty soon we'll all be living in paradise.

From certain points in the borough of Hackney you can see the tower of Canary Wharf, a great landmark in London's Docklands. Not long after the election, Olympia and York, the international property company which owns it, went bust. It was not the end of the world: hardly anyone used the office space it provided in any case. Docklands was once held to represent the triumph of the enterprise culture. It is now a bit of a joke.

As the sun came up on the morning of Friday, 10 April, Neil Kinnock said on the steps of Walworth Road that the whole country deserves better. He was right. Will someone please provide it.

17 August, 1992.

BIBLIOGRAPHY

Anderson, Bruce: *John Major – The Making Of The Prime Minister*, 4th Estate, 1991

Ashdown, Paddy: *Citizens' Britain*, 4th Estate, 1989.

Burk, Kathleen, & Cairncross, Alice: *Goodbye Great Britain – The 1976 IMF Crisis*, Yale, 1992

Butler, David: *British General Elections Since 1945*, Blackwell, 1989

Carvel, John: *Citizen Ken*, Chatto & Windus, 1984

Coates, Ken, ed: *What Went Wrong – Explaining The Fall Of The Labour Government*, Spokesman, 1979

Cockerell, Michael: *Live From Number 10*, Faber & Faber, 1988

Collins, Martin, ed: *Ireland After Britain*, Pluto, 1985

Coogan, Tim Pat: *The IRA*, Fontana, 1980

Critchley, Julian: *Britain – A View From Westminster*, Blandford, 1986

Critchley, Julian: *Heseltine – The Unauthorised Biography*, André Deutsch, 1987

Davis, David: *The BBC Viewer's Guide To Parliament*, BBC, 1989

Derbyshire, J. Denis and Derbyshire, Ian: *Politics In Britain – From Callaghan To Thatcher*, Chambers, 1990

Donnachie, Ian; Harvie, Christopher; Wood, Ian S.: *Forward! Labour Politics In Scotland 1888–1988*, Polygon, 1989

Foot, Paul: *Words As Weapons*, Verso, 1990

Foot, Paul: *Who Framed Colin Wallace?*, Macmillan, 1989

Gamble, Andrew: *Britain in Decline*, Papermac, 1981

Halsey, A. H.: *Change In British Society*, Oxford University Press, 1986

Harris, Robert: *The Making Of Neil Kinnock*, Faber and Faber, 1984

Harris, Robert: *Good And Faithful Servant – The Unauthorized Biography Of Bernard Ingham*, Faber & Faber, 1990

Hattersley, Roy: *A Yorkshire Boyhood*, Oxford University Press, 1983

Hattersley, Roy: *Press Gang*, Robson, 1983

Herington, John: *The Outer City*, Harper and Row, 1984

Heseltine, Michael: *Where There's A Will*, Arrow, 1987

Hirst, Paul: *After Thatcher*, Collins, 1989

Hobsbawm, Eric (and others): *The Forward March Of Labour Halted?*, Verso, 1981

Hobsbawm, Eric: *Politics For A Rational Left*, Verso, 1989

Hughes, Colin and Wintour, Patrick: *Labour Rebuilt*, 4th Estate, 1990

Jack, Ian: *Before The Oil Ran Out*, Flamingo, 1987

Jenkins, Peter: *Mrs Thatcher's Revolution*, Pan, 1987

Kavanagh, Dennis and Seldon, Anthony, eds: *The Thatcher Effect*, Oxford University Press, 1989

Kellner, Peter and Hitchens, Christopher: *Callaghan – The Road To Number Ten*, Cassell, 1976

Kinnock, Neil: *Making Our Way*, Blackwell, 1986

Lane, Tony: *Liverpool – Gateway Of Empire*, Lawrence and Wishart, 1987

Lawson, Mark: *Bloody Margaret*, Picador, 1991

Leapman, Michael: *Kinnock*, Unwin Hyman, 1987

Leigh, David: *The Wilson Plot*, Mandarin, 1988

Livingstone, Ken: *Livingstone's Labour – A Programme For The Nineties*, Unwin Hyman, 1989

Livingstone, Ken and Ali, Tariq: *Who's Afraid Of Margaret Thatcher?*, Verso, 1984

Major, John: *The Power To Choose, The Right To Own – Selected Speeches*, Conservative Political Centre, 1991

Marquand, David: *The Unprincipled Society*, Fontana, 1988

McKie, David, ed: *The Election – A Voter's Guide*, Guardian/4th Estate, 1992

Neuberger, Julia, ed: *Privatisation*, Papermac, 1987

Pearce, Edward: *The Quiet Rise Of John Major*, Weidenfeld & Nicholson, 1991

Pearce, Edward: *Election Rides*, Faber & Faber, 1992

Ponting, Clive: *Breach Of Promise – Labour in Power 1964–1970*, Penguin, 1989

Ponting, Clive: *1940 – Myth And Reality*, Cardinal, 1990

Press Association: *John Major – Prime Minister*, Bloomsbury, 1990

Samuel, Raphael; Bloomfield, Barbara; Boanas, Guy, eds: *The Enemy*

Within – Pit Villages And The Miners' Strike of 1984–5, Routledge and Kegan Paul, 1986

Saville, John: *The Labour Movement In Britain*, Faber & Faber, 1988

Scruton, Roger: *The Meaning Of Conservatism* (second edition), Macmillan, 1984

Selbourne, David: *Left Behind – Journeys Into British Politics*, Jonathan Cape, 1987

Seyd, Patrick: *The Rise and Fall of the Labour Left*, Macmillan, 1987

Short, Clare: *Dear Clare – This Is What Women Feel About Page 3*, Radius, 1991

Shrapnel, Norman: *The Seventies – Britain's Inward March*, Constable, 1980

Silk, Paul: *How Parliament Works*, Longman, 1987

Smith, Keith: *The British Economic Crisis – It's Past And Future*, Pelican, 1986

Smyth, Gareth, ed: *Can The Tories Lose?*, Lawrence and Wishart, 1991

Tyler, Rodney: *Campaign – The Selling Of The Prime Minister*, Grafton, 1987

Waller, Robert: *The Almanac Of British Politics*, Routledge, 1991

Wapshott, Nicholas and Brock, George: *Thatcher*, Futura, 1983

Wilson, Des: *Pressure – The A to Z Of Campaigning in Britain*, Heinemann, 1984

Wilson, Des: *Battle for Power*, Sphere, 1987

Young, Hugo: *One Of Us*, Macmillan, 1989

Various Authors: *Manifesto for New Times – A Strategy for the 1990s*, Communist Party/Lawrence and Wishart, 1990

Various Authors: *Thatcher's Britain – A Guide To The Ruins*, Pluto/New Socialist, 1983

Numerous articles in *New Statesman and Society*, *The Spectator*, the *Guardian* and the *London Review of Books* also provided valuable information, stimulation or both.